The
Totalitarian
Temptation

Books in English
by Jean-François Revel

THE TOTALITARIAN TEMPTATION

WITHOUT MARX OR JESUS

THE FRENCH

AS FOR ITALY

ON PROUST

The Totalitarian Temptation

By Jean-François Revel

TRANSLATED BY DAVID HAPGOOD

Doubleday & Company, Inc., Garden City, New York
1977

LIBRARY OF CONGRESS CATALOG CARD NUMBER 76–48604
ISBN 0-385-12274-8

La Tentation Totalitaire
ⓒ EDITIONS ROBERT LAFFONT, S.A. 1976

CONTENTS

Foreword to the American Edition   7

ONE: *The Communist Counterrevolution*
1   Socialism and Its Foes   15
2   The Totalitarian Urge   23
3   Why Stalinism Is Advancing in the World   30
4   The Democratic Misunderstanding   38
5   The Socialist Misunderstanding   51

TWO: *Of Docility Toward Stalinism: Its Manifestations and Its Consequences*
6   The Fear of Anti-Communism   63
7   Unofficial Stalinism or Pidgin Marxism   98
8   The Excommunication of Social Democracy   127

THREE: *The Suicide of the Socialists or The Indirect Justification of Totalitarian Solutions*
9   Excesses in the Economic Critique of Capitalism   143
10   Excesses in the Moral Critique of Capitalism   173
11   The Myth That Democratic Liberalism Is Utterly Bankrupt   191
12   The Refusal to Analyze the Causes of Failure   213

FOUR: *State and Reaction*
13   The State as Narcissus   239
14   Uniting the Nine Powers   252

5

Contents

FIVE: *National Totalitarianism or Global Socialism*
     15 Of Docility Toward Stalinism:
          An Essay in Explanation   261
     16 Toward a New Socialism?   285

     A Note on Eurocommunism
          The "Historical Compromise" and the
          Democratization of Western Communists   297

FOREWORD
TO THE AMERICAN EDITION

Usually one does not need a foreword to explain what a book is about. Sometimes it's wise to point out what a book is *not* about.

In Chapter 15 of *The Totalitarian Temptation,* I said that a book, however widely circulated, read and reviewed, may be misunderstood. This is partly due to the "pars pro toto" (the-trees-for-the-wood) principle: some formations or ideas remain in most people's minds. Secondary views disconnected from each other, isolated from the main thesis often turn into lasting memories of a book.

Looking back at reactions provoked by *Without Marx or Jesus* (1970; American edition, 1971), I can't deny that it was correctly understood. Nevertheless, many misconceptions got the better of some readers. Some critics missed its central, quite obvious meaning. "Once more unto the breach . . ." A few words about *Without Marx or Jesus* before commenting on what *The Totalitarian Temptation* is not, because there is a strong link between the two essays.

Here are a few typical mistakes. Error number one: "It's mainly a book favorable to the United States of America." No. It's neither a pro- nor an anti-American book. I merely said that throughout many historical periods, one comes across a "laboratory society." England, France, Italy were such societies, one, two, or five centuries ago. So is the U.S.A. today. And it is not alone. Sweden may be another laboratory, but it cannot have the

7

worldwide impact of American culture in exploring the future of democratic-capitalist societies, at their best or at their worst.

Error number two: "You said that a revolution would soon come to America. But the New Left and George McGovern were heavily defeated in 1972. In the seventies the young are in a pretty conservative mood." No. I never suggested that a revolution was on the point of breaking out in the United States; I said that it had already occurred. But I also insisted that I was using a modified version of revolution as a concept. As a matter of fact, that definition is the hard core of *Without Marx or Jesus*. Four times at least, I suggested that the new American revolution will probably fade away since history shows that most revolutions end in failure. To me, revolutionary success is the fact of *not* implementing the very opposite (as the Russian Revolution did) of what the revolution was supposed to achieve. If it accomplishes, say, half of its initial plan, it's a triumph. I now think that the American revolution is still on the move but on different paths. That, for a revolution, is perfectly proper since it cannot be an imitation of the past. If students of the seventies had indulged in a remake of what their elders had achieved in a different situation, that would have been a symptom of decline.

Finally, the objection about George McGovern and the New Left is simply irrelevant. Again and again, in *Without Marx or Jesus* I contend that a real revolution, in other words a *major* and not only a *minor* change, rarely begins at the political level. Rather, it starts at the grass roots of the sociocultural system. Although McGovern's astonishing rise during the primaries and his apotheosis at an extraordinary convention were an expression and a confirmation of the American metamorphosis, I never predicted that a radical President would soon be elected. History is not that simple. A revolution is not simply a new political orientation. It works through the depths of society. It writes the play in which political leaders will act much later. Besides, a complex "developed" revolution is likely to be slow. Indeed, if it is a democratic revolution, it can only be slow because it is democratic. Fast revolutions always go with civil wars, repressions, violations of the law (when it survives). And so they end in counterrevolutions or the Gulag.

Enough about *Without Marx or Jesus.* My excuse for those retrospective remarks is that they also apply to *The Totalitarian Temptation,* rooted in the previous book.

In what sense? This new essay attempts to answer the following question: of the two types of revolution now fighting each other in the world, which one will win in the end, knocking the other out? The first type is the democratic model I described in *Without Marx or Jesus.* It is the only truly revolutionary one: it leads to an improvement of mankind's happiness. The second type is the Marxist-Leninist-Maoist model, with all its little brothers in many countries not strictly belonging to the Communist camp—but still implementing a brand of totalitarian socialism which I call "unofficial Stalinism." This second type involves a phony revolution, cleverly using leftist incentives to build reactionary totalitarian states under the false guise of socialism. Today, throughout the world, it seems to be more attractive, to find more supporters than democratic countries. In this book, I try to explain how this has happened, and why. That is my central theme.

Therefore (to reply to the question often put to me) the new American revolution, or the new world revolution that started in America, will probably fail—not because of the United States but because the world steadily rejects democracy.

Now, a few items about which this book is not. *It is not a book about France or the French Left.* Many Europeans read my book through that prism because political passions have been stirred up by the increased weight of the Socialist and Communist parties' coalition in France. Of course, the totalitarian temptation is very strong in Western Europe. Both official and unofficial Stalinism are quite powerful in that area. But this book deals with a world situation in which Europe is important, but not alone. I tried to devote as many pages to Latin America, Southeast Asia or Africa as to that part of the world where I happen to live.

It is not a book about current affairs in 1975 or 1976. Of

9

course, the examples used are picked mainly (but not only) from recent years. They are there as illustrations of theoretical paradigms, not for the sake of reportage. I make that quite clear, because the agony of the political commentator is that people start asking him, five weeks after his book is out, whether it does not need a little "updating." I try to bring out patterns and trends valid over long periods not dependent upon small or local variations, like the fall of the Swedish Socialists or the outcome of the Rhodesian crisis. Every day, throughout the human tragedy, *more* events occur which are not necessarily *new*. The only relevant question is whether *one* fact makes it necessary to change global interpretations. And not that it turns out to be more or less recent than another. In politics many things seem new just because they are put in a new way—say, "Eurocommunism" (see "A Note on Eurocommunism," page 295). Politicians and columnists genuinely labor over the novelty of last-minute facts or issues, because it makes their job more exciting.

It is not a eulogy of capitalism any more than it is a eulogy of socialism. Economically, morally and politically, I compare capitalism with 1) pre-capitalist systems, 2) earlier phases of capitalism itself (to see if it has demonstrated a capacity for improvement) and 3) present Communist- and Marxist-oriented societies.

In the long run, the balance is less horrific for capitalism than usually assumed. In contemporary political scholarship, to suppress evidence seems to be a normal way of showing which side you took; since I did not, I have sometimes been labeled a "supporter of capitalism." True, the habit of generally hearing about the shortcomings of capitalism makes a fair appraisal of the system look weird.

It is not an encouragement to go back to the cold war. It is pretty paradoxical that the United States is accused of "cold-war mongering" if you try to assess exactly what the Communist countries are doing and whether or not détente is a failure for the West. Should democratic countries now become biased in favor of communism, just because Americans feel guilty about McCarthyism and the Vietnam war? Such an approach is irrational. I am not interested in demonology: I care about what's going on. Indeed, the subtitle of this book could be "Why Is U. S. Foreign Policy Failing Almost Everywhere?" Why is Soviet totalitarianism popular in Africa? Why is Castro a star and Kissinger a villain, in spite of his brief initial lionization and notwithstanding his credentials as a détente maker. Why does the President of the United States have to be heavily protected in Rome, Tokyo, Paris, or Stockholm against hostile demonstrators while in some Western cities any Eastern statesman walks or drives peacefully through friendly or indifferent crowds? Abroad, the only violent demonstrators that a Communist head of state fears are usually refugees from his own country.

It is not a book about communism, or, at least, it is only indirectly a book about communism, Communist countries and parties. I read an American review, commenting on the French edition of my book. The reviewer wrote that on the Communist system I was accurate but not very original. This is precisely what I said about myself in the very first chapter. My purpose is not to add anything to our gigantic knowledge of communism. I attempt to explain why we know so much and use so little of this knowledge. Why did the huge amount of evidence available for decades on Communist states have so little impact on so many Western minds, third-world people and the mainstream of historic evolution? Why are democratic societies, inside and outside their area, vilified much more than totalitarian states? The reason would be clear if Communist or authoritarian socialist regimes had been successful in the pursuit of collective happiness over a long period; and capitalistic-democratic ones, or those based on a mixed economy, colossal disasters. In the long run, things have worked exactly the other way round. Why then is the philosophy of the less attractive and less affluent of the two systems becoming more and more popular? (Except of course among its own "beneficiaries," who, anyway, are not allowed to change their minds.) The more "socialism" is discredited and ridiculed at home, the more influential and glamorous it seems to become abroad. So, in a way, this is more a book about what's going on in those parts of the world where totalitarianism is *not* yet ruling, in those countries where, sometimes, a strong Communist party does *not* even exist.

As the title clearly implies, it's a book about the temptation, not about its object.

J.F.R.

One

THE COMMUNIST COUNTERREVOLUTION

1

SOCIALISM AND ITS FOES

The world today is evolving toward socialism. The main obstacle to socialism is not capitalism but communism. The socialist society of the future can only be worldwide and it can only be brought about at the cost, if not of the abolition of nation-states, at least of their subordination to a global political order.

Such are the three central ideas of this book. The question is whether the socialists will succeed in eliminating the two primary barriers that prevent the building of a socialist world: the state and communism. Or will the socialists insist on serving their rivals' interests, helping them to help each other, continuing on a suicidal course that will end in their own destruction and the creation of new totalitarian states?

The objection will be raised that asking such a question requires that I define what I mean by socialism. My reply is that no definition is needed. We have a surplus of definitions of socialism; what is lacking is examples of socialism. Socialism is like freedom: if we feel we still need to define them, after all that has been said and all the social experiments that have been made, it simply means we have no intention of putting them into effect. When sects or parties engage in such academic hairsplitting, they do so to mask, and to justify, their authoritarian intentions. A French writer—I think it was Jean Cocteau—once said: "There is no such thing as love, there is only evidence of love." Similarly we can say: there is no such thing as socialism, there is only evidence of socialism. And no such thing as democracy, only evidence of democracy. All too often, if one tries to define love, socialism or freedom in the abstract, the effort results only in philosophical platitude, juridical abstraction, Stalinist dogma or liberal verbiage. But the difficulty vanishes and the task becomes easy once we set out to list the specific manifestations of what we are trying to define. Politics is a behavioral science.

In 1975, at a time when the Spanish were discussing "after Franco" and theorizing on their country's "passage" to democracy, I spoke with a high official of the dying dictatorship who made this elementary observation: "All our quibbling about the nature of democracy serves only to delay its return. A ten-year-old can understand what democracy is. If you run down a list that includes free elections, universal suffrage, freedom of assembly, free speech and so on, he will realize right away that in any political system those are conditions whose existence or lack of it demonstrates the existence or absence of democracy." To complete the thought of that rightist official, who was fed up with the shilly-shallying in his own circles, I would add the fact that quibbling, as he put it, about the essence of democracy is a way of rejecting democracy just as true of those who call themselves "leftist" as it is of those on the "right." I do not see why the sorry pretexts by which one may try to avoid the light of the sun should be considered reactionary in one case and progressive in the other.

It is obvious what makes up the "evidence of democracy." Simply eliminate one or another aspect of that evidence and, as their absence begins to be felt, it will be clear that they do indeed constitute the fact of democracy.

When some self-righteous preacher sets out to explain to me that only a state monopoly—that is, a state monologue—of the news can make the press and television serve the people, because we all know about the "false objectivity" of the New York *Times, La Stampa* or NBC, I understand that he wants to eliminate news in favor of propaganda. Of course there is "false objectivity," but it can only exist where the real thing is also allowed to exist. According to Bertrand Russell, some propositions lack even the capacity to be false, by which he meant that they are too shapeless to be refuted, that they have not been worked out sufficiently to stand as statements, whether true or false. Karl

Popper argues along the same lines: only a statement that has a minimum degree of coherence can be proved false.

Similarly, societies where news is censored cannot enjoy the luxury of false objectivity because they do not have the true variety. In free civilizations, false objectivity must be fought by true objectivity, not by some alien bureaucracy. Prejudiced history is eliminated, or at least combated, by serious history, and corrupt journalism can only be defeated by honest journalism, not by a government commission whose first act may be to distribute some secret subsidies. A free press isn't always right and it isn't always honest, any more than a free man is always right and honest. If literature could not have been authorized without first learning how to ban trash, we would still be busy correcting the first set of proofs to come off the printing press. Those who do not understand that freedom has value in itself, though its expression necessarily produces evil as well as good, are poorly suited to the culture of democracy.

I have lingered over this classic example of freedom of the press because it is one of those fundamental tests that separates those to whom democratic culture is congenial from those to whom it is not. The first find it easy to define a free press, while for the second the question is tortuous and complex, because, in their innermost souls, they tend to conclude that only a press that affirms their beliefs to the exclusion of all others can be considered "free." The frank dogmatism with which they propose to liberate us from the pluralism that characterizes the "repressive" capitalist press, forcing on us in its place a monotonous diet of their opinions and their laundered news, is the antithesis of what I call "evidence of democracy."

Evidence of socialism is far harder to find than evidence of democracy, because democracy is in existence, which is not the case with socialism. With each passing day socialism gains ground—but as an ideal, not in practice. The literature of socialism is the most abundant we have seen since that of the medieval theologians, but the ideals of neither are reflected in the real world. I observed earlier that there have been experiments in socialism, but those experiments have everywhere failed, which has not been the case with political democracy. Of course some socialism does exist, notably in the capitalist countries—indeed, *only* in the capitalist countries. But these are fragments of socialism; there is not a single socialist society. The study of political democracy can draw on a rather ample historical record, but the study of socialism is an exercise in futurology. Naturally the totalitarians trumpet the flaws of democracy, but to be flawed is quite different from not existing at all. The democratic society has its flaws but it exists. Socialist society may be perfect, I agree—but it doesn't exist.

Most debates about the "definition" of socialism result less from the desire to implement socialism than from quarrels among factions struggling for power either in office or within the opposition parties. Having little to do with the needs of mankind, these debates merely provide the language in which political elites and their authoritarian leaders contend over the future disposition of the spoils of office. But the goal of politics is human well-being, the greatest good for the greatest possible number, not the success of a few professional politicians who seek to impose their views on the majority (while claiming to follow its wishes). Despite their leftist vocabulary, their goal is the ancient one of power for a minority, not the well-being of the masses.

In order to dispense with foggy sectarian disputation, let us cautiously say that one can define as progress toward socialism, as "evidence of socialism," any change, reform or revolution that results in making the economic system work a little more for the benefit of man, and man a little bit less for the benefit of the system; that makes the system work for a greater number of people and that brings it a bit more under their control. Anything that makes men serve the economy, giving its needs priority over theirs, is anti-socialism; socialism, therefore, subordinates the economy to the needs of the greatest number, but *without ceasing to improve the economy.*

The economy must be brought more under the people's control *because no socialist economy is possible without socialist political democracy.* What is the value of a supposed socialization of the economy if political power remains in the hands of an oligarchy which is free, for example, to decide to spend 40 per cent of the gross national product on weapons and prestige projects, those tools of the state imperialism of a "Great Power," which simply means the power of the oligarchy itself?

The parallel growth of economic and political democracy presupposes that the output of the economy will be maintained or, better, increased. What difference in practice is there between those irresponsible "socialists" who, as soon as they come to power, impose their untested ideological principles on the management of the nation, with the result that production drops by one half—and, on the other hand, those irresponsible capitalists who permit an economic crisis in which a fall in production is accompanied by inflation and unemployment? There is in fact no difference, except that the damage done by the capitalists is often less extensive and less permanent, and that they spare us the sanctimonious sermons of the "socialists." At least capitalism is not satisfied with itelf except in good times when it is performing successfully, whereas socialist boasting need not be based on any performance at all. Failure raises the socialist morale—luckily, since if its self-esteem had to based on success, socialism would live in a state of constant humiliation.

When I wrote that the world is evolving toward socialism, I meant that the sheer listing of the world's necessities makes a powerful case for a globally managed economy, under a political order capable of that global management, in the interest of all mankind (in theory no longer a stupid idea) and with the greatest possible equality among people.

But I don't mean that this evolution will come about by itself. All too many of us have accepted the illusion of fatalism, derived from a simple-minded historical determinism inherited from Hegel and Marx, which excludes any possibility of creative invention. History in this view occurs automatically. Politics however is action, not a journey through a predictable future. All that has proved inevitable in history is that problems get worse: the solution never springs from the worsening of the problem. Humanity will never achieve socialism unless we proceed in a spirit of realism that analyzes and corrects its own mistakes—virtues hardly cultivated by present-day socialists. Thus when I referred to evolution, and even to a necessary evolution, I meant that it had to happen, not that it would happen.

Indeed, the two main obstacles that stand in the way of achieving socialism—communism and the nation-state—seem almost insurmountable. On a purely rational level, it is pretty generally agreed that the traditional nation-state is incompatible with the creation of a worldwide economic and political order. It is also agreed that this new order is the only framework in which solutions can be implemented to problems that, because of the interdependence of the groups that make up humanity, can no longer be resolved on a national basis. Socialism, therefore, can neither be conceived nor brought into being except on a global scale. But at the same time, the more that fact is realized—at least by those who are not employed in the service of one of the existing national orders—the more the nation-state grows rigid instead of flexible. The more we talk of international co-operation, the more we reinforce the nation-state, an institution that excels only at stirring up and exacerbating rivalry among nation-states.

The natural inclination of the nation-state is to subordinate domestic affairs to foreign policy, that is to everything which serves to compete with and to weaken other nation-states. Obviously this does nothing to promote either global co-operation or human well-being. But the nation-state is incapable of acting otherwise. We may even offer as "evidence of socialism" any reversal of this natural tendency. When a country subordinates foreign to domestic policy, to the well-being of its citizens, we can consider it more socialist than when it does the contrary. This is the case with Sweden, or Japan since 1950 (whether willingly or by necessity). And when a nation sacrifices its internal development to seek power and prestige abroad, it is moving away from socialism. Notable examples are the Soviet Union, Egypt under Nasser, Gaullist France, and India under Indira Gandhi. Since these are nations at quite different levels of development, it is clear that their behavior is determined not by their economies but by the nature of political power and the use it makes of the state.

As for making common property of the earth's natural resources—a necessity if the human species is to survive—it cannot come about, it cannot even begin, as long as the nation-state exists. The state by its nature can only use whatever resources fortune places within its reach to increase its power and diminish that of other states. This has nothing to do with a wise use of the earth's riches for the benefit of all mankind—indeed, any such ideal is aborted by the nation-state. Thus the growing frustration of nation-states seeking power and "independence" makes the problems of mankind ever more difficult to resolve.

The increasing rigidity of the nation-states must not be confused with another important phenomenon of our times: the renewed aspirations of ethnic groups. The confusion arises because the effort of ethnic communities to assert, or recapture, their cultural identities is often called nationalism. But it is not the same as the nationalism of the nation-state. As long as they do not conflict with the rights of mankind, the rights of ethnic groups or "nationalities" must be respected in the same manner as the rights of individuals. But just as granting the rights of the individual in civilized society does not mean he has to build a fort and acquire an arsenal, recognizing the rights of ethnic groups need not always result in the creation of another armed sovereign state. This simple-minded equating of cultural autonomy with nationhood can only contribute to the anarchy that plagues our poor planet by placing the power to do harm in the hands of a whole gang of local political hoodlums who seize control of the new states, and some not so new states, to satisfy their despotic ambitions. We must consider ourselves fortunate when they do not call themselves socialist, which, alas, most of them do. How often in the course of the last twenty or thirty years have we seen the leaders of a national liberation movement, worthy men and even heroic, fight for independence and, when it was won, capture the new state and subject their people to their own obsessions, their lust for power and the megalomaniacal fantasies of their foreign policies. Becoming masters of that plaything the nation-state can draw from the purest of hearts the excesses of tyranny, though when the state is more or less disguised as a republic and wears a socialist façade that tends to make it immune from criticism by world opinion.

Still more formidable is the statist influence of communism, whether of the Soviet, Chinese or Indochinese variety. There are several reasons why communism in alliance with the nation-state is an adversary of socialism. The first is that communism gives birth to the most powerful and secretive nation-states the world has ever known, thus setting mankind back by several centuries in its evolution toward a civilization freed from the state. Secondly, communism uses the progressive themes of socialism in propagating its own expansion. Thus communism can exploit the discontent that results from the "contradictions of capitalism" (which surely exist) in order to destroy political democracy in the name of socialism, and thereafter install a political order that is neither democratic nor socialist and is, in terms of economic performance and respect for human rights, vastly inferior to capitalism.

Confusion is fostered by the systematic use of the word "socialist" as a synonym for "Communist"—the "socialist states" being those Communist nations ruled by a totalitarian bureaucracy, and "socialist revolutions" being those in which a minority has seized absolute power and has no intention of ever relinquishing it. It is easy to understand why the Communists have a stake in promoting this confusion in terms. It is far harder to understand why so many "socialists" and "revolutionaries" are willing to follow their lead, and thereby help the Communists make socialism forever impossible.

THE TOTALITARIAN URGE

Does there lurk in us a wish for totalitarian rule? If so, it would explain a great deal about how people behave, about the speeches they make and the times they remain silent. Within what I shall call for the time being the "Left" in non-Communist nations, the faults of free societies are so magnified that freedom appears to mask an essentially totalitarian reality, while the faults of totalitarian societies are so minimized that those societies appear to be free, in essence if not in appearance. Such societies are pictured as being fundamentally good, though for the time being they do not honor the rights of man, whereas free societies are evil in nature, even though their subjects live in greater freedom and less misery. If one were to believe some of the commentaries published in those (rare) nations where freedom of expression prevails, a Communist society, even though it was no more than an immense concentration camp whose inhabitants were struggling painfully for sheer survival, is a society that is bettering itself. But a free capitalist society is to be destroyed, no matter how one may judge the quality of the lives its citizens actually lead.

Doubtless this differential treatment is, first of all, the result of the difference in political regimes. In societies that permit domestic criticism, the continual denunciation of injustice soon piles up a mountain of grievances, while the silence imposed on totalitarian societies precludes any similar daily listing of their liabilities. Of course these liabilities are revealed from time to time, but only by foreign observers or by refugees, which does not produce the same effect as harassment by a domestic opposition which is part of the system it is attacking. Nor does it carry the same weight as a free election in which, for example, a substantial percentage of Poles or Romanians were allowed openly to cast their ballots against socialism. In practice, only the failures and the crimes of liberal capitalism and social democracy are ruthlessly tallied every day; only these societies are constantly being indicted by their own members.

Thus members of democratic societies get a view of their own regimes that is unfavorable compared to others, while the same kind of systematic disparagement, either constructive or destructive, cannot manifest itself in Communist societies, where criticism is either stamped out at birth or prevented from spreading by the power of the bureaucracy. It is like a football game in which the only points registered on the scoreboard are those lost by one of the two teams.

Still, while this explanation may account for the pro-communism manifested in some third-world nations where the masses are ill-informed and have never known political freedom, it does not tell us why there is a growing trend in the West to discount freedom as compared to justice (which in any event the Communist regimes do not provide either). For there lies the typical nonsense. If it could be proved that by renouncing freedom and dignity one could achieve social justice, the choice would be a painful one, but it would be a choice. But that is not the case, and we all know it, though it is seldom taken into account.

This paradox in East-West "dialogue" seems to result from the refusal (rather than the inability) of the Western Left to draw the necessary political, economic and moral conclusions from the realities of life in socialist societies. Indeed, they do not even perceive those realities except in brief flashes. On the contrary, one who bears witness to Communist oppression is often dismissed as a reactionary—after all, don't the fascists say the same things he does? If a tramp denounces the plague, then all those who denounce the plague are tramps. Self-censorship is in the long run more effective than the official kind. As a former professor at the University of Prague put it: "Self-satisfied, condescending, listening to its own voice, the West recites to itself its own version of socialism . . . what has not been experienced is made into dogma."[1] Since it is impossible to remain totally and forever ignorant of the realities of Eastern Europe, China and some "socialist" states of the third world, the refusal to judge them doubtless reflects a decision to approve them no matter what.

If a substantial minority in the West thus deliberately closes its eyes to obvious reality, the explanation may well lie in an unacknowledged desire to live under Stalinism, not in spite of what it is, but because of what it is. Some want to wield the power of a tyrant, a wish from which none of us is free; for others it is the need to submit to a tyrant's rule, and none of us is free from that murky impulse either. After all, if tyranny had never enjoyed the complicity of its victims, the history of our times—and many other times—would have been quite different.

Perhaps we need not plumb the depths of human psychology to explain these favorable views of totalitarianism. Common sense is enough to tell us that the small groups that rule the Communist parties and unions in the West would like to extend their power to the whole society. Certain personalities bloom only when exercising absolute power. Some know they are incapable of reaching the top, or indeed any position of influence, except in a society where zeal in the service of tyranny can substitute for talent; others, endowed with great talent, cannot bear any limits on the authority that accrues to them because of that talent. The desire to escape pluralism, rather than its acceptance, is the norm in man's history. Besides, what we agree to, when we do agree, is never pluralism itself, with its constant daily scraping on the nerve ends of our power and our pride, but rather a political system that makes pluralism inevitable. We choose, through both reason and morality, the mutual limitation under law of our desire for power. But, following our natural inclination, what person would not choose absolute power, if he could

[1] I. Yannakakis, quoted by C. Jelen in *Les Normalisés* (Paris: Albin Michel, 1975).

be sure it would always be his own and never another's? To pretend otherwise is just hypocrisy.

As for the masses, who in a future totalitarian state will be excluded from power and dominated by a bureaucratic minority and the official intelligentsia, what do they know of that future condition until it happens to them?

Even in the best-informed societies, there exists a domestic third world of ignorance. Having been told over and over that the free societies of the industrial West are history's most horrendous cases of oppression and misery, that any change is preferable to the awful present, those who vote for the Western Communist parties lend their support to totalitarianism, not through any desire for Stalinism, about which they know nothing, but because they believe this is the only route to reform and improvement in their lives. And, once they experience Stalinist rule, it will be too late to escape it should they change their minds. The transition to totalitarian rule is by definition irrevocable, except in the case of some cataclysm like a world war. From the moment that people are in a position to evaluate totalitarian rule from their own experience, they no longer have the ability to abolish it, or criticize it, or alter it, or even to escape it. Then, after a generation, a people subjected to a totalitarian regime has scarcely any means of comparing their society to others. More consistently strict than old-fashioned dictatorships, the totalitarian powers forbid free travel by their citizens abroad and by foreigners on their territory. News having been entirely supplanted by propaganda, it becomes impossible for residents of a totalitarian state to conceive of, or to remember, a society different from their own. Their capacity to dream as well as to think begins to fail. Their spirit is battered by propaganda and enfeebled by cultural isolation; nostalgia for the past and the utopian dream of the future are both beyond their reach. Such people can no longer imagine either past or future.

There is to this day not one bit of evidence for the liberal Left's eternal hope that communism will evolve toward democratic pluralism, that Communists will accept the principle of rotation of power, that is that they will agree to let themselves be voted out of office.

The distinctive characteristic of communism, its very reason for being, is to eliminate the possibility of any challenge to its rule, thus to deny to the people, and indeed to the ruling minority itself, any opportunity to change their minds, once the regime is in power. Communism would lose its meaning if Communist governments agreed, after a "frank and cordial discussion" with their liberal allies, to add to their system a codicil stipulating that pluralism was permitted and they would give up power, once they had gained it, if that was the will of the majority. For a Communist government, once it is in possession of the state, to enter into such an agreement would be as contrary to its basic nature as for the president of a multi-national corporation to give its competitors the right to expropriate it whenever they choose. Accordingly, all proposals to liberalize Communist rule have been rejected by the logic of the system.

It is in the nature of a democratic pluralist system, based on free elections, that government is supposed to pay for its mistakes, while in Communist states the people pay for government's mistakes. Of course the people in a democracy suffer the consequences of their government's errors. Nonetheless, the system provides as a penalty for a failure in policy that those in office can be replaced by others. By contrast, the logic of Communist rule is that a series of failures results in tightening the oligarchy's grip on the people, even though some individuals in the oligarchy may be purged. In Stalinist jargon this is called "normalization."

Such is the nature of communism in power. As for communism in the opposition, in the Western democracies, the discipline it imposes on both its leaders and its rank and file can only be justified if its goal is the attaining of absolute and permanent power. Without that goal Communist behavior becomes absurd. Why use tactics that in the short run are both repulsive and politically ineffectual, unless the ultimate purpose is to gain power that need not be shared with others? The Italian Communists, as is well known, can allow themselves to be more tolerant than, for example, French Communists, because they can plausibly hope to win an over-all majority and thereby come to power by democratic means, which is not the case in France. But it would make no sense if they did not pursue the logical next step: after becoming one of the parties in power, eliminate the other parties. If that were not their goal, they would be social democrats; and it is possible that they are in the process of becoming social democrats.

The Communists' goal is the taking of power. That is the goal of all political parties, granted, but what distinguishes the Communist party is the use it makes of power once it has it. And, as with all political parties, we must distinguish between what Communists say to justify themselves and their actual use of power—where they have it and when they have it, of course, not *before* they have it, or where they do *not* have it.

Pro-Communists of the liberal Left suffer from the illusion that there exists some variety of communism other than Stalinism. But Stalinism is the very essence of communism. What varies is not the Stalinist system but the harshness with which it is applied. You cannot shoot or imprison all of the people all of the time. Nor is it necessary every day of the week to send tanks to re-establish Stalinist order in a friendly country. At times when pressure from above plus a rising standard of living are enough to forestall rebellion, repression need not be spectacular: it is part of the daily routine. But it is nonetheless Stalinist. Khrushchev and Brezhnev have been no less Stalinist than Stalin himself, in the sense that they maintained the order he created. They sent their troops into the satellite countries when it was necessary. They were just less bloodthirsty than Stalin, and they put an end to murder camouflaged in judicial robes. But the Stalinist order remains: the police apparatus, the arbitrary arrests, the concentration camps, the whole totalitarian system of controlling people and ideas. That is how it had to be. Whether in Moscow, in Peking or in Hanoi, a Communist regime that was not Stalinist would destroy itself. The "independence" from the Soviet Union, such as it is, that Romania enjoys in foreign policy was accompanied by a strengthening of the local Stalinist grip within Romania itself, in order not to provide the Soviets with a pretext for armed intervention on the grounds that socialism was threatened in Bucharest. However pleasing that foreign policy may be to the leaders' egos, its consequence for the Romanian people was still heavier totalitarian rule. Yet Romania is not 90 miles from the United States nor a victim of "imperialist embargo"—the standard excuses given for Cuban totalitarianism. Titoism has provided Tito with a certain amount of freedom of action with regard to Moscow, but far less freedom for Yugoslavs from Tito. All in all, there is now available a rather large body of historical experience from which we can conclude, by observation not speculation, that there is not today and there never has been a non-Stalinist Communist regime. Let us not mistake an effort for a system, or books people write, for societies in which people live.

Thus the totalitarian urge is made up of two components.

The first component is not really a desire for totalitarianism, since it is based on the people's ignorance of Communist regimes, understandable enough in countries where no one has experienced those regimes. It is a political expression of the class struggle, of the struggle for economic justice and the improvement of life in general, without a clear picture of the future form of government implied by support for the Communist or Marxist party. Among the people as a whole, the Communist alternative is simply seen as the opposite of the faults of the society in which they are living.

By contrast, the other component, the desire for totalitarianism among elites, is based on a clear knowledge of the kind of society they are choosing, in spite of the massive defects of that society, and in spite of their reluctance to concede that those defects are inherent in such societies rather than accidental deviations. This calls for a more complex psychosocial interpretation.

3

WHY STALINISM IS
ADVANCING IN THE WORLD

In most parts of the world, the advance of Stalinism can be easily explained, for its causes are both massive and few in number. Acting together they set in motion a force to which nothing can offer lasting opposition.

The three internal factors that lead to Stalinism are underdeveloped economies, hatred of foreign domination, and the lack of any experience of democratic pluralism. To these must be added an external factor: the influence of the Soviet Union or China, as the case may be, each of which seeks to set up satellite systems to serve the interests of their rivalries with the United States and with each other. But the efforts of the Soviet Union and China would remain fruitless without the three main internal causes: poverty, nationalism, and the historical absence of democracy. The last of those three makes irrelevant any Western sophistry about the difficulties of reconciling democratic politics and socialist development. Why should people fear the loss of something they have never had?

I do not propose for the time being to discuss the merits of those factors. In my view they are of dubious validity. From the point of view of man living in the poverty of underdevelopment, centralized bureaucratic control appears to be the only political means to attain prosperity, even if that belief turns out after the fact to have been in large measure an illusion. Blaming all one's misfortunes on foreign domination speaks to a basic and universal instinct; during a war for independence, that instinct produces discipline and self-sacrifice, but in peacetime its results are less salutary. No matter how great the ultimate cost may be, any demagogue finds in nationalism his easiest and most fruitful theme. Finally, though it is by definition true that those who have never lived under freedom do not feel its absence, would not the creation of democracy where it is now absent stimulate an awakening of the human spirit that is necessary to economic development itself, and more: is not democracy indispensable to the liberation of people as well as nations?

Whether or not those observations are pertinent, they will certainly not be heeded. In circumstances of poverty and humiliation, the advocates of nationalist, socializing dictatorship speak the only language that is now understood. What they do after they gain power is another matter. Before that day, it is only natural that people listen to them, especially when there is a vacuum of news and opinion, a vacuum which by the way most of them will subsequently perpetuate in order to protect the state they have created.

It is far harder to understand why the case for Stalinism should find favor in developed, well-informed civilizations, and particularly among the most prosperous and informed classes in those civilizations.

Stalinism in the developed democratic nations is quite limited, both by area and in the vote it attracts. The number of prosperous nations in which the Communist party, thirty years after the Second World War, amounts to more than an insignificant sect is only three: Italy, France and Japan. I listed them in descending order of the Communist vote: about one third of the electorate in Italy, one fifth in France, one tenth in Japan. The Communists also played a part in the political history of democratic Chile, until the coup that ousted the government of Salvador Allende. Chile is not a rich country, yet it is not part of the third world either. Similarly, we should add to the list two countries which lived for many years under conservative, clerical dictatorship, Portugal and Spain; in each the Communists seem likely in free elections to be able to draw a stable and lasting 10 per cent of the vote, or somewhat more.

But elections are one thing and parties are something else. The Communists have never been able to come to power where honest elections are held under circumstances where the vote has meaning: where most citizens enjoy the benefits of freedom of assembly, a free press, the right to an education, and where people can travel and ideas circulate in equal freedom. Never have the Communists won a majority under these conditions, nor even a plurality of the vote, although many had expected them to do so in the Italian general elections of June 20, 1976.[1]

By contrast, wherever it attains a minimum critical mass, the Communist party, with card-carrying activists numbering only no more than 4–5 per cent of the party's vote, can wield influence far out of proportion to its electoral strength and can even set the conditions for the nation's political life. In the countries listed above there is a Communist "dynamics" that results in the party's having a political productivity greater than its percentage of the vote. This dynamics has three main causes.

It is due, first of all, to the efficiency of the party organization and the fidelity of its staff and followers; so rigid is the faith of the party's rank and file that, aside from occasional minor defections, they are always ready to carry out the leadership's ideological and political orders. Of course they are also willing, though sometimes reluctantly, to follow the most unexpected changes in the party line.

Secondly, the Communist dynamics is due to their hold on the labor unions. There is a contradiction here, for in countries with a strong Communist presence the union movement is both controlled by the party and at the same time much weaker numerically than it is, for example, in social democratic states, or even in a free economy like that of the United States. (It is far from true that the American economy conforms entirely to the classic free-enterprise model, but we shall not argue that point here.) The unionized part of the working class amounts to 15 to 20 per cent in France, 20 to 30 per cent in Italy, 30 per cent in West

[1] The Communists got 34.4 per cent of the vote, an increase of 2.4 per cent from the regional elections of June 1975. But the Christian Democrats also gained ground, and more than the Communists. The difference between them, only 1.9 per cent in 1975, rose to 4.3 per cent. The *sorpasso*—that is, the Communists becoming Italy's largest party—has not as yet taken place. (See Foreword.)

Germany, 50 per cent in Britain and Denmark and 70 per cent in Sweden.[2] In a word, Communist control of the unions strengthens the influence of the party while weakening the labor movement.

During this century the working class has been better represented by the social democratic unions of northern Europe than by the Communist unions of southern Europe. To understand why this has happened, we must bear in mind that the goal of Communist unionism is not to improve the conditions of the workers in the capitalist system, but to exploit conflict in order to undermine that system.

It is true that the rule is not always followed. The Communists often adopt a reformist line (earning them jeers from the ultra-Left) at times when they fear that more militant tactics will boomerang, driving the petty bourgeoisie and the peasants to the Right or even to fascism. But, whatever the tactics of the moment, the principle remains that unionism to Communists is a political weapon.

This is of course indignantly denied by Communist (or, more generally, Marxist) unions, and it is on this ground that they are always attacked by government and management. Both sides lie with enthusiasm, describing as political a strike called on economic issues and vice versa.

To cut through this confusion, we must distinguish between the political *consequences* of a strike or any other union action, and the union's political *ties* which cause it to base its tactics on the strategy of a political party: it is the difference between unionism as a political reality and unionism as a political instrument.

There can be no such thing as totally non-political unionism.

[2] The percentages of unionization are from J.-D. Reynaud in *Les Syndicats en France* (Paris: Seuil, 1975). Note the suspiciously vague figures for France and Italy. It seems hardly compatible with modern census techniques for the CGT, the French Communist union federation, not to be able to state within a million how many members it has—i.e. whether its membership is 1.5 or 2.5 million. It is as if the French government were able to give no more precise a figure for the nation's population than to say it was somewhere between 30 and 50 million. In such cases, the more pessimistic figure is usually the more accurate one.

Even the narrowest of union demands has economic consequences and political aftereffects. Politics in a democracy
expresses conflicting interests. Any major strike has a political aspect, because if it is important the strike cannot be settled between union and management without involving elected office-
holders, whether national or local. As we saw as early as the
nineteenth century in Great Britain, when the growth of the
labor movement led to the creation of the Labour party, the unions, expressing the will of the working class, put their stamp on
the nation's politics.

But when the union is controlled by a political party, it is the
party that puts its stamp on the union movement—and hopes
that it will be the only union movement. The British example
can be described as union politics; the latter example as politicized unionism. Whether a politicized union movement is
unyielding or moderate in its demands will depend not on the
economic situation but, for example, on the date of the next elections, or even on the party's desire to harass the government for
foreign policy reasons. That is why the leaders of such unions are
sometimes more aggressive, sometimes less so, than the workers
themselves. At times we see them launching an artificial strike
decided upon by the leadership, while on other occasions they
are busy trying to suppress strikes begun by the members.

The politics of an independent union movement grows out of
its experience, while the politics of a party-controlled union
movement is determined from the beginning. Yet it is the first
kind of union movement, which has its origins in working-class
needs, that is politically the more powerful. The socialist governments in West Germany, Britain and Sweden really emanate
from the major unions in those countries. In southern Europe, it
is the opposite: the major union movement emanates from the
Communist party.

Union membership is relatively small when its political align-
ment is a precondition rather than a consequence of joining the
union. The CGT, the French pro-Communist union federation
(whose secretary-general by tradition is a member of the politburo of the French Communist party), had in 1976 no more than

2 million members out of a working-class population of 22 million. (See footnote 2 in this chapter.) The other Marxist or radical-leftist union federation, the CFDT, which advocates socialist worker management, could claim at best 800,000 dues payers. Communist unions often call a strike simply to demonstrate how many workers will follow them. Since it only represents a small fraction of the working class, the union's bargaining power is weak when times are quiet. Its power increases when some social conflict makes its cause attractive to non-union workers who will then follow the union members out on strike. But if things go wrong the union lacks the means to support the strikers at a time when only the ability to hold out will enable the workers to win the test of strength.

The two forms of unionism produce quite different results for their members. By the end of the 1950s, German workers enjoyed higher pay and a shorter working day than the French; and so we see French workers who live near the border crossing the Rhine for jobs. In the same period worker co-management was instituted in many German firms: employee delegates and union representatives from outside the firm both sit on the board of directors, a true first step toward the sharing of economic power.

These political changes are far more basic than an electoral "surge to the left" in which all that happens is that the Left picks up a few more seats in the legislature. In Britain the Trades Union Congress often is in effect the government. It can guarantee the defeat at the polls of Labour and Conservative governments alike, and does so with the most serene impartiality—the first in 1970, for example, and the second in 1973—when they dare to oppose its demands; the TUC pursues its interests as it sees them with a rather dangerous indifference to such other national priorities as the fight against inflation and the need to reduce the balance of payments and foreign trade deficits. These unions do not say they want to change the society, but they have changed it and are still doing so.

The unions of the Latin nations, on the other hand, proclaim their desire to change the basic nature of society, but in fact they do not even succeed in altering the surface. They even make of their impotence an article of faith, and with good reason since they live on their revolutionary future, or, at least, their revolutionary rhetoric. Grimly they deny the possibility of any progress within the existing system, which presumably has remained unchanged since the dawn of capitalism. When the lot of the working class improves, they refuse to recognize the fact, and they remain silent when a law is adopted benefiting employees. According to them, the discontent of the workers is forever increasing, their purchasing power forever diminishing. So one is tempted to ask these union leaders: "What have you been doing for the last thirty or forty years? If it is true that the situation of 'the manual and intellectual workers of city and country'—to borrow a generously broad definition dear to the Communist party—has only worsened over all those years, then this hardly speaks well for your efforts. You are condemning yourselves in your own words. Either you're incompetent or you don't mean what you say."

But this kind of southern European unionism is very effective in carrying out the political objectives assigned to it, which are to subordinate union objectives to Communist strategy, and most of all to prevent the growth of a strong reformist union movement, because this would deprive the Communist bureaucracy of its role as virtually the only spokesman of the working class in dealing with management and the political authorities. This strategy was carried to its logical conclusion by the Portuguese Communists when, after the army had overthrown the heirs of the Salazar dictatorship, they convinced the ruling armed forces movement to impose a single labor union, despite the protests of the socialists, the social democrats and the centrists. Their control of the single union federation enabled the Communists, with a handful of well-trained activists strategically placed in each firm, to control the nation's economic life and to use that power for political purposes, especially in the press, radio and television. Thus, although they only won 13 per cent of the vote in the April 1975 elections, the Portuguese Communists could at will paralyze the economy and manipulate the news—they had, indeed, more actual power than the Socialists and the Social

Democrats together, who represented 64 per cent of the electorate. This is a fine example of the Communists' "dynamics" in
which thanks to their monopoly of organized labor they won a
share of political power far beyond their share of the vote. The
fewer the workers that belong to unions, the easier the monopoly
is to maintain. Exactly the Leninist model: the organized minority appoints itself as spokesman of the unorganized majority, and
employs any means to preserve its monopoly of that role. Thus
the numerical weakness of the union makes the political strength
of the party.

Finally, the third reason for the advance of Stalinism lies in
the meek response of the non-Communist Left. The Left's attitude toward Stalinism ranges from overt complicity to timid in-
action. The effect has been to discredit social democracy and
gradually to bring people to consider as transient and unimpor-
tant the basic characteristics of totalitarianism, and in any event
to see them as far less serious than the evils of capitalism. As a
result it is assumed—and for the Stalinists this is a dream come
true—that any criticism of communism must necessarily emanate
from the Right. Aside, that is, from communism's critics on the
ultra-Left, whose message usually boils down to attacking the
Stalinists for not being Stalinist enough. Thus the whole social
democratic school of thought, the socialism that saw itself as the
next step after the achieving of political freedom, has let itself be
placed on the defensive. Social democracy allows itself to be
viewed as a sort of watered-down Stalinism, or a variant form of
rightist paternalism, rather than as a distinctive political and intellectual movement. Having lost its faith in itself as the only
true leftist movement, social democracy fails to articulate a creative criticism of the Communists, except on those occasions
when, having been kneed particularly hard in the groin by the
Stalinists, it bleats forth an appeal for human rights—to no avail,
of course. Thus the silence, the absence of effective response to
Stalinism, that we see in democratic societies.

4

THE DEMOCRATIC
MISUNDERSTANDING

Before describing the symptoms of complacency toward Stalinism and searching out its causes, notably among those who
neither vote Communist nor are party members, we must stress
the reasons why there is not nor ever can be such a thing as "free
communism." This legendary beast is used by those who abet the
progress of Stalinism to deny any responsibility for the consequences of their position. They believe, so they say, in free communism—which they prefer to call "socialism"—and not in totalitarian communism.

But in reality it is always the second that gains ground, never
the first. Instead of asking what law of history is suggested by
this uniform outcome so often repeated, they tell us it is unfair to
judge "socialism" on the basis of experience. Indeed, what else
could they say? For history tells us this and this alone: to advocate the expansion of communism is to advocate the only kind of
communism there is, not the opposite variety.

For public relations purposes, Western Communist historians
describe Stalin's crimes—in the open-minded moments when
they even admit those crimes exist—as "accidents of history."
This rather unimaginative intellectual dodge simply demonstrates that these historians are scarcely Marxist. How, from a
Marxist point of view, can one explain so many accidents and deviations over so many decades without finding their causes in either the economic system, the social system or the political
order? Or, if one prefers, how can it be explained that this despotism has endured for more than half a century if it is not
rooted in a historically determined process? Surely it would be

the first case of its kind since the beginning of time, and it is ironic that the spokesmen of "scientific" socialism should be the first to offer us this odd application of Marx's historical materialism: one constant, Stalinism, long-lived and showing no sign of decay, in two such different nations as the Soviet Union and China, equally present in all their satellites and imitators—this constant is said to be the result of mere chance, a simple accident, bearing no relation to the system of which in fact it is an integral part.

To make plausible the notion of a history consisting entirely of a series of exceptions, one would have to be able to point to some moments, no matter how brief, at which the rule, not the exception, prevailed. But no such moments can be found in the history of the Soviet Union and Communist China because, to repeat, the essence of Stalinism lies not in its crescendos of murder and exile to labor camps but in the system that makes those abuses always possible, though they need not always be applied with the same degree of harshness.

No Communist state has ever been other than Stalinist. As for Communist parties in democratic states, they behave like missionaries in a pagan land. They have to come to terms with local superstitions and accept a degree of religious syncretism. But their tolerance is only temporary. Why submit to democratic decision-making if one knows the ultimate Good and has a scientific theory that determines how a society must be managed? Democracy is based on uncertainty. If the people believe the leadership is in error, they can replace them with other leaders. The opinion of the majority determines the society's direction because no one is totally committed to belief in an unarguable Verity. Thus the ability to convince others is the essential talent of political man in democracy. But if those in power are convinced they hold the absolute Truth and represent the only legitimate political interest, inevitably they will consider it their right and duty to impose their truth by any means, no matter what the public may think, or better still, by preventing the public from thinking at all. That is how most states throughout most of history have behaved, without any qualms of conscience. The abnormal in history is respect for pluralism, both of values and interests, within the social group and in its relations with foreign groups. The norm is intolerance and its corollary, legitimized violence. If I am certain of the truth of my doctrine, why should I permit freedom of opinion when it will only propagate error and impede the functioning of the one true social and moral order? The Catholic Church followed this principle for centuries, emulated in most cases by the Protestant sects that rebelled against its rule. Nor could the Church have acted otherwise in its role of guardian of the One True Faith. Similarly, the verbal endorsement by Communist missionaries in the West of human liberties and rotation in office can only be considered tactical concessions —useful to them since Communists are always in the minority in the democracies. Political pluralism has drawbacks only when one is in power, but in the opposition it is a pure asset. Why not exploit that asset? But the rights of the individual and of the opposition, instruments of the struggle against those in power, cannot be preserved in a socialist society, for no one can be permitted to oppose a righteous regime. Thus those rights are only temporarily conceded. If they held otherwise, the Communists would be untrue to their own beliefs.

The Chinese Communists and their European disciples were thus justified when they contested Khrushchev's "revisionist" condemnation of Stalin in 1956. The social democrats miss the point if they do not understand that "liberalization" and self-criticism in the Communist party has no more meaning than the in-and-out movement of an accordion. The accordion can be stretched to a certain point, but not beyond or it will break, and after being stretched it must once more be tightened. Maurice Thorez, the orthodox secretary-general of the French Communist party in Stalin's time, accurately conveyed the essence of Marxism-Leninism when he said: "The third cause of the errors committed by our party is that until very recently we were still very attached to democracy, we were not able to free ourselves, we could not break its hold on our party. Our party has grown in a nation which has been infested with democracy for fifty-seven years. This party has yet to lead any revolutionary battles, any serious struggles."[1]

The comparison may surprise, but to understand Leninism-Stalinism we must recognize that it is based on the same hypothesis (though with regrettably less literary merit) as Plato's political philosophy. Both assume there is an abstract model of society whose truth has been demonstrated once and for all. Reality must copy that ideal model as faithfully as possible. Politics consists of bringing the society as a whole, and each individual in his person, in behavior and in thought, as closely as possible into conformity with the ideal. Under both doctrines the people are to be led by a minority that alone comprehends the ideal in its entirety: in Plato, these are the philosopher-kings; in the Communist party, the Politburo and the Central Committee. Orders from the top are implemented and explained by a class that grasps their general purpose though they do not understand the ultimate theoretical principles of the ideal: Plato called them the warriors, and under communism, it is the rank and file of party members. Finally, in both systems, the peasants and the workers —Plato's artisans—labor to support the first two classes; they take their orders from above, though they are incapable of seeing how their work fits into the over-all plan, much less of understanding the theory from which that plan was derived. They are the majority of the people, and force may legitimately be used to compel their obedience. The people must be kept on the proper path; the rulers entertain no doubts about that path, for it is derived from a doctrine that has been definitively proved. The art of government therefore includes constant education and re-education and the permanent surveillance of the people—for their own good. In *Laws,* Plato provided for secret agents who would eavesdrop on conversations; citizens are required to

[1] From Thorez's speech in *Classe contre classe, la question française au IXe congrès exécutif et au VIe congrès de l'Internationale communiste* (Paris: Bureau d'éditions, 1929). Thorez was not officially made secretary-general of the party until January 1936, but by then he had been for at least ten years one of the most important French Communist leaders and one of Stalin's most faithful echoes.

denounce each other's deviations, and those who cannot be redeemed must be discreetly "liquidated."

Under Plato, just as under Stalin and Mao, culture is carefully regulated. Music, drama, dance, art, poetry and architecture, even gymnastics and dress, are in *The Republic* the topic of minutely detailed prescription and prohibition, just as they were to become in the twentieth century under the control notably of Zhdanov in the Soviet Union and Madame Mao Tse-tung in China, who were of course implementing the supreme theory: the thought of the philosopher-kings Joseph Stalin and Mao Tse-tung.

Given that state of mind, neither democracy as it is understood in the West nor even a flabby sort of "liberalization" can be an essential part of the system. Rather they are its opposite, its mortal enemy, just as dictatorship is the opposite and the mortal enemy of democracy. Do we let schoolchildren vote on whether they prefer Aristotle's cosmology or that of Copernicus? André Bonnard, a great Hellenist and also a great Stalinist sympathizer, summed up the logic of totalitarian censorship: "Any society that is aware that it embodies and protects precious values will take care not to allow a writer to use what he calls his talent to undermine those values. Thus censorship exists in the Soviet Union, as is natural in an organized society." That reasoning is invoked to some degree in all kinds of societies: what distinguishes the totalitarian states is the universal system of censorship that results from it.

Totalitarian ideology is used like any other to justify power. But it is not just a lie told by the masters, nor does it produce only liabilities for those to whom it is applied. If the masters were not in large measure sincere, the system would not be so implacably enforced: the cynic is more tolerant than the fanatic, and greed more accommodating than faith. If Stalinism worked only to the disadvantage of those it governs, repression would not suffice to keep it in power. But in the view of its administrators and their Western apologists, Stalinism must not be judged on a balance sheet, listing assets and liabilities from the point of view of the consumer. Even if you were to demonstrate with chapter and verse that the number of liabilities for those who are worst off is less in the Netherlands than in the Soviet Union, and that the average Dutch citizen enjoys more assets, this calculation would not shake their confidence any more than does information about the poor quality of Soviet life, or the trumped-up trials or the concentration camps. As Proust said in *Swann's Way:* "The facts of life do not penetrate to the sphere in which our beliefs are cherished; as it was not they that engendered those beliefs, so they are powerless to destroy them." To a Stalinist, the Netherlands or the United States is not a *real* society. It is to prevent such unseemly empirical comparisons that Stalinist governments forbid their citizens to travel abroad, reserving that favor for incorruptible party activists who are reliably equipped with ideological blinders. As the Czech cultural weekly *Tvorba* observed in 1972: "It is in our interest that those who travel to the West be worthy representatives of their socialist fatherland and not fall apart politically the first time they see a woman's sweater in a department store." Sometimes the government must allow out certain kinds of citizens for propaganda reasons—dancers, athletes, scientists—whose Leninist orthodoxy falls regrettably short of their talent, with the result that a steady percentage defect while they are abroad. But the average citizen must not be permitted to know any society but socialism. Unlike the advanced capitalist societies, socialist states have no problems with immigration, only emigration.

The price of a ticket on the Moscow subway has stayed the same for many years: one may respond by pointing to the chronic shortage of potatoes, but to no avail. (For that matter, the bus fare in Rome stayed at 50 lire, or $.15, for many years too—but what under socialism is a triumph, under capitalism is mere hypocrisy, to which the proper reproach is silence.) The socialist says that under capitalism people are crushed by the rising cost of transportation; that they also enjoy abundant supplies of low-priced potatoes is irrelevant, because their societies are basically corrupt. The stable subway fare in Moscow is a normal product of socialism; the shortage of potatoes is a momentary mishap. Under capitalism it is the opposite: whatever functions poorly is due to the basic laws of the system, while anything that works well is accidental and transient. It serves no purpose in such a debate to recall the facts of Russian history: industrialization largely under way before 1917; peasants worse off under Stalin than in the late nineteenth century; industrial working conditions amounting to serfdom; industrial production geared to the service of the state—weapons, aircraft, space travel —not to the goods that would have raised the people's standard of living. But suppose we discern, in certain socialist countries, the first tardy birth pangs of the consumer society? In that case consumption, which in the West was always a decoy, just another way in which the workers were alienated, now in the East suddenly becomes a liberating force. But how did the dishwasher, which in Paris is a toy of the oppressors, a tool for alienating and subtly exploiting the workers, how did that machine in Moscow become the symbol of socialist success and the good life? Silly question! In Paris the "contradictions of capitalism" produce the inevitable evils of a free society, while what happens in Moscow results from a basically correct line.

Even with a correct line, however, unessential mistakes will happen, as Communists "admit." But the "criticisms" of socialist living conditions published in the Eastern European press, cited often by Communists in the West as proof that the East is not totalitarian, always attack the erroneous interpretation or incompetent execution of orders from the summit, never the summit itself nor its system. Error, when it is publicly recognized, is always error in execution, never error in leadership and still less in principle. Errors in general policy are recognized and possibly punished, by the purge of those responsible, only in secret within the oligarchy itself—and of course without questioning the basic principles of Stalinist socialism.

That's why Nikita Khrushchev's famous speech on Stalin's tyranny, delivered at the 20th Party Congress in 1956, did not and could not initiate a real de-Stalinization. Khrushchev denounced only Stalin's crimes against party leaders and the Communist bureaucracy, not his oppression of the people. Furthermore, Khrushchev delivered his speech behind closed doors and only to the party hierarchy; it was never published in the Soviet Union nor willingly in the Western Communist press, where only brief excerpts appeared after the speech had been published all over the world in the "bourgeois" press. In Khrushchev's eyes, Stalin's crime was that he broke faith with the ruling oligarchy to make himself king over the barons, tyrant over the tyrants, assassin of the assassins and torturer of the torturers. It was not that Stalin enslaved the Soviet people, for they remained enslaved: under Khrushchev Gulag was still there with its tens of millions of prisoners; so were the mental hospitals used as political prisons, and police surveillance, and censorship. Six months after his speech, Khrushchev the de-Stalinizer was sending tanks to shoot down Hungarians rebelling against Stalinism. Orthodox in his dialectical materialism, Khrushchev even inflicted once more on Soviet science the rule of Stalin's geneticist Lysenko, the charlatan whose theories had already done so much damage to both basic research and agricultural production.

What many failed to see was that Khrushchev's speech was directed against Stalin but not against Stalinism. It was intended to enable the Stalinist system to survive by ridding it of those pathological excesses that would eventually have destroyed the regime itself. Stalin was leading Russia toward ruin by slaughtering or intimidating the ruling bureaucracy and exterminating ever larger sections of the working population. It was vital to put the system back in working order by instituting what one might call a healthy totalitarianism. The "thaw" was just that, and not a move toward democracy. Today the Khrushchev 1956 speech is officially buried, and in the history books the time of "subjectivism" (Khrushchev) is more severely condemned than the time of the "cult of personality" (Stalin).

Just as we cannot find even the embryo of a tendency toward liberalization in the history of Communist regimes, we find that Communist parties in the democracies have never renounced Stalinist practices long enough and in sufficient degree for us to conclude that they have undergone a metamorphosis. All we find are minor changes that in no way alter the basics of the system. The liberal socialists keep mistaking a swing of the pendulum for

The Totalitarian Temptation

the beginnings of continuing change. The return swing of the pendulum always comes as an unpleasant surprise to the Communists' allies, for they cannot find a rational explanation for the sudden softening and hardening of the party line. But there is a rational explanation from the Communist viewpoint. If the socialists cannot find the explanation, it is for the valid scientific reason—Marxists will understand this point—that they are operating on a false hypothesis. Socialists insist on diagnosing as the symptom of some future democratization what in fact is only a classic Communist tactic: the so-called Popular Front, or Union of the Left. This tactic has two goals: to postpone the conflict with the "Right" when it is in the party's opinion too strong to be overcome by frontal attack; and above all to prevent the development of a reformist or social democratic movement by dividing into two camps the social groups and the voters that would make up such a movement. Those in one camp are rendered ineffective by their alliance with the Communists, the others by their alliance with more conservative forces.

Communist "liberalization" reflects neither good will nor broad-mindedness. The temporary and purely verbal concessions Communists are forced to make for the sake of their electoral alliances never go so far as to question the methods of communism, which when it triumphs will eliminate both allies and elections, nor its ultimate goal, which remains "bureaucratic centralism": the irreversible creation of a state under the authoritarian rule of the single party.

No matter how Machiavellian its intentions, the party in opposition must not compromise itself to the point that it is not in condition to carry out that eventual responsibility. The party in a free society must reflect the future, must be the miniature prototype of the society to come; it must be kept ready to be inserted in working order into that society, as the motor is inserted in the chassis or the soul into the body. If the party ever ceased being the "model" of the order it seeks to impose on society, its future could not be realized and its present behavior would make no sense.

The "liberal" concessions Communists can make are neces-

46

sarily very limited if they are not to repudiate their own policies. One can give up communism, but one can hardly change one's way of being Communist. That is why the most substantial concessions Communists make to democratic ideals apply always to the future, never the present; they are promises rather than deeds. The Communists will promise to respect human rights should they come to power with the Socialists or the Christian Democrats. There are many ways in which the Communists could—but do not—demonstrate that respect for human rights now, while they are in the opposition. Thus only the Communist press refuses to implement legislation guaranteeing the right to reply, and only that press consistently mounts personal attacks on those who express opinions differing from its own. If the Communists believe that anyone who now criticizes them is "selling out" or "playing the imperialists' game," why would they believe otherwise when they are in power, even power shared with other parties? Is it not the duty of the state, for which they would share responsibility, to stamp out corruption and punish those who serve foreign interests? The justification for a future elimination of freedom of expression can be read in the polemics of Communists in the democracies. According to the Communists, no one differs with them in good faith. Therefore, to silence a critic of the Communists, or an opponent of a government in which they take part, is merely to punish a servant of monopoly capital or an agent of American or Chinese propaganda. This will be defined as a criminal proceeding against conspiracy, not interference with free speech. One may argue that the Communists' allies will prevent any such outcome. But the question once more is why don't those allies force the Communists to respect human rights today? If democratic socialists are unable to make the Communists give up their totalitarian practices, of which the socialists are often the primary targets, when both are in the opposition, how could they do so if the Communists were sharing in the powers of government?

Those who do not understand how Communist parties operate understand nothing of contemporary politics.

The Right and the cold warriors made the mistake of equating communism with pre-war Nazism and Fascism, whereas all the three have in common is their organization and their savage methods. Nazism and Fascism, limited by their identification with the national interest of their respective states, did not enjoy the ideological appeal that has made communism a global force. The cold warriors counterattacked with military preparations, intelligence, counterespionage and propaganda, not realizing that the Communists were more effective than they on that terrain, and, moreover, that the West had to provide an ideological response to communism. If indeed such a response is possible. One faith is best countered by another faith, not by a solution, and a response made up of a package of solutions and unresolved problems is still less likely to prevail.

The non-Communist Left has either rejected Stalinist dogma and chosen social democracy, as in West Germany, Britain and northern Europe, or, in the countries where Communist power is the determining fact of political life, it has alternately allied itself and broken with the Communists. Each time such an alliance is at issue, the non-Communist Left proclaims that socialists and Communists agree on the basics but differ on details, whereas the truth is precisely the opposite. Each time the Left feels the need to believe that the Communists have changed, are changing, will change. Each time their hopes are disappointed as they learn of some fresh proof of totalitarianism, either in the East—in Budapest, in Prague, in the Gulag—or at home in the ranks of their Communist allies. And each time the Left fails to make the connection between this latest event and all the similar events that preceded it. The event that has upset their theorizing is depicted as an accident, to be followed by a period of convalescence during which the party will examine its conscience and emerge with its moral fiber definitively restored.

It is characteristic of the neurotic—and I am using the word in its literal sense—that he responds to reality with behavior based on fantasy. He is unable either to adapt to reality or to understand it. That is why his behavior is ineffectual.

Neurotics always forget the last episode in which their neurosis manifested itself. The person who is always late to appointments, the businessman who always falls into the same traps, the con man's victim who knows better but is always available to be swindled once more—when misfortune strikes, each can offer a unique explanation for something he believes has never before happened to him. Yet to everyone else their behavior follows a pattern that has manifested itself many times in the past. Similarly, the debates between Communists and leftists in 1973 that followed the publication in the West of the writings of Soviet dissidents—Maximov, Sakharov, Jaurès and Roy Medvedev, Sinyavsky, Amalrik and above all Solzhenitsyn and his *Gulag Archipelago*—were carbon copies of debates that had taken place more than twenty years earlier, when the European Left first heard reports about the concentration camps in the Soviet Union. Among French intellectuals the earlier debate centered on the polemics between Camus and Sartre, in which Camus was right but Sartre won. The political point to observe here is that everything that happened on the earlier occasion—the horrified reaction of the non-Communists; their effort to maintain a dialogue with the Communists while firmly condemning Soviet behavior; the furious response of the Communists, who accused the Left of playing the reactionaries' game and compromising the cause of peace (later it became détente); the Left backing down in shame; the final surrender in which the Left despite a few grumbles expressed its hopes for the future—all this was repeated word for word, argument for argument, during the Solzhenitsyn affair of 1973–74. But none of the actors were aware that they were working from the script of a melodrama that dated from twenty years earlier, and which itself was no more than a revival of the performance staged in the West at the time of the Moscow trials of 1937.

Lessons are never remembered in this land of ignorance and forgetfulness. The same classic situations recur, but no one recognizes them. The same quotations, the same names, the same arguments are recited as if discovered for the first time. The historical memory of the Left is like that of a pillow: it changes shape when pounded by a fist, but it doesn't know how to avoid the blow, and it always peacefully regains its original shape, ready for the next pounding.

If the non-Communist Left had remembered and analyzed the past—which should be the minimum responsibility of political leaders and intellectuals alike—it would not have failed to observe that all those scenarios were the same. Then it could not for long have maintained the myth of "regrettable incidents" and "deviations that have now been corrected," nor could it have escaped the conclusion that these various events taken together constitute a clear historical pattern. But on the whole the non-Communist Left everywhere has failed to view events in that way; it prefers to forget rather than to understand.

That understanding would have forced the Left to give up its hope that communism and democratic socialism would in time draw closer together. It would have been forced to recognize that the Communists advocate (and in power, implement) a social design that categorically excludes democracy. The design may not be a bad one: that's another issue. But it will neither preserve nor institute democracy. Communism does not destroy democracy where it had once existed—Czechoslovakia before 1948—in order to revive it at some future time. When communism destroys democracy, it does so because that is its intent. And when it fails to create democracy, that is because it is not in its nature to do so.

THE SOCIALIST
MISUNDERSTANDING

Except when it opts for social democracy, as it has in northern Europe, the non-Communist Left persists in the mistaken belief that communism is a form of socialism. It is nothing of the sort. The goal of communism is to destroy capitalism, but not to install socialism, which means to make the economy serve the people. Communism's goal is to make both the economy and the people serve what Milovan Djilas called "the new class"—the ruling bureaucracy. Power under bureaucratic rule is based not on property, as under capitalism, but on holding office. Workers are more rigorously subjugated under bureaucratic than under capitalist rule and the methods by which they are "exploited" (which, in Marxist terms, consists of expropriating the surplus value they produce) are more direct and authoritarian. Since the ruling bureaucracy controls the labor unions, the workers have no way of defending their interests, except perhaps by malingering. The rule of the new class necessarily requires a system of government under which citizens have no political rights and are constantly subject to police surveillance, and a purged and censored cultural life peopled by eunuchs who have surrendered any thought of resistance.

Culture being a cause of friction between the two Lefts, the Stalinists have always claimed that cultural repression was aimed not at freedom of thought but at the political manipulations that are supposedly concealed in artistic opinions. At the time when the French Communist party was trying to impose the dreary and ludicrous aesthetics of "socialist realism" on its members and sympathizers, it promoted an artistic disaster named Fougeron, a painter whose torpid pretentiousness was too much even for some party activists. One of these went so far as to complain to a party leader: "I am being persecuted because I don't like Fougeron's painting." That party leader, Laurent Casanova, replied, "You don't understand at all, for the basic question is that the reservations about Fougeron were *expressed in such a way that they constituted a political attack against the party.*" This revealed the vicious circle: since Fougeron's promotion was motivated by the politics of Moscow's aesthetic "line," it was impossible to judge him purely on his artistic talent. In any event, without the party's sponsorship, Fougeron would never have reached a standing in the world of art where his talent was worthy of discussion—any more than Lysenko would have in the world of genetics.

Totalitarianism politicizes all areas of life by definition, and subsequently smells out politics behind any form of cultural dissidence. The same sophistry was employed, and with more than a little success, to try to prevent the Left in the West from fighting for Solzhenitsyn's and Sakharov's freedom of speech in 1973: according to the party, the issue of freedom of speech only camouflaged an attack on détente.

Thus do the Communists ingenuously admit that they are totalitarian. For it is in the nature of a totalitarian regime that it believes no human activity can exist independently of itself, with its own set of values, but must rather be judged merely as an aspect of the ruling political system. Totalitarianism does not condemn a work of art because it conceals a political motive. It is because the regime is totalitarian that in its eyes a work of art always has a political dimension—more accurately, *only* a political dimension: for or against the regime—none of whose parts can be considered independently of the whole.

These facts have been well known for a long time, for the nature of totalitarian regimes has been abundantly documented. The real question is why the information has had so little impact on political thought and on people's feelings.

It no longer needs to be demonstrated that Communist regimes are opposed both to Marx's form of Marxism and to (or *therefore* to) the ideals of democratic socialism. What we need to know is why so many refuse to acknowledge that proof and act accordingly—for that refusal is perhaps the greatest single impediment to all efforts to solve the world's political and social problems. The revolution that the world so urgently needs cannot be brought about until the socialists realize that communism rather than capitalism is their most formidable foe. A society can make the transition from capitalism to socialism, never from communism to socialism. The fact that socialists and Communists find the same faults in capitalism does not mean that they both intend to replace it with the same political order. Though the efforts of the future new class to seize power from the present owners of capitalist society may parallel for the time being the complaints of working-class citizens against those same owners, nonetheless the goal of the new class is still power for itself, not for the workers. Marxists should have no trouble understanding that elementary historical analysis.

That is why there is no validity to the familiar contention that liberal socialists must be careful to stand aloof from defenders of capitalism in making their case against Stalinism. Representatives of capitalism combat Stalinism because it wants to destroy them; socialists need feel no shame in doing the same, and for the same reason: because Stalinism wants to destroy them too. Socialists simply give away something for nothing whenever they allow Stalinist propagandists to put them in the same category as capitalists because both oppose Stalinist methods; Stalinism threatens socialists just as much, though in a different way, as it does capitalism. Furthermore, one finds in capitalist societies many democrats who reject Stalinism on the same grounds as the socialists: because they believe in political democracy and pluralism. Those who deny the importance of such people, on the pretext that to recognize it would be "playing the reactionary game," are in reality playing the Stalinist game, for the Stalinists always try to evade the issue of democracy so they can use the socialists to destroy capitalism, and later destroy democracy at the expense of the socialists.

Nor is there any excuse for the illusion that socialists and

The Totalitarian Temptation

Communists can wage a common struggle up to a certain point, after the demise of capitalism, when the choice will be made between democracy and totalitarianism. Communism will always be stronger when that time arrives, even if it wins fewer votes (as indeed has always been the case) than the democratic parties. Should the Communists ever win more votes than the others they will be invincible. Why should a party that acts as if it had unanimous support when it is in the minority change its bahavior when it wins a plurality of the vote? And, once communism is in power, the cause of socialism is lost beyond any appeal: an effective opposition can be organized against capitalism, never against bureaucratic rule. It is easier to correct economic and social inequity than to win freedom from political despotism.

In addition to this historical record, we may invoke the testament of the founders of socialism, whose will has been violated to such an extent that one of the experts in the field could call as a witness *Marx critique du marxisme* (*Marx Criticizes Marxism*), the 1974 book by Maximilien Rubel, who has edited the best French edition of Marx's works. In a chapter whose title, "Marx and Democracy," suggests that it is more funeral oration than political program, the author even suggests that the term "Marxism" be abandoned. The term is useless or even harmful, he contends, because "Marxism" is either associated with regimes that have destroyed Marx's ideas, or it is just a synonym for socialism in general.

Other equally qualified authors can cite numerous texts showing that Marx held the idea of party, and even more the single party, to be incompatible with the proletarian revolution, and that, notably in his polemic with Bakunin, he virulently condemned that already Leninist party of "priests of a secret science" whose code of conduct can be summarized in the formula "those who are not with us are against us," that party which "aspires only to perpetuating dictatorship" of its "barracks communism."[1] If the words were not those of Marx, the cry

[1] Quoted by Kostas Papaïoannou in *L'Idéologie froide, essai sur le dépérissement du marxisme* (J.-J. Pauvert, 1967). See Chapter I: "Marxisme et orthodoxie."

would be raised that they were vehicles for the "obsessive and vulgar anti-communism" of the enemies of détente and of the Union of the Left. After all, one could denounce in the same terms the anti-communism of Lenin, who in 1895, before he had become completely Leninist, wrote in his obituary article on Engels: Marx and Engels "both become socialists after being democrats, and the democratic feeling of hatred for political despotism was exceedingly strong in them. This direct political feeling, combined with a profound theoretical understanding of the connection between political despotism and economic oppression, and also their rich experience of life, made Marx and Engels uncommonly responsive politically."

But what is the use of these quotations, or the thousand others that could be cited to make the same point? Knowledge of the original texts, while necessary to understanding them—for those few who are concerned with understanding—has never affected the behavior of sects or rulers. The history of the heirs of Aristotle, Jesus and Freud—as well as Marx—demonstrates that the more they make a fetish of the founder's words, the less they can agree on the meaning of any given statement, no matter how clear the founder's thought may seem to an outsider. What a paradox! The clearer the thought appears, the more it is generally necessary to use force, ranging from a monopoly on education through brainwashing to capital punishment, to make everyone understand the orthodox interpretation of the founder's words.

If the contrast between Marx's thought and the actions of the regimes that call themselves Marxist causes more scholarly debate than political change, it is because it is easier to bend philosophy to fit reality than to do the opposite. Deposing Stalin is a risky undertaking, while any one with an adaptable conscience can justify him—and Mother Nature has made adaptability more common in the human conscience than in the world of facts. Thus those who take an indulgent view of totalitarianism are discouraged neither by the fading historical image of that ghost known as the "original and authentic inspiration" of Marxism nor by information on the reality of life in Communist nations. I am aware that the ideological spokesmen of those countries emphasize that they have not yet reached the state of communism, but have only achieved socialism. Let us say then that Communist states can be defined as those in which all power is in the hands of a single political party that calls itself Communist.

Those nations are in no manner socialist. Western leftists are blocked from perceiving Communist reality by their obsessive clinging to the belief that those countries represent a first step on the road to socialism. That pious belief cannot, I repeat, be refuted even by libraries full of information showing that Communist regimes resulted from revolutions that, while anticapitalist, were neither proletarian nor socialist. These regimes make sense in their own terms; they are not in transition, successful or otherwise, to socialism. As the author of one of the best studies of bureaucratic totalitarianism wrote: "The bureaucracy doesn't keep the promises of socialism, but it keeps its own promises."[2]

Shamefaced sympathizers with totalitarianism can always avoid facing the uncomfortable facts of communism by shifting the discussion to the "essence" of socialism, "essence" being easier to manage than reality. Or else they will say that communism as rule by the new class or state capitalism is an old theory that made the rounds long ago. That's true, which is what makes that response so interesting. That the earth is round is also an old theory that made the rounds long ago. But if a billion people were still navigating as if the earth were flat it would be fascinating to search out the reasons for their cosmological belief and their nautical behavior.

[2] Marc Paillet, *Marx contre Marx* (Denoël, 1971). Paillet is at the heart of the phenomenon when he says: "The fundamental dispossession of the capitalists can take place through the state taking over the apparatus of production without that causing the realization of socialism . . ." This dispossession entails "a new organization of society . . . an economy which warrants, at the level of the state and of the firm, a new ruling class which appropriates the surplus value in an original way, that is, precisely through institutional mechanisms: such is the reason for the surprising appearance of the ruling bureaucracy. Its place had been vacant. It was installed there by the socialist revolution. People became aware at once of the place and of its occupant. Hence, the reaction of surprise."

Since no example of Leninist socialism is other than totalitarian and bureaucratic, one wonders how the doctrinaire ideologists can dismiss so disdainfully those who point out that the promise of socialism in freedom, while surely praiseworthy, remains a promise only, not something experienced in reality. The utopia of socialism with human face has been crushed everywhere even before it could be born. (How distressing that *becoming* humane, which should be the least we could expect from a regime dedicated to liberating humanity, should present for socialism a problem as impossible as squaring the circle. A Marxist-Leninist, that is to say a "scientific" socialist, surely should seek out the cause of this recurring failure. In science a law is that hypothesis which is verified by all experimental observation. Perhaps present-day Marxists are going to stage still another of their many epistemological revolutions by offering this innovative definition: the law shall be that hypothesis which is verified by none of the experiments. It would seem more "scientific" to consider the possibility that the hypothesis is wrong, that there is no inherent democratic tendency in communism, that communism is not akin to but incompatible with what we can call (without too much black humor) socialism—or, more precisely, the ideal of socialism, for, if Communist states are a reality, socialism has never existed except as an ideal.

Neither serious discussion of the totalitarian nature of Communist states nor rigorous evaluation of their economic performance is possible as long as Communist reality is confused with the socialist ideal. Failure to distinguish between facts and intentions is very convenient for those who would prefer not to recognize the former or define the latter. Thus they can escape both the overwhelming verdict of history and the intellectual requirements of formulating any serious program for the future. According to the "progressive" interpretation, poverty, disorganization, waste, even the purges are all merely blemishes on a socialist economy that admittedly is still functioning poorly.

But actually Communist societies function marvelously well, at least from the point of view of their ruling oligarchies. Seldom has a political system so adequately fulfilled its expectations. For the bureaucracy, the priority above all others is to preserve its power. Once that is assured, the bureaucracy has no objection to a rise in the standard of living provided it is not incompatible with the bureaucracy's authority. When there is a conflict of interest—should some form of material progress require or threaten to produce greater freedom for some workers—the bureaucracy will maintain its power at the expense of material progress.

But it would prefer not to have to choose, and it is a vile slander to accuse the bureaucracy of deliberately keeping its people's standard of living below that of the capitalist countries. But it can permit no breach in its authoritarian centralized control of the economy, for that is the very cornerstone of its political power. Such a system produces poor economic results but is politically indispensable. However, the bureaucracy presumably would be glad to improve the economy on any occasion when it could do so without compromising political stability.

It is because economics is subordinated to politics that the rulers do not have to pay for their mistakes. As I observed earlier, whereas in democracy errors in management are supposed to be paid for by those in office, under communism they are paid for by the people. The expiation of error usually requires purges which, while they lop off a few heads among the oligarchs, strike most heavily among the party rank and file and the masses. In other words, those who participated least in the misguided policy are the most heavily punished. One of the best observers of China, Lucien Bianco, described Mao Tse-tung's "irresponsibility" during the Great Leap Forward of 1958 and again during the Cultural Revolution several years later, in a 1975 series of articles in *Le Monde* that stirred an angry response in certain philanthropic Parisian circles (their anger naturally being directed at the author, not Mao). In both cases the economy was thrown into disorder and millions into misery by arbitrary, seemingly crazy decisions taken in the capriciousness of absolute power. These acts were certainly "irresponsible" toward the Chinese people, but not with regard to their real purpose, which was to re-establish Mao's dominant political power at the top of the bureaucracy. Andrei Sakharov, in his terrifying description of daily life under totalitarian rule,[3] described in detail how the poverty and degradation of the masses were favorable to maintaining the police state and therefore were politically necessary. Thus what to the people seems a calamity, and to the lower ranks of the bureaucracy a series of incoherent events, will be viewed at the top of the oligarchy as proof of the logic and the smooth functioning of the system.

On the other hand, the fact that such a system is viewed by so many in other countries as only a somewhat overly energetic version of socialism is one of the strangest political and cultural enigmas of our times.

[3] *My Country and the World* (New York: Knopf, 1975).

Two

OF DOCILITY TOWARD
STALINISM:
ITS MANIFESTATIONS
AND ITS CONSEQUENCES

6

THE FEAR OF
ANTI-COMMUNISM

In July 1975 the Soviet press agency Tass put out a communiqué attacking the French Minister of the Interior, Michel Poniatowski, for his "anti-Communism and anti-Sovietism," which Tass blamed on Poniatowski's desire to attract attention after failing to advance his career by other means. Thus personal insult was added to the political point. Note that the supposed Communist change of style in honor of détente is, like other Communist changes, in practice hard to discern. Secondly, while Poniatowski had indeed frequently attacked the French Communist party during the previous year, he had not similarly criticized the Soviet Union except for its past. Thus the charge of "anti-Sovietism" was just vituperation. Of course to describe the French Communists as "fascistic and totalitarian" may suggest that the same adjectives could be applied to the nation that is their model, but this hardly constitutes an attack on the Soviet state in its international role. As Soviet leaders are forever reminding us, the principle of détente is better relations among nations without any relaxation of "ideological vigilance," indeed with renewed vigilance to prevent contamination through contact with the infidels. Why should the capitalists relax their vigilance while the Soviets are increasing theirs?

Besides, when Communist leaders denounce capitalism, they do not receive in return a note from Western foreign ministries charging them with "obsessive anti-capitalism" and sordid self-seeking, and even lowering themselves to playing on totalitarian prejudices against the West, all this to make up for the terrible mediocrity of their own professional lives. Any such statement would be condemned and derived as narrow-minded and stupid by most of the Western press itself. Certainly it would arouse more lively protests than greeted the message from Tass, which —as a French radio commentator euphemistically put it—"often" expresses official Soviet views.

The incident highlights the difference in the means of action available to East and West in the defense and promotion of their respective political systems. When you think about it—and considering only the interaction between the two systems without making any value judgment about their respective merits—the Communists have the right to be represented in the rival camp by parties, newspapers and unions, while the West has no similar rights in the East; and a spokesman for a Western party cannot even attack the local Communist party for purely domestic reasons without being charged with "anti-Sovietism" and endangering international relations. Those interested in logic and consistency will also note that the umbilical cord that links the Soviet state to the Western Communist parties, which must not be mentioned when the independence of those parties is questioned, becomes a part of international law when the Soviet Union feels it has been disparaged through one of those parties. This is flagrant interference by Moscow in the domestic affairs of another sovereign state, and it is surprising how passively it is accepted by that state. If to be anti-Communist is to be anti-Soviet, the Soviet Union's right to enter into our domestic debates grows out of our respect for democracy, and those who are offended when the Soviets do so are themselves opposed to democratic principles.

Doubtless it was in that spirit that French officials hastened to let it be known that Tass's rebuke to Poniatowski would not affect Moscow's benevolent attitude toward Paris. The proof was that the French Minister of Finance, in Moscow at the time to negotiate a commercial agreement, was not asked to leave by the Soviets. Détente was not halted.

But, someone will say, Poniatowski is a right-wing conservative, a reactionary, who really does preach anti-communism. So he just got the rebuke he deserved. How often have I heard this sort of reasoning, even from non-Communists. It only goes to show the extent to which Stalinism is accepted.

Yet why on earth should it be reprehensible for a right-wing conservative to be anti-Communist? Is it considered contemptible or lacking in style for the Communists to attack the parties and institutions to which they are by definition opposed? The Communists are forever denouncing "an unprecedented anti-Communist and anti-Soviet campaign" (since they have been discovering one a day for the past sixty years, one wonders how they can all be "unprecedented"), this campaign being "orchestrated" by "unrepentant anti-Communists" (the word "unrepentant" striking a theological note of sin and repentance). It would of course be reprehensible in a democracy to deny Communists the right to participate in politics, but they in turn attempt to deny the same right to others. Political parties are not usually asked to praise their opponents. No one demands that the British Labourites and Tories stop attacking each other, and no one shouts "obsessive anti-Democrat" when that party in the United States comes under the usual campaign fire.

Thus we can conclude that the Communists have already demonstrated, in democratic systems and before coming to power, in spite of all they say, especially since their recent profession of "liberalization" and acceptance of "pluralism," that they are incapable of conceiving of politics as anything but a monopoly—their own. They arrive at this conclusion by claiming, and ultimately believing and even making others in part believe, that no one becomes anti-Communist because he has honest reservations about communism, or serious reasons for not wanting to live under Communist rule, or has had unfortunate experiences in his dealings with Communists, but only through innate anti-communism. He expresses those reservations, states those reasons, exploits those experiences only because he was already anti-Communist. His belief predates any observation of reality; anti-communism is thus not an effect but the original cause. Anti-communism in this view is never a result of historical observation, only an evil predisposition. Thus the publication in the West of *The Gulag Archipelago* was the result of an international plot "knowingly orchestrated" by "enemies of détente." It was the duty of readers of the book to ignore the facts that it revealed, for otherwise they would reveal themselves to be stained with "visceral" anti-communism. Readers could not reach conclusions unfavorable to communism based on the facts related by Solzhenitsyn, but only because their souls were already contaminated with anti-communism. That is why they gave credence, and still worse, echoed Solzhenitsyn's rumors, thus taking part in the international plot that, by no coincidence, was being hatched at that very time.

If anti-communism is unacceptable coming from an outright reactionary who is shamefully proud of his beliefs—the party would grant his right to be reactionary if he was not anti-Communist, which is to say he is entitled to his opinions as long as he abandons any views that might damage the good repute of his adversaries—the Communists are incomparably more intolerant of criticism emanating from actual or potential allies who claim to agree with them in principle. Rightist criticism is automatically discredited as based on blind prejudice serving class interests. When it is muttered on the Left, criticism is also rejected as "playing the rightist game" and revealing in those who express it the same venomous anti-Communist prejudice, all the more insidious, all the more venomous, for being better concealed. So it is that there can be no such thing as honest and objective criticism of communism.

The Communists also believe that any criticism coming from the Left arises, not from an analysis or even just a perception of the facts that differs from their own, but rather from the secretly persisting presence in their psyches of that toxic, mysterious and baleful substance: anti-communism. This maleficent and corrosive substance is akin to the "virtues" or "entelechies" of the Schoolmen, who explained the phenomena of nature not by the relation of cause and effect, but by properties inherent to bodies. According to them, a stone falls, not due to weight and gravity (of which they were unaware), but because of the stone's inherent tendency to go downward, or, as in Moliére's satire, the poppy is a soporific "because it contains a dormitive virtue which has the capacity to induce sleep." The souls of outright reactionaries are totally stained in black with this kind of innate property of anti-communism, which predates any knowledge, but at least one knows what to expect from them. It is far more pernicious among friends and allies, whose refusal to submit entirely to party doctrine despite their similar ideologies sends the Communists into fits of exasperated suspicion.

Members of the non-Communist Left often learn this at their own expense. Thus, right after the signing in June 1972 of the joint platform that sealed the alliance between France's Socialist and Communist parties, Georges Marchais, the Communist secretary-general, made a report to the Central Committee of his party in which he condemned their new allies as incurable reformists. Most notably, Marchais said: "It is true that the platform is not socialist, that it could only be agreed upon by eliminating any ideological confrontation, that we made our [Socialist] interlocutors acknowledge that we must limit ourselves to a common plan of action; that we have accepted no compromise that infringes on our principles, on the line set at our congresses, on the rights of the workers or on our international duties; and that we will be vigilant in promoting our own party's position and its independence of opinion and action, and in reinforcing its influence and its organization." Long kept secret, Marchais's report was only made public three years later (by Étienne Fajon, another Communist leader, in his book *L'Union est un combat*). Stung to the quick, Socialist leader François Mitterrand reacted with a vigor uncharacteristic of the forbearance with which he had previously accepted the blows dealt him by his allies. He proclaimed himself saddened by the duplicity of the statement "adopted by the Central Committee of the Communist party two days after we drank the champagne of friendship at the Place du Colonel Fabien" (where the Paris headquarters of the French Communist party is located). Mitterrand spoke with bitter sarcasm of the Communist strategy as "based on an alliance with a partner whom they deem incapable of being other than a traitor and a relapsed heretic." But anyone who fails to understand that the partner must inevitably be so judged merely shows that he was not raised on a diet of Marxist tradition, or else that he has fallen prey to the old illusion of believing that a Communist party can repudiate Stalinism without destroying both its internal cohesion and its public façade. The Communists can repudiate some of the manifestations of Stalinism—its "excesses"—but never its essence.

That explains the ambiguity of the Western Communists' condemnation of the Warsaw Pact military intervention in Czechoslovakia. The French Communist party undoubtedly disapproved of the intervention, almost as much as did its Italian counterpart, but at the same time it forbade all other political and union groups from joining it in that opinion. Granted the Soviet invasion was to be deplored, but it must not be used as a pretext for anti-Sovietism. Though the Communist newspaper *L'Humanité* at first dissociated itself from the invasion, it ran no less than eleven articles justifying the Soviet action between August 23 and September 8 of 1968. It scolded the Left to the effect that no one should be allowed to draw anti-Communist or anti-Soviet conclusions from those admittedly regrettable events. Should we therefore understand that scientific political analysis must not be permitted to derive the cause from its effects? The fact that the water is bad never suggests that the well from which it is drawn is poisoned.

The Communists' allies must, if they want the alliance to last, at least pretend that they believe that fine example of magical reasoning. Often they find themselves in the schizoid situation of having to put up with Stalinist brutality while proclaiming that this in no way slows the inevitable process of Communist liberalization. Once they have let Stalinist terror box them into its system of contradictory logic, men of the Left are haunted by the fear of being accused of that sinful property of the soul—anti-communism. For example, in July 1975, the Portuguese Socialist leader Mario Soares appeared on television with the Communist secretary-general, Alvaro Cunhal, at a time when the Socialists, though Portugal's largest party, were constantly being hoodwinked and threatened by the much less numerous Communists. Soares is no dupe, in fact he is among the toughest in the Socialist flock, and yet his first words were: "We don't practice anti-communism." Note that it is the victim of aggression and duplicity who has to exonerate himself while the perpetrator, magnanimous and for the moment affable, would not dream of saying, "We don't practice anti-socialism." That would sound ridiculous, but more importantly, neither he nor his adversaries believe he has anything to account for. By contrast, socialists and reformers all over the world feel they have to preface any daring statement with this absurd disclaimer: "We sometimes criticize the Communists, but we are not anti-Communists."

That is absurd because one is "anti" something to the extent that one finds fault with it, neither more nor less. If one is opposed to the Soviet Union's concentration camps and denial of human rights, then one is to that extent anti-Communist. At the same time, one can be pro-Communist to the extent of approving Communist support elsewhere on a working-class issue. If the Communists campaign for equal rights for immigrant workers in France, I am pro-Communist. If they want to nationalize the news media, I become anti-Communist. I am anti-Communist at the time of the Hitler-Stalin Pact of 1939, and pro-Communist when, in 1941, the French Communists began to participate in the Resistance against Nazi occupation. I become anti-Communist once more when the Communists began infiltrating the Resistance to prepare for postwar politics. Similarly, the Communists and a number of socialists were anti-Gaullist in domestic politics, and more or less openly pro-Gaullist in foreign policy. One could oppose the Vietnam policy of the American Democratic party during 1964–68 and therefore be anti-Johnson, while backing the President's domestic reforms in the same period. Capitalism has both positive and negative aspects. One can be both pro- and anti-capitalist, as are the social democrats, in proportions that will vary over time. A pluralist system contains many shades of agreement and disagreement in the relations among its member groups. There is nothing wrong with saying: I am pro-Labour on this issue, anti- on another, pro-Christian Democrat in Italy on this, anti- on that. One may revise or reverse one's opposition to a party as circumstances change. It seems impossible to oppose one or more of a political party's policies without to that extent being "anti" that party. Yet concerning the Communists we are forever hearing statements that would startle us in any other context because their logic is roughly as follows: I disapprove of 40 per cent, or 60 or 90 per cent of what the Communists do, but I am not at all anti-Communist.

The reason for this incongruity is that the Communists demand total commitment and never recognize any value in the domestic policies of any party other than their own or those controlled by them.[1] Their denunciations of others are based on these two assumptions: the part equals the whole—that is, you cannot disagree with the Communist party on a given issue without being "anti-Communist"; if you attack the Communists you attack the entire Left and have therefore gone over to the reactionaries. The worst of it is that these crude methods of intimidation are effective. The Left reacts in cowardly fashion with the most obsequious sort of self-censorship, while the Communists are accorded the right to spread lies and slander and insult about the most respectable of democrats, nor do their victims respond with anything like the vigor they display if similarly attacked from any other political quarter.

When one rereads the press clippings on Solzhenitsyn and other Soviet dissidents, or the invasion of Czechoslovakia, or the behavior of the Portuguese Communists since the end of the dictatorship, one can only shake one's head in disbelief at the seemingly unshakable spirit of appeasement displayed by the leaders and the publications of the non-Communist Left. They make every possible concession short of utterly repudiating themselves, and their softness muffles the impact of revelations detrimental to the Communist image. Worse yet, they pick up the Stalinist habit of lying, sometimes by omission, and of denigrating anyone

---

[1] "Domestic policies," because the case of foreign affairs is different. For example, during the 1960s the Communist leadership covertly supported de Gaulle's anti-American, anti-NATO and anti-Common Market foreign policies. But that support was not clearly visible to the party's rank-and-file militants, whose faith was fed with large helpings of anti-Gaullist propaganda.

who does not follow their leadership. They could not be any more partial to the Communists without openly renouncing their oath of allegiance to basic human rights and their belief in the eventual and necessary reconciliation of socialism and democracy—a belief that is the only excuse for their behavior. One step more down this road would bring the Left to Stalinism and the suicide of socialism. And yet their willingness to go the edge of the precipice earns them no gratitude from the Communists. Dismissing the political Stations of the Cross already traveled by the Left, the Communists take note only of their refusal to make the final leap into Stalinism. Thus the socialists find themselves most vigorously denounced at the very times when they have been least honest with themselves and with history. Doubtless because they feel themselves doubly guilty: of having fudged the truth, and of being all the more subject to the shameful charge of anti-communism. If they remain silent under Communist attack, things just get worse, but if they were to rebel they would have to confess publicly that they were wrong about the Communists. Thus are they nailed to the cross of "alienation"—the most exquisite torture that could be invented for disciples of Marx.

The Communists in their polemical onslaught are much harder on the misguided socialists and reformers than on the representatives of free enterprise. The dialectic is always the same: yes, socialist legality was violated in the past in the Soviet Union, but that's over, those violations have been properly condemned. The violations of human rights currently alleged just do not exist—neither Gulag nor the murder of dissidents in psychiatric hospitals. Or maybe they still exist in the Soviet Union, but they will not exist in the *new* socialist countries, the *next* socialist societies, where freedom, human rights and pluralism will flourish. Of course some might say that Communists have always said that before they came to power. But any such statement or any reference to violations of human rights is a myth, and anyone who spreads them is ipso facto an "official spokesman for anti-communism." He is "repeating word for word the slogans shouted by Franz Josef Strauss [leader of the right-wing

Christian Democrats] in order to revive the German desire for revenge." Such people are providing Solzhenitsyn and Sakharov with "an audience they don't have in the Soviet Union." True enough, and with good reason—and perhaps a less dense syco-phant would have avoided an argument that contains such an obvious boomerang. And—the line goes on—Soviet critics want to increase international tension and rekindle the cold war. Reproaching French Communist intellectuals for abandoning dissident Soviet intellectuals is part of the "anti-Communist cam-paign waged against the Union of the Left" in France.

One might better say the campaign against the Union of the Left waged by the Union of the Left against itself. For the state-ments quoted above, all from *L'Humanité,* the official French Communist organ, are in each case aimed at political figures and publications that support the Union of the Left between So-cialists and Communists. We can see that the lexicon of Stalinist invective against "social traitors" never changes.

Why indeed should it change? It works. Stalinist invective effectively deters the party's critics. A mere glimpse of its clenched fist is usually enough to make the leaders of the non-Communist Left swallow their words. Thus it was soon made clear in the independent leftist press that Solzhenitsyn was a "rightist," a believer in the religious values of the worst kind of Slavic obscurantism. The strategy involved in this sort of reac-tion—and in this case the Left was truly "reactionary"—is imper-ceptibly to nudge the debate over a troublesome piece of evi-dence from the grounds of fact to that of opinion. The "impossibility of verifying" each of Solzhenitsyn's allegations re-sults in evaluating his description of Soviet oppression as "testi-fying at least as much to the state of the author's mind and that of his associates as to the nature of Soviet society as a whole." "At least as much!" And why not "more," while we're about it? That example from a French leftist publication (which is savaged by the Communists whenever it gets out of line) shows us how a major historical document, worthy of critical analysis, is reduced to the level of personalities. Instead of discussing the accuracy or lack of it of Solzhenitsyn's testimony, the information he offers is treated as the hallucinatory projection of the author's own feelings, which we are to accept or reject on purely emotional grounds. Doubtless the author of *Gulag* is a truthful man, it is conceded, but his testimony is impugned by his religious "values." Besides, once he is in the West, Solzhenitsyn will write only what pleases his new capitalist masters. And if what he writes displeases them, a university professor predicted, he will be silenced "as so many others have been prevented from writing." Too bad for Solzhenitsyn, but that's the way it is. Furthermore, is not the use made of Solzhenitsyn by the Right enough to make him suspect? One of the statements quoted above reminds us of a similar statement made by Jean-Paul Sartre twenty years ago in his response to Camus on the Soviet concentration camps: "Like you I find these camps intolerable, but I find *equally* intolerable the use made of them every day in the bourgeois press" (emphasis added).

We find the same reasoning in the great British liberal paper *The Guardian,* whose American correspondent wrote on July 15, 1975: "Solzhenitsyn believes that all international relations should be forged on the basis of an intense personal morality—his own—and firmly believes communism to be foully evil and that even the remotest evidence of warmth expressed towards it and its protagonists is morally wrong. That kind of talk has gone down extremely well with this society's more Neanderthal brothers and sisters and overnight, it seems fair to say, this man who, via the Book-of-the-Month Club (which has insured that millions of unread copies of the *Gulag* lie on coffee tables from Scarsdale to Sausalito) and the kind of media blitz so popular in this country, has become the darling of the redneck population." Here we see in outline the dialectic that leads to docility toward Stalinism: 1) The nature of the Soviet concentration camps is a personal belief of Solzhenitsyn's, an article of his faith. 2) He wants to bend international relations to his own whim, to sabotage détente. 3) His beliefs gratify the reactionary Right, and so are false and nefarious. 4) Solzhenitsyn has made a lot of money out of his sensational book by palming off on the Americans—who else?—a lot of copies that no one has read. (But if no one reads it, why all the fuss?) Meanwhile, the issue of the historical reality of Gulag has long since vanished from sight.

Because of its fears of committing the sin of anti-communism, the goals of the liberal Left become so modest that it deceives itself into thinking it is conducting a fruitful "dialogue" with the Communists when all it is doing is avoiding their anathema by practicing preventive self-censorship. While the Communists never separate anti-communism from anti-Sovietism, their partners in the Union of the Left do not permit themselves to refer to policies made in concert within the Communist International, still less to the financial ties between Moscow and the Western Communist parties. For example, foreign journalists in Lisbon between April and December of 1974, and even some Portuguese Socialists, could not help noticing the extraordinary proliferation of personnel in the Soviet Embassy and its tourist and cultural services. Frank Carlucci, the hapless American Ambassador, so carefully watched he could hardly leave his office, was constantly accused of meddling in Portugal's affairs. But no one seemed to feel the need to explain why Portugal suddenly needed several dozen Soviet vice-consuls and attachés, all of whom spoke Portuguese remarkably well.

These same observers were so spiteful as to point out the contrast between the Portuguese Communist party's small popular base and the amount of money it was lavishing on its propaganda operations. Since the party had only a few thousand card-carrying members, it would have had to collect dues on the order of perhaps $20,000 a year, suggesting that its membership mainly consisted of directors of multi-national corporations. Some middle-of-the-road Italian and British papers dared to report that the party received about $50 million from the Soviet Union, by well-known if indirect conduits, between April 1974 and April 1975. Naturally this libel was promptly denied, and none of the "independent Marxist Left" publications made the slightest investigation of the matter. One of these papers went so far as to omit from the text of a speech by Henry Kissinger a reference to the Soviet subsidies received by the Portuguese Communists. (The editor had every right to disclaim responsibility for what Kissinger said, but no right to omit the statement.)

Should a leftist publication dare to refer openly to Moscow's subsidizing of Western Communist parties, it would by virtue of that fact cease to be considered a leftist publication. That is how bit by bit the news is bowdlerized. Otherwise, the guilty party would have to endure the verbal onslaught of the Communists plus the sorrowful bleating of its leftist colleagues, shocked by this display of poor taste and the inopportune digging up of old clichés from the "anti-Communist arsenal." But in that April of 1975 the "with human face" socialist press was getting its ears boxed daily for supporting—without much conviction, and of course with no success—the right of the Portuguese Socialist paper *República* to continue publishing. Having just found itself involuntarily involved in a "campaign of slander against the Portuguese Communist party," the Left needed a respite in which to lick its wounds and obtain absolution.

Paradoxically, the Communists, though forever claiming they are victims of systematic prejudice, in fact enjoy privileged treatment in the independent press, which takes from their leaders and their press the kind of abuse it would not accept from any other parties or publications. Many Left independents have become "Finlandicized" within the borders of France, or Italy, or Latin America, or even Spain—a condition that manifests itself by excessive praise of the Communists, when the occasion arises, as well as by the muting of criticism. "Finlandicization" was of course coined around 1960 by Richard Lowenthal and Willy Brandt to describe the situation of Finland after World War II, when the independence of its amputated territory was guaranteed only by docility toward the Soviet Union in its diplomacy and even at home (in news coverage, for example). In a broader sense, "Finlandicization" designates all forms of docility and self-censorship for the benefit of Stalinism, beginning with the claim that Finland itself is not "Finlandicized."

Thus, when the first secretary of the French Socialist party, François Mitterrand, announced upon his arrival in Moscow in April 1975 that he would not bring up Czechoslovakia because

75

"that is a subject to be dealt with in Prague, not Moscow," that amounted to saying that both the invasion and the continued occupation were to be decided upon by the aggressor, not the victim. That single phrase shows us who is the moral loser in the association between socialists and Communists, which partner must keep his thoughts to himself for the alliance to survive. This moral abdication is all the more deplorable because in this case it concerned the ultimate purpose of politics, human freedom, and was not even reciprocated by the Communists. Mitterrand's silence in Moscow did not prevent Boris Ponomarev, the Soviet leader in charge of relations with other Communist parties, from casting anathema on "the nefarious role of the Socialist International" where the French Socialists sit with their European counterparts, all of them being guilty of supporting the Portuguese Socialists, of advocating the economic integration of Western Europe and of failing to condemn Israel with sufficient vigor. Thus, while Mitterrand remained silent on Czechoslovakia, Ponomarev was energetically meddling in the internal affairs of other nations by deriding the basic policies of the Western socialists.

The non-Communist Left had not foreseen the events that took place in Czechoslovakia in 1968. On November 22, 1967, *Le Nouvel Observateur* printed an article entitled "Meeting in Prague" in which Claude Estier, who in 1972 was to become the official spokesman of the renewed French Socialist party, described the visit he and Mitterrand made to the Czech leader Novotný in these terms: "Antonín Novotný has been presiding over his nation's destiny for ten years. With a new leadership generation that is energetic and straightforward, he has changed the country politically and has transformed its economics." Three months later this "straightforward" man and his team were to be ousted by their own party as the most odious incarnations of immobilism and Stalinist obscurantism.

The European Common Market calls forth lengthy Soviet condemnations and censure of the socialists for favoring an organization said to present a threat to détente, especially if economic integration should lead to political integration. But imagine how shocked the Soviet leaders and the Western Communist press would have been had Mitterrand taken advantage of his visit to Moscow publicly to censure Comecon. He would have been told in no uncertain terms to mind his own business. Yet the economic integration is far more advanced in Eastern Europe through Comecon than it is in the West, especially since the Budapest "summit" meeting of summer 1975, when Mongolia and Cuba were admitted to membership (while Moscow forbids Finland to enter into agreements with the Common Market). As for political integration, that has been a reality in Eastern Europe for a long time.

European and "non-aligned" socialists are not the only ones to be morally Finlandicized. It was a Republican President of the United States who thought it better not to receive Solzhenitsyn during his Washington visit in July 1975, for fear the Russians would take offense. Kissinger had advised Ford not to receive Solzhenitsyn because the meeting might have compromised détente. But, as the New York *Times* accurately observed on that occasion, the Soviets themselves have insisted that détente as a means of economic co-operation and of reducing the risk of war does not imply that they will relax their ideological vigilance. Why shouldn't that work both ways?

Eastern European leaders regularly receive delegations of Western Communists who eloquently describe the hellish conditions of life under free enterprise—and no Western government makes it a condition of détente that those visitors be shown the door. Such a demand would be considered an inadmissible act of interference in the Soviet Union's domestic affairs. But for a Western chief of state to receive Solzhenitsyn would have been deemed "cold war" behavior. Docility toward Stalinism has become such a habit in the West that hardly anyone even notices these contrasts in behavior. When for example the French Foreign Minister was to meet his Spanish counterpart in 1973, *L'Humanité*, suddenly concerned with human rights, accurately observed that "a report made public by the organization Amnesty International provides a timely reminder that M. Jobert is going to negotiate with the representative of a fascist state." In its report Amnesty International condemned the "brutality and discrimination endured in Spanish prisons by opponents of the Franco government." It reports testimony that the "practice of torture in police stations is general, regular and virtually without restriction." However, that same week, when Russian dissidents denounced the same abuses in Soviet prisons, *L'Humanité* had this to say: "On the pretense that they are displeased with the domestic regime of the Soviet Union, not only do they oppose détente, but they call on reactionary forces in Western nations to come to their rescue; under the pretense of obtaining 'democraticization' [strange quotation marks!] of the society in which they live, they call for renewal of the cold war. Senseless demands! Demands that are absolutely in contradiction to peaceful coexistence *of which a fundamental principle is non-interference in the domestic affairs of others.*"[2] (Emphasis added.)

Fear of committing the sin of anti-communism, of being considered "reactionary," no matter how unlikely the description, even when it is the Stalinists who are reactionary, counterrevolutionary and anti-socialist, has produced among leftists and progressive liberals all over the world the habit of minimizing or passing over in silence any facts or ideas that might be disagreeable to the Communists. They avoid emphasizing the truth about the history of communism in Western nations as well as the truth about life in the Communist states. The task of telling those truths is left to those who are indifferent to the charge of anti-communism, that is, to the conservative Right. This tends to make the Communists invulnerable because they can argue that the source of any "pseudo-revelation" is evidence enough that it consists of mere slander. Should the revelation happen to come from a source on the Left, it is easy for the Communists to claim that the lone individual who dared to break step with his fellows has "gone over to the reactionaries." The process of discrediting him is facilitated by the fact that his progressive and humane socialist brothers will usually abandon him with the most hasty and virtuous cowardice. Has he not "after all" played into the hands of the Right?

2 *L'Humanité*, August 27, 1973.

Thus the question of determining the validity of historical information and testimony is answered by never being asked because 1) if the information comes from the Right, it is tendentious, and there is no point verifying it, and 2) if it comes from the Left, it so resembles what usually comes from the Right that one can only feel sorry for the person who undertook the distasteful task of circulating it, which in any event he probably did to settle some personal score.

Accordingly the Communists can punish with impunity any insubordinate socialists who displease them, knowing that their fellows on the Left will come very slowly to the rescue of the offender if indeed they do not gladly join in lynching him.

Oliver Todd, a leftist writer known since the beginning of the sixties for his reporting on both North and South Vietnam, expressed the belief in 1974 that North Vietnam after its victory would create a Stalinist state "representing the most obscurantist form of communism." Todd had made several long visits to Hanoi, and he had sympathetically described both the nation's wartime suffering and its leaders' points of view. But once his articles contradicted the official Communist version of reality, his reporting was no longer deemed worthy of discussion on its merits. He also made the error of observing, during several weeks spent with the Vietcong guerrillas, that the Provisional Revolutionary Government of South Vietnam was a creation of the North Vietnamese army, and that it was the Communists who were violating the Paris accords by constantly crossing the cease-fire line. Certainly the South Vietnamese government was overthrown in 1975 by North Vietnam's armed divisions, not by a popular uprising, as the official mythmakers would have us believe.

Todd's credentials—his knowledge of Vietnam, his unique contacts with the guerrillas, his political sophistication—should have been reason enough for his articles to cause a serious debate on Vietnam among leftists. Learning what had actually happened—such a daring ambition!—even if it did not conform with Hanoi's official version, would not necessarily have implied condemning the actions of North Vietnam and the Provisional

Revolutionary Government, for many deceptions can be justified by that long and bloody war of independence. But the desire to know the truth played little part in what followed.[3]

Now, although we know from the gasps of delight with which for sixty years their allies have greeted each new and encouraging symptom that the Communists have made miraculous progress in their respect for others and their thirst for objectivity, that indeed they have been sighted rising toward the heavenly seat of freedom of thought, on this occasion they nonetheless were able to remain true to their own imperishable souls. They applied their infallible formula: forget facts, forget ideas, spit on the person.

The Communist press resigned itself to the necessity of burning the master heretic though, as *L'Humanité* nobly put it, it is "never pleasant" to have to "report a man's degradation." This beast, "more Nixonian than Nixon," had "justified the past crimes of imperialism" and his behavior was comparable to that of the Nazi who had supervised the execution of French Communist members of the Resistance thirty years earlier at Châteaubriant. This measured critique, an honor to the profession of journalism, was then subject to the multiplier effect of the Union of the Left. The victim could not defend himself. Not in the Communist press, which does not apply the absurd provision in the bourgeois code guaranteeing the right of reply. Nor yet in the publications of the non-Communist Left which, cowed by Stalinism's

[3] The cult of willful ignorance is so advanced in the French Left that the official Socialist paper, *L'Unité,* hired as its specialist on Indochina and Southeast Asia in general an Australian Communist, a notorious agent of the Communist International, who even traveled for quite a time on a North Vietnamese passport! The readers of the paper were unaware of that, of course, and doubtless believed they were drinking from the pure spring of objectivity. But how about the editors of *L'Unité?* Were they equally ignorant? Should we attribute to simple-mindedness, or to deliberate malice, their eagerness to open their pages without verification to someone who, in the vocabulary of infiltration, is known as a "submarine?" This correspondent, Wilfrid Burchett, later surfaced, doubtless by pure coincidence, in Angola: always in the right place, always ready to offer the French Socialist readers of *L'Unité*—and many others—reassuring interpretations of any Communist leap forward.

wrath, buried the subject under a pall of silence, in the interest of course of unity on the Left.

This was one more case of the non-Communist Left giving up its right to freedom of opinion and information on a subject that had nothing to do with the objectives of democratic socialism. Once more the Communists had imposed censorship on their allies with the threat of ending the alliance, a threat that is never reciprocated. (The Socialists point to the concessions made by the Communists in their joint platform. But those are promises for the future; Stalinist behavior is in the here and now.) Some will say that the facts and opinions in Todd's articles were questionable. That is their opinion. But suppose they are right—what difference does it make? Freedom of speech does not apply only to unquestionable opinions: quite the contrary. But totalitarianism begins when, questionable or not, opinions are no longer questioned; tomorrow they will not even be mentioned.

Granted that the discussion of current events, especially events as tragic as those of Indochina, is likely to be inflamed by emotion. But what happened in this case was not emotionalism but terrorism and submission to that terrorism. Stalinism is not just concentration camps, the Moscow trials, the psychiatric hospitals. It is how Stalinists behave in their everyday political, personal and intellectual relations with others—and it is how the Left allows itself to be subjugated by that behavior. Nor are current events the only ones to be censored by this alliance of fanaticism and servility. Here is a case where history was the victim.

At issue was a biography of Maurice Thorez, the most representative of French Communist leaders to date. (In the decade of the fifties the party called itself "the party of Maurice Thorez.") It was published in 1975 under the title *Thorez, vie publique et vie privée*. Its author, Philippe Robrieux, is a professor who is a professional historian. He was secretary-general of the Young Communists in the early sixties; the book is his doctoral thesis. Thorez had been dead for eleven years, and much of this lengthy book deals with the period before World War I. I would add that it is a serious scholarly work that reveals many previously unpublished facts and interprets the Communist International in the setting of sixty years of European politics. It is also a work of great literary merit.

Here is the "review" that appeared in *L'Humanité* on May 21, 1975, under the headline TO GET ATTENTION: "There are people who amount to nothing themselves who, in order to make people notice them, will set out to write—anything—about someone who has left his name in history. Thus an obscure professor, who was once briefly a member of the Union of Communist Students, has chosen to offer a thesis on 'the secret and public life' of Maurice Thorez. A louse tries to climb on a lion's mane. To get attention."

Anyone in publishing or journalism can only admire the subtlety with which the author of this choice morsel managed to avoid making any reference to the name of the author and publisher and the correct title of the book—no danger of promoting its sale! Note also that Robrieux's motive is the same as that attributed by Tass to Poniatowski: to lift himself out of obscurity and to attract public attention. Only one way either of them could do that—anti-communism. One wonders also how Stalinism's sympathizers can go on believing and saying that today's Communists have nothing in common with those of yesteryear in their intellectual scruples, their tolerance, their concern for objectivity. On the contrary, they are as prolific as their fathers and grandfathers in their production of statements and articles that honor the human spirit every bit as much as that paragraph from *L'Humanité*. The subtle zoological observation of *L'Humanité*'s anonymous reviewer became frankly worrisome when it was learned that those wretched lines had panicked the editors of the non-Communist Left. When the party frowned, it became necessary, if not to ignore—that was a bit difficult—at least to blunt the impact of this sinful book. A major publication, *Le Monde*, hastily canceled the major front-page article it had commissioned from one of its star contributors, and in its place got a less-known hack to turn out a lukewarm piece which it then relegated to the no man's land of the inside pages, somewhere between the weather report and the latest news on constitutional reform in Ruanda.

The game as usual consisted of treating as an expression of one man's opinion what in fact was a scholarly investigation whose value lies in its research and its contribution to the understanding of events. Most notably, the author demonstrates irrefutably the French Communist party's total submission for half a century to Stalin. The game also consisted of slipping in here and there the thought that this life of Thorez brought "grist to the mill of the Right." Now, either the facts reported in the book contradict the party's claims, in which case the Right's view is correct, and there is nothing to be done about it; or else the party is right—but that has to be shown. In any event, on the various occasions when the veils concealing the reality of Communist history were torn away, the scene that was revealed exceeded the worst "slanders" of the Right more often than it confirmed the illusions of the Left. On would think that might incite the Left to a bit of humility, or at least caution. But the criterion of validity, once more, is not historical truth, but the misuse that anti-communism might make of that truth.

The Left is now applying to China the same dogmatic assurance and imprudent optimism that it previously applied to the Soviet Union. The few books that contradict the triumphant picture of contemporary China painted in most of the current literature are passed over in silence, scornfully condemned, or discredited as "settling personal scores," even when the authors are Chinese or are foreign scholars who have managed to penetrate beyond the standard official tour.[4] Obviously it is our duty to try to evaluate objectively Communist China's successes and failures in confronting the economic problems of this most immense of third-world countries. But we should not forget, as so many euphoric visitors seem to do, that China lets us see just what she wants us to see so that we will think what she wants us to think about her accomplishments. No serious investigator, no economist who cared about his reputation, would take the respon-

[4] Recent examples are Jean Pasqualini and Rudolf Chelminski, *Prisoner of Mao* (Coward, McCann & Geoghegan, 1973); Lai Ying (translated and adapted by Edward Behr and Sydney Liu), *The Thirty-sixth Way* (Doubleday, 1970); and Simon Leys, *Les Habits neufs du président Mao* (Champ libre, 1971) and *Ombres chinoises* (UGE, 1975).

sibility of evaluating the economic situation of Australia, say, or Brazil or Canada, if he could see only what the authorities chose to show him and if the only statistics available came from the government. Let us remember that the Soviet Union managed to conceal completely from the West the mass starvation that followed the collectivization of the land in the 1930s; that as late as 1950–55 established economists were writing that the industrial and agricultural production of the Soviet Union was about to surpass that of the capitalist nations, and that Eastern Europe would soon become the breadbasket and workshop of the Western world.

That they had burned their fingers with those forecasts did not cause the same observers to improve their methods when they transferred their attentions to the Chinese economy. The same is true of the subject of repression and totalitarian discipline in China. When Solzhenitsyn predicted during a round-table discussion on French television (on April 11, 1975) that in twenty or thirty years the world would doubtless learn of the existence of Chinese and Indochinese Gulags, he was sarcastically asked (by Jean Daniel, editorial director of the Socialist weekly *Le Nouvel Observateur*) if he was taking up fortunetelling. Given the history of other Communist states, the sarcasm seemed misplaced: the same causes are more likely than not to produce the same effects. Shortly after that, the authoritative French demographic journal, *Population,* published a study that concluded that China had 150 million fewer people than it should according to even a conservative estimate of the normal rate of increase. The authors could find no explanation for that statistical difference, even after accounting for a reduction in the birth rate and the (unlikely) possibility that China suffered a major famine in the early sixties. This demographic gap is disturbingly reminiscent of the similar gap that appeared in the Soviet Union with the census of January 1959. The total population reported at that time, 208,827,000, was about 20 million short of the figure projected by Western demographers, even taking into account the lives lost during the war and during Stalin's repressions before the war.[5] If Communist statistics are considered plausible when they report good news, should they not also be believed when they suggest pessimistic conclusions?

Besides, we need no insider information to know that "violation of socialist legality," supposedly a thing of the distant past, still flourishes in the Soviet Union. The main violation, which causes all the rest, is that the Politburo has robbed the Russian people of sovereignty by usurping the powers of the soviets. Nothing in the Soviet constitution provides that the nation should be ruled by the Communist party.[6] It is also obvious to all who care to see that the Soviet Union and China display the primary characteristics of totalitarian states: a single official political party; no free elections; monopolistic economic and political power; ideological control of news, culture, education; citizens forbidden to go abroad or even travel freely within the nation; citizens work and live where assigned by government; foreigners not allowed to travel freely; citizens under surveillance of political police force; opposition to the government, i.e. the Communist party, a crime; a crime, also, to spread news harmful to socialism, for example news of shortages or workers' revolts[7]; justice subordinate to the party; and, of course, concentration camps. These are merely the most obvious totalitarian characteristics of the major Communist powers, conditions often being worse in some of their satellites. Even their most benevolent allies do not deny those traits of Communist civilization. But any such admissions by Western Communists—though such concessions are always predicted and frequently announced, the announcements always proving premature—are superficial and

[5] Robert Conquest, *The Great Terror* (Macmillan, 1968). See Appendix A: "Casualty Figures."
[6] See especially *Mémorandum du mouvement démocratique soviétique au Soviet suprême d' U.R.S.S.*, which appeared in "samizdat" form in the Soviet Union in December 1970 and was published in the West by the periodical *Droits de l'homme en U.R.S.S.*, No. 4, 1972, Brussels.
[7] After five years in the camps, Andrei Amalrik, author of *Will the Soviet Union Survive Until 1984?*, was again arrested in September 1975 on the double-barreled and supremely totalitarian charges of spreading false information and residing in Moscow without authorization. He was finally expelled from the U.S.S.R. in 1976.

meaningless. And the few concessions to reality made by the Communists are simply used by them further to intimidate the liberal socialists, especially in Europe and Latin America.

Let me offer among many examples the press conference held by the secretary-general of the French Communist party on August 29, 1973. It was a classic case of self-contradiction. At the very time that the secretary-general was declaring that the charges made by Soviet dissidents had been made meaningless by the 1956 20th Congress, when Khrushchev gave his secret speech, the secretary-general himself was behaving just like the Communist leaders before the 20th Congress. In those earlier Stalinist days they denied the existence of the concentration camps and the psychiatric hospitals and the rest of the totalitarian arsenal—which is just what Marchais did at his press conference. Of course in those earlier days they would have raised their voices against violations of socialist legality—had any occurred. Fortunately they did not, except in the propaganda "orchestrated" by "the worst reactionaries." A Communist leader who speaks like his predecessors—that is, denies the facts and calls those who report them unscrupulous saboteurs and enemies of peace—scarcely seems to represent progress. In what way is he less than Stalinist? What real, meaningful, painful concessions has he made to democracy?[8]

After denying the facts comes the disciplining of "allies." *L'Humanité* two days later selected as its main target a journalist who is a supporter of the Union of the Left: "During the press conference held by our party on Wednesday, the correspondent of *Le Monde*, Thierry Pfister, asked the following question: 'Why in the Communist party's sharpest responses concerning the press does it single out *Le Monde* and *Le Nouvel Observateur*, both of which support the non-Communist Left?' 'Very simple,' Georges Marchais told him, 'because *Le Monde* and *Le Nouvel Observateur* present a caricature of the policies of the French Communist party, which is one of the essential components of the Union of the Left. For the rabid adversaries of the joint plat-

[8] See "A Note on Eurocommunism" concerning the new turn taken by the Western Communist parties in 1976 and their alleged liberalization.

form and the Union of the Left, anti-communism is in the nature of things. But it is different in the case of *Le Monde* and *Le Nouvel Observateur,* which claim to belong to the Left. They are free to choose their camp. But let them not claim to be helping the Left when they are joining the camp of the adversaries of the Union of the Left.'"

Le Monde replied that the joint platform did not contain sufficiently clear and unequivocal guarantees of human rights in a future French socialist society. As usual *L'Humanité* answered by citing statements in which the party had solemnly promised that freedom would flourish in socialism *à la française*—tomorrow. But today, in the present, *L'Humanité* went on in standard totalitarian fashion: "We have confirmed within the last twenty-four hours that *Le Monde* wants systematically to damage the Communist party—and therefore the joint platform of the Left—by misrepresenting its policies."

L'Humanité concluded by displaying its usual respect for the individual: "What makes Pfister lie?"[9] If the Communists' partners are to avoid being described as traitors, they must follow the party line in each detail. Only at that price can they know peace and enter into a state of grace.[10] The Communist strategy consists of granting in theory that others have the right to disagree with them, but in practice denying that right in each particular instance. Thanks to what evidently must be incredibly bad luck, in no case does it ever turn out to be a sincere criticism, always a sinister maneuver secretly mounted by the enemies of so-

[9] On August 31, 1973.
[10] Jean Daniel, editorial director of *Le Nouvel Observateur,* the most important weekly of Socialist tendency in France, exclaimed, after a particularly unworthy attack on him by the Communists on the subject of Portugal: "It will become known that you answer ideas with insults . . . Is it dishonest to disagree with you?" (*Le Nouvel Observateur,* July 14, 1975). But is there any question about that? The Communists *always* answer ideas with insults when one disagrees with a position the party has decided to uphold. Only the everlasting illusion of the "liberalization"—i.e. the self-destruction—of Stalinism can lead one to expect otherwise. Some time later, following a second and even more venomous article in *L'Humanité* (Jean Daniel was accused of urging the "fascists" to massacre the Portuguese Communists), the editorial director of *Le Nouvel Observateur* brought a charge of libel against *L'Humanité*. Shortly thereafter he withdrew the charge.

cialism. It is a familiar Stalinist game, and it remains unchanged despite the recent promises of liberalization. Stalinism, once more, does not consist only of its worst extremes, of killing and arresting its critics. It begins with tactics of hypocrisy, intimidation and dishonesty intended to disconcert its allies and (with considerable success) weaken their defenses with the constant menace of excommunication, so that eventually they no longer react to the insults to which they are constantly subjected.

In the days preceding the episode just described the French press contained several examples of the way the Communists are able to dominate the free socialists, even when the socialists outnumber them. Indeed, ever since 1917 Bolshevism has practiced the art of dominating others when it is in the minority, which means it must use undemocratic methods.

Thus on August 23, 1973, *Le Monde* published an article, mentioned earlier, on "The Communist Party and the Intellectuals." The article, though written in the awareness of what had happened to Solzhenitsyn and the other Soviet dissidents, was generally optimistic about the Communists. The next day *L'Humanité* wrote that the article was a "falsification" and that it was part of the "anti-Communist campaign against the Union of the Left." That afternoon *Le Monde* published excerpts from the Communist article and its editorial director, Jacques Fauvet, concluded after expressing some reservations that "the important thing is that the dialogue be opened and remain open."

As its form of dialogue, *L'Humanité* said the next day that *Le Monde* was "recidivist," a term with criminal connotations. Two days later the editorial director of *Le Nouvel Observateur*, Jean Daniel, wrote, after some moderate criticism of the Communists, that "we would rather exchange ideas than insults." The lover of ideas was informed the next day by *L'Humanité* that "even in leftist disguise, anti-communism belongs to the Right" and that "before a dialogue could be held, *Le Nouvel Observateur* would have to stop practicing distortion and lies."

After having greeted comments that were moderate, courteous and conciliatory with this avalanche of insult, the Communists adopted the role of pilgrim of unity and chanted in the unctuous voice of its secretary-general, "The French Communist party is not only willing but anxious to engage in debate with all who want to launch our country on the socialist path."[11]

By its intimidating tactics the Communist party had succeeded in turning the situation around: although it was originally at fault, it ended by granting the "anti-Communists" the favor of a dialogue. It cleverly established a power relationship in which it is acceptable for the Communists to heap reproaches on their partners, but unacceptable for them to suggest the slightest reservations about the Communists' behavior. Note that these vintage Stalinist polemics came more than a year before October 1974, when political seers professed to discern a mysterious "hardening" of the Western Communists' position toward their socialist allies. How naïve! Eternity did not, by definition, begin in October 1974, nor in 1976, the year the Communists adopted the new "Italian" line: independence from the Soviet Union and democracy at home. But it was not new at all: in 1946, and even earlier, in 1936, that same "new" line had been proclaimed—and subsequently rejected. At no time have the Communists ever planned political action with any goal other than obtaining a monopoly of power. While they are in the opposition they get their allies in shape by making them jump through the hoops: those are the training methods of the Union of the Left, i.e. Communist domination.

The Communists are so used to enjoying this "most favored party" treatment that they use the joint platform or any other kind of alliance to justify calling their allies "prevaricators" and "liars." How, they argue, can one claim that the Communists in power would eliminate human rights, when Georges Marchais has said: "With the Communists in the government tomorrow, Solzhenitsyn could publish his books." It would seem that we are supposed to give words precedence over facts, and that the French Communist party is to be the only political party in the world whose promises are to be considered, under threat of sacrilege to the Left, as chiseled in granite. Besides, what Marchais in fact said was this: ". . . Solzhenitsyn could publish his book,

---

[11] *L'Humanité*, August 31, 1973.

provided, of course, he could find a publisher." My bet is that he would not easily find one.

This disruptive aggression, as unjustified and even clownish as it may appear, has served international communism well, for—to take a recent example—it has enabled the French Communists to make their Socialist allies unwitting (or, alas, at times conscious) accomplices in the persecution of the Portuguese Socialists after the April 1974 revolution. Mario Soares is the only Socialist since the death of Stalin who has remained Marxist and has tried to collaborate with the Communists in the creation of a new government without making the slightest even verbal concession on basic democratic principles. His experience does not speak favorably of the alliance between democracy and Marxism. Soares conducted himself with an intelligence and courage that stand in vivid contrast to the cowardly hypocrisy and idiotic guile of those who in order to achieve their ideals begin by repudiating them. But the best one can say of the non-Communist Left, except for the social democratic parties, is that their support of Soares was flabby, tardy, brief and halfhearted. They showed far more inspiration in the ingenious arguments and excellent rationalizations that they diligently spun out to justify the cynical and well-plotted effort to install national military communism in Portugal.

The first signs of a plot against democracy in Portugal, evident in September of 1974, were scornfully denied by the Left as the hallucinations of fearful minds or of interests threatened by the prospect of an advanced form of socialism. Granted certain minor precautions had to be taken against fascist conspirators, in order to establish freedom. When these minor precautions became major ones, when the Communists and their allies in the armed forces movement imposed a single labor movement and infiltrated the news media, the international Left suddenly discovered that it would be risky for a nation that "had known fifty years of dictatorship" to make too rapid a transition to democracy, that it was to be expected that its shepherds would for some time hold the nation on a short leash. Besides, what right had they to speak, those who were now denouncing small blotches on the Portuguese revolution, when they had never raised their voices against the dictatorship of Salazar and his successor Caetano? The "hypocritical" international press was far slower to become disturbed over fascism in Salazar's time!

This objection holds no water for two reasons. The first is that the international press and public opinion in the democratic nations, with the exception of the extreme Right fringe, have always condemned the dictatorships of Salazar and especially Franco. Of course regimes that endure that long do not make the news every day. But each time those dictatorships attracted attention with their periodic brutalities, it was hard to find a European or American publication, from the center Right through the extreme Left, that excused their behavior. In fact, agreement on the subject was so general that there was scarcely any debate. Of course, the real question is why Europe gives birth to so many dictatorships and why it is so difficult to get rid of them. But unfortunately that question in the twentieth century is not limited to Spain and Portugal.

The second reason that invalidates the objection I cited above is that criteria have changed, or so I would hope. After Salazar we judged events in Portugal according to a new standard, that of the effort to establish democracy. And now we were being told: "You must not judge Portugal according to the democratic ideal, but by comparison with Salazar." A fine idea: since the Portuguese people were used to dictatorship, put them back under a dictator as fast as possible. I wonder if that reasoning does not reflect contempt for the Portuguese and Spanish people. Suppose after the Liberation that the French had gone from one dictatorship to another with a different ideology, and suppose the British or the Swiss had offered us this consolation: "After Vichy, another authoritarian regime is good enough for you French. You're not qualified to want true democracy." Would we have been flattered by the zeal with which our neighbors resigned themselves to our destiny as a lesser people? It was strange also to see the argument that a people is "not ready for democracy," that smelly old adage proclaimed by every colonizer and usurper of power, sailing under socialist colors. Democracy is learned by the practice of democracy, no other way.

Another game consisted of exclaiming that the dispute between Socialists and Communists in Portugal was somehow so intrinsically evil that it must not be mentioned because it was "exploited by the adversaries of the Union of the Left in France." Again, either that "exploitation" was founded on fact, and the behavior of the Portuguese Communist party cast a sinister shadow on any collaboration with Communists, in which case it was no exploitation but a legitimate historical inference; or else it was unfounded, the Communists were not trying to use the army to establish totalitarian rule, in which case that fact should be demonstrated as soon as possible for that would mean the dispute with the Socialists was without purpose.

That demonstration became rather prickly on the day that national military communism imposed its own platform on all the non-Communist parties, regardless of the outcome of the elections, so that the regime subsequently was able to act as if the elections had never even taken place. (In that election, let us remember, Soares' Socialists won 38 per cent of the vote, and the Social Democrats 26 per cent, for a free socialist total of 64 per cent, compared to 17 per cent for the Communist party and its allies.)

Now the foreign socialist Left, eager to serve the public relations needs of the Portuguese Communists, conceived the idea that true "revolutionary legitimacy" was incarnated in the army, because it was they, not the parties, that had won a majority of the vote, that had overthrown the dictatorship. To such lengths are people willing to go to avoid giving offense to the Stalinists. Of course no coup d'état can succeed without the military, or at least part of the military. But what characterizes right-wing coups, like those of the Greek colonels in 1967 or General Pinochet in Chile in 1973, is that they abolish popular sovereignty, which is what leftist coups are intended to restore. It might also be observed that had the socialists and liberals tried to overthrow the dictatorship prior to 1974, they would have been crushed—by that same Portuguese army, which at that time was fascist.

The capacity of the Portuguese military to govern was never at issue among all these political notions. No matter how often the military demonstrated by their supreme incompetence their mastery of the art of ruining a nation's economy, no one bothered to ask by what right they dictated when the sun was to shine and the rain to fall, nor what price the Portuguese people would have to pay for enjoying the benefits of the military's talents.

Except that troublemaker Soares, who would not keep quiet and who, instead of parroting the line that the "proletarian revolution" had priority over "formal democracy," the latter benefiting only "moneyed interests," remained impervious to Marxist science and insisted with dreadful tactlessness on brandishing the old-fashioned scarecrow of totalitarian communism and the police state.

On July 12, 1975, after the Socialist ministers resigned from the legal government, which had been made impotent, François Mitterrand made an angry speech on the Portuguese situation, pointing an accusing finger at what he denounced as the "Olympic games of hypocrisy." This hypocrisy, we were told, was that of those who protested *against* the murder of socialist democracy perpetrated by Stalinists in uniform in the name of revolutionary legitimacy. The French Socialist leader's diatribe was on the theme mentioned earlier: he was exposing those who "never said a word" against Salazar, and today said nothing against Franco.

At that time those who opposed the effort to implant a police state in Lisbon included many of the long-time opponents of Salazar and Franco—people like Mario Soares himself, and Raul Rego, editor of *República,* the paper confiscated by the Communists, who was a lifelong anti-Salazar activist. We could also present to the French Socialist leader those Spanish Socialists who risked their lives in combat against Franco, paid for their beliefs with thirty years of exile and now were among the bitterest opponents of the military-Stalinist plot in Portugal, if only because they had witnessed the evil doings of the Stalinists on the Republican side during the Spanish Civil War. Those who pretended that only the Right worried about the Portuguese crisis, that only from a rightist point of view was there cause for concern, were merely paving the road to dictatorship. Is anyone who calls himself a leftist entitled to be a tyrant since the brilliant discovery of the "dictatorship of the proletariat?" And should socialists be promoting that line? I am well aware that Mitterrand later wrote (in *L'Unité* of July 25) that he would be greatly angered if democracy in Portugal was imperiled. His article developed the idea that the Portuguese Council of the Revolution was mingling Lenin and Cavaignac. Other than the fact that Lenin was never reluctant when it came to practicing repression, who on earth remembers Cavaignac, especially outside France? (Cavaignac was the French general who crushed the revolution of 1848, killing several hundred demonstrators in the streets of Paris.) Hitler or Mussolini would have carried more weight as comparisons to Lenin—but imagine how *L'Humanité* would have reacted! In any event, Mitterrand's belated article seemed to have the effect of a thunderbolt, for the very next day the triumvirate of Costa Gomes-Carvalho-Vasco Gonçalves (the latter being the Communist agent imposed by the Communist party although the people had been demanding his ouster for two weeks) claimed absolute power and launched once more the Stalinist counterrevolution. A few weeks later Mitterrand addressed a very firmly worded letter to the secretary-general of the French Communist party. Now, in August 1975, Mitterrand for the first time underlined the Communists' responsibility for the disintegration of Portugal, thus agreeing retrospectively with those critics whom he had dismissed as rightists for the past fifteen months. It was too late in the day. He should have forced the issue with the French and Russian Communists at least six months earlier: "Stop perverting the democratic process in Portugal, or no more Union of the Left in France." But right up to the last moment Mitterrand restricted his fire to "the Right that did not condemn France." As if that were the problem!

I do not know if Mitterrand was aware that, by shifting the subject of the debate, he was quietly going along with the most classic type of Stalinist counterattack. The old Stalinist trick is, whenever the Communists have tried to grab something by force, to distract attention by shouting from the rooftops about "reactionaries" who are profiting from events or "pseudo-revelations" to "orchestrate an anti-Communist campaign."

Even if the military-Stalinist "permanent coup d'état" in Lisbon had been condemned only by former Nazis, the point was not who was protesting but what was going on there. The job of a political leader is to inform himself and express an opinion on the basic situation, not the opinions of others.

The basic situation was that the French Socialists during the winter of 1974 and the first half of 1975 could not speak their minds on Portugal, except in brief whispers soon drowned out by Communist anathema about "hypocrisy," because the Union of the Left was at stake. Contrary to the current phantasmagoria, the problems of Portugal were not blown up by enemies of the Union of the Left, but rather were minimized and prettified by the non-Communist members of the Union, who were afraid of coming to the moment of truth with their Communist partners, a moment they may postpone but which they cannot evade forever.

In fact, support for the armed forces movement was not a policy decided upon just by Alvaro Cunhal, the Portuguese-Communist leader. The decision was made by the Communist International, and thus it is an issue on which the French Communists can make no concession. A Reuter's dispatch dated July 4, 1975, provides confirmation, if any is needed: "Moscow—Boris Ponomarev, alternate member of the Politburo of the Soviet Communist party, has advised Western Communists not to give up their revolutionary goals, despite the strategy of making common front with leftist forces. The Soviet Communist party intends to continue its struggle against social democracy, Mr. Ponomarev declared at a meeting. He said: 'While aiding the common actions of Communists and social democrats whenever it is necessary and possible, the Soviet Communist party is developing and will continue to develop a concrete and carefully argued critique of the ideology and policy of social democracy.'"

"Mr. Ponomarev made the statement in a commentary on what he called 'the harm caused by the actions of certain social democratic leaders, *notably in relation to the events in Portugal.*'"

But Boris Ponomarev did not want the Communists at that time to share power alone with the military: that would have been too obvious. That is why the Portuguese Communists tried on the one hand to prevent the Socialists and Social Democrats from leaving the government and on the other to ensure that the government (which resulted from elections) had no power. Still, following the legal route in politics is only coincidental for the Communists, and that is the essential point of conflict between socialists and Communists everywhere in the world. Thus the conference of Latin American and Caribbean Communists, meeting about mid-June of 1975 in Havana, while calling on other leftist Latin American parties to join in "mutual respect" in "arriving at a frank and complete analysis," also put out a concluding document according to which all the conquests of the "revolutionary movement" had to be "defended by force of arms." This is their general strategy: make promises to the democratic parties, then seize power by force as soon as possible. That is exactly what the Portuguese Communists tried to do again in November 1975. The failure of their attempted coup preserved the possibility of democracy in Portugal; their success would have ended that possibility for good.

For the moment let us pass no moral or political judgment on that strategy. My own opinion is that it results in regimes that are not only anti-democratic but also ineffectual from the point of view of the economic and social revolution that supposedly justifies them. But perhaps I am mistaken. The mistake no one should make, however, is to close his eyes to the fact that this strategy means the certain sacrifice of representative democracy.

Thus the docility toward Stalinism that characterizes the parties and press of the non-Communist Left systematically undermines resistance to the advance of Stalinism in the world. Without as yet suggesting reasons for that docility (some are rational and others irrational, or rational for reasons that cannot be admitted), I have simply described some of its manifestations and its consequences. Later on I shall offer some hypotheses about the causes of that docility. But its manifestations and consequences are not hypotheses—these are facts.

Docility toward Stalinism confers on the various Communist parties a privileged status that is quite the opposite of the supposed handicap of omnipresent anti-communism that they claim to labor under. Non-Communists tolerate from the Communists a brutality and dishonesty in political and intellectual debate that they would reject in any other political group. Communists benefit also from a benevolent censorship of anything that might offend them: information about the methods practiced by Western Communists, and information about life in Communist nations. The latter kind of information is first of all extirpated whenever possible at the source by the totalitarian state, and then what manages to reach the West is adulterated and sugarcoated by those in the press who fear to be branded with the guilt of "anti-communism." Thus people are distracted from the real question—how Communist societies function—in order to pay attention to how Western Communists react to embarrassing news from those societies. There is a great imbalance between the constant pitiless denunciation of the crimes and errors of free capitalist societies and the double or triple filtering that sanitizes information about Communist societies. In this soft environment, Stalinism advances without meeting any effective opposition—opposition, that is, not from the conservatives but from the Left, whose critical role and popular themes have both been usurped by communism.

UNOFFICIAL STALINISM
OR PIDGIN MARXISM

Docility toward Stalinism is not found only in those nations where the presence of a strong Communist party leads the Left out of respect for democracy, to accept the fact that this party does not respect democratic rules. Nor is it found only in the nations that adjoin the Communist powers, where in Europe this docility takes the form of "Finlandicization," and in the Asian countries bordering on China the form, one might say, of "Thailandicization" or "Burmacization": formal independence, territorial integrity (or, at least, the absence of territorial annexation), but also diplomatic and military subordination. In 1975 Burma and even the Philippines of dictator Marcos made the journey to Peking to be Thailandicized. Other Asian states will either follow their example or, like India, be able to resist Chinese imperialism only by opening their doors to Soviet imperialism.

But a sort of unofficial Stalinism—we could also call it lay Stalinism, or Stalinism once removed from its political cousins in the organized Communist parties—weighs increasingly on societies that are under neither domestic nor foreign Communist pressure. This form of Stalinism is a mishmash of Marxist-Leninist as well as Marcusian and leftist ideas accompanied by third-world postulates according to which the industrial nations are responsible for all the past and present ills of this planet.

The first of these postulates is that there is no possibility of improving the "system"—a vague concept that seems to refer to capitalism in its Swedish as well as its Brazilian variety, and to the capitalism of the first quarter of the nineteenth century as well as to that of the last quarter of the twentieth. Such historical and regional differences are all wiped out by the intrinsic and uniform evil of the "system." When the "system" is hard on the workers, it is exploiting them; when it provides them a relatively good living, it is "co-opting" them. Thus all attempts at reform are absurd. There never has been and there never can be any real improvement, unless it is a seeming improvement that conceals some new trap. It is necessary to "destroy the system"; otherwise, all the rest is in vain. Another way of stating this postulate consists of saying that "nothing is possible without changing the form of society." However, this aphorism applies only to capitalist societies. Despite the massive flaws of Communist societies, the same people do not say that in those societies it is impossible to correct the flaws except by "changing the form of society," that is by first abolishing the present economic system itself. It seems that cause and effect are linked only in capitalist societies.

The second postulate is that first priority goes to the destruction of the system, the system of course being capitalism and capitalism alone. This abolitionist mission takes precedence over freedom, democracy, law, elections and the rights of man. In any event, Marx and Lenin have already informed us that freedom is only "formal" as long as "money" holds sway, and Herbert Marcuse has added that the greater the degree of tolerance in a society, the more "repressive" it is.

The third postulate is that the only imperialism that exists derives from capitalism, and that of course means, above all, American imperialism, aided by a few neocapitalist pseudo-democratic puppets. Almost everywhere in the world "imperialism" today is synonymous with "United States."

The credo summarized in those three postulates constitutes a kind of pidgin Marxism that holds sway in many parts of the world where communism in its officially organized form is still a small minority. This basic credo, which in some cases can no longer even be debated, is a kind of political and intellectual master key: it encourages the Stalinization of economic and political power. It serves, in effect, to justify any authoritarian

The Totalitarian Temptation

form of rule as long as its promoters proclaim a vaguely socialist platform—even if they later prove unable to put that platform into effect or, more prosaically, prove themselves incapable of governing the nation. But, even after the ensuing collapse, in which both human freedom and the beginnings of economic progress are lost, this archaic *caudillismo* dressed in Marxist rhetoric now pleads not guilty because imperialism is there to take blame for its failures. It doesn't matter whether imperialism tried to bring on the collapse or whether it is in fact American (not always the case): "imperialism" is not subject to critical analysis. And the causes of failure are never to be found at home.

Furthermore, the three postulates of pidgin Marxism serve the cause of nationalism, that damper of critical thought and servant of the nation-state, for which they provide new arguments to justify even the most primitive versions. When democratic liberal ideology prevailed, a regime was judged primarily according to its legality, according to the ways in which power was achieved and exercised. Under the three postulates of pidgin Marxism, the regime is judged above all by its anti-imperialism, as measured by the intensity of its nationalism and by its socialist intentions— the implementation of which soon becomes virtually impossible to verify because where such regimes flourish the news has been freed from the sinister influence of "money" with such skill that it has not been heard from since. Since, moreover, nationalization or, more exactly, state ownership of the economy is the only socialism known to centralized authoritarian regimes, this kind of unofficial or lay Stalinism is, under a pseudo-revolutionary pretext, a throwback to the so to speak prenatal stage of political power, when no distinction was made between control of people and ownership of things.

All the ingredients of the confused ideology of pidgin Marxism contribute to paving the way for the entrance on stage of orthodox Stalinism: thus the idea that "democracy is a luxury," that "freedom of information serves no purpose"; or the idea that capitalism can neither remedy the poverty of the third world nor the wealth of the developed world, since it perpetuates misery in the former, alienating overconsumption in the latter and injustice everywhere against a background of constant crisis; and, finally, the idea that social democracy is a bastard, contemptible solution that does not "break with the system." In this mentality, then, everything works together to create the pre-conditions for Stalinism, for the Stalinist type of state, an omnipotence floating on amorphous, silent masses, soon isolated from the world, and to build society on two levels only, the bureaucracy and everyone else.

Receptivity to unofficial Stalinism is, moreover, increased by some ideologies or forms of political action which in theory oppose but in practice favor it. This is often the case with leftism, rival as it is of Stalinists and detested by them: the past-worshiping ideological leftism of Ivan Ilyich, as well as the "revolutionary terrorist" leftism of urban or rural guerrillas.

The ideology of worshiping the past, found mainly in rich countries with advanced technology, feeds, like any worship of the past, on forgetting what actually happened in that past. It is disturbing to see, at a time when a university education is available to an ever larger proportion of youth, when students determine an increasing proportion of political orientations, that ignorance of history, though there is less excuse for it than ever, is still at the root of so many opinions. The sanctimonious evocation of a "conviviality" and a harmony with nature that we supposedly destroyed through the twin sins of education and medicine can hardly stand up under informed historical examination. Only yesterday the average life expectancy was twenty-five years, and famine and epidemic regularly wiped out one third or half or more of the population—was that harmony with nature? A world in which might made right and the weak fought each other implacably—was that conviviality? Ancient Greece in which a war between city-states—large villages for the most part —ended with the "convivial" epilogue that the victorious army put the losers to the sword, women and children and old people included—was that conviviality among peoples? The world of Europe in the seventeenth century when hundreds of thousands of women were burned at the stake as witches—was that a convivial society? The times when a family of six labored in the fields for fifteen hours a day in order if they were lucky to harvest the same six kilograms of bread that the worst-paid immigrant laborer today can earn in less than an hour—was that a convivial way to earn a living? Granted we should not swallow whole the pessimistic picture of the past that was widespread in the eighteenth century—though it was discredited by today's worshipers of the past whose ideology, under its syrupy and sanctimonious surface, is both reactionary and misanthropic. The pre-industrial past was not so harsh a time as it was pictured by the men of the Enlightenment, who contrasted it with the brighter future they foresaw for the generations to come. But far, far less was it the golden age portrayed by contemporary obscurantists, who, if they do not invent the past a priori, assemble a composite image including only the happiest fragments of past societies. After all, those eighteenth-century authors lived before the industrial revolution, when the agricultural revolution was just beginning, in a world that except for a tiny minority was spiritually emptier, more monotonous and more punishing than our own. They were born into that world and they looked upon it every day of their lives, so when they described it with such aversion they perhaps felt and knew better than we what they were talking about. Furthermore, what they wrote is more often confirmed than contradicted by serious contemporary historiography. The work of modern historians like Georges Duby, Pierre Goubert, Peter Laslett, Pierre Chaunu or Emmanuel Le Roy Ladurie, firmly grounded in scientific demography, makes ridiculous the prettified picture painted by those who idealize the past.

That doesn't abolish or excuse the suffering and abuse inflicted on humanity today. At least we do not make that suffering a model to be emulated—except in the case of Stalinism, which many appear to consider quite "convivial."

This ignorant, vague and deluded transformation of the past into Utopia devalues the present by contrast and lends credence to the notion that all the troubles of mankind began with the first world revolution, the eighteenth-century revolution that gave birth to the modern world: the revolution in science and industry, in education, democratic politics and capitalism—in a word, the "system." The idea that economic production, knowledge and freedom are the true scourges of mankind was already being circulated 150 years ago by the old extreme Right.

It follows that any form of totalitarianism would be a lesser evil, provided it begins by ridding us of the system. This belief cannot be countered with logic, for it flourishes on confusion and internal contradiction. An example of the latter is the common practice of eulogizing the way of life of past underdeveloped societies (in most ways pre-industrial Europe belonged in that category) while condemning the present underdevelopment of the third world as one of the great evils produced by the system. But, alas, mental confusion and internal contradiction are the crutches of faith; those who linger in the swamp are bound to catch malaria. As for the past-worshiping ideology of conviviality, it merely adds its sidestep to the gloomy cavalcade of prophets according to whom the jailer is definitely the best physician to treat the ills of free societies.

At the opposite pole from the Utopians of the past, "revolutionary" terrorism also contributes to the advance of Stalinism, for it also holds the premise that existing societies cannot be reformed. "Death and resurrection"—in this view, that is the only law for those who want to change human societies. In a word, *progress does not exist.* Thus opposition to the system must be total, it must aim at the system's destruction.

The guerrilla whose goal is liberation of the national territory has entirely different and completely logical motives.[1]

Here I am referring to purely political terrorism, in inde-

[1] Note however that nations of the third world, for whom wars of national independence or resistance to imperialist invasion have so often and so rightly been sacred struggles, are as capable as others of imperialist aggression among themselves and against their own minorities. We need hardly be reminded of the ethnic genocide practiced by West Pakistan against East Pakistan (now Bangladesh) and by China against the Tibetans. More recently "socialist" Ethiopia threatened to boycott the meeting of the Organization of African Unity, in Kampala in July 1975, if observers from the Eritrean Liberation Front were invited. One rarely perceives one's own imperialism.

pendent nations, of the sort now raging in third-world countries afflicted by economic insecurity and dictatorship as well as in prosperous and democratic West Germany, Canada, Japan, Italy, France and the United States (with its Black Panthers and Symbionese Liberation Army, among others). Its ideology consists of rejecting any method of changing society except a merciless battle against all of society's institutions and all its members, a battle waged by any means, including random killing by bombs in public places and the taking of innocent hostages. Law is a delusion, and nothing can be hoped for from any action taken within the rules of the social contract.

Yet when terrorists of this school of thought are arrested, they immediately appeal to that same law whose futility supposedly excuses their resort to violence. They cry out: "We want our attorney! We want to be treated as political prisoners! We call on the Minister of Justice to remove our prosecutor! We demand the right to communicate with the press and with our friends! We denounce the shameful police brutality to which we have been subjected! We make an appeal here, we make a motion there, and we call on the masses in five continents to denounce any violation of due process in our case!"

Now, either West German society (for example) is as the terrorists described it before their arrests, a society without law that can *only* be changed by violence, and therefore violence is legitimate; or else it is the society presupposed by the terrorists' defense, a society under the rule of law, and therefore the justification for their terrorism disappears and they are no more than murderers under the criminal law. But one cannot claim to have been transported as in a fairy tale from a land without law to a land ruled by law at the moment of one's arrest. The members of the Resistance caught by the Gestapo knew whom they were dealing with: the organization that arrested them was the same as it had been while they were struggling against it before their capture, and they did not expect from the Gestapo impartial judges, press conferences or obliging radio broadcasts.

Unfortunately the terrorists drive democratic nations, which are poorly equipped to cope with them, into taking emergency measures and bit by bit to transform themselves into semi-authoritarian societies. We have seen it happen in France and Italy. It is one of the main ways in which freedom is diminishing. A growing climate of illegality makes democratic institutions progressively less workable, and leads inevitably to competition between fascism and Stalinism, and their alternation in power. The Uruguayan poet Ricardo Paseyro accurately stated why such terrorism results not in revolution, that is in a new state founded on a new social consensus, but rather renders impossible any kind of state and any kind of consensus. Paseyro wrote, in *Le Monde* for February 12, 1971: "Playing the game, directly or indirectly, of those forces that incite civil war, violence outside the law and destruction of the social fabric is a poor service to Europe, to Latin America and especially to Uruguay. The issue in Uruguay, a country which above all values freedom, is not left or right in the French sense; nor is it good or bad government; the issue is simply the survival or the destruction of the rule of law. Whatever the viewpoint of some Europeans—whose attraction to the guerrillas is all the greater because at home they themselves are peaceful citizens—the resurgence of the guerrillas can only retard progress in Uruguay and Latin America. We forget that Nazism began as packs of armed men calling themselves socialists; the fact that there is a considerable number of former pro-Nazis among the theoreticians and sympathizers of the Tupamaros and other terrorist groups is hushed up; nor is it emphasized that the working classes do not participate, even from afar, in these movements."

Besides, without sharing Stalinist or rightist obsessions with the eternal "foreign plot," it is clear (only the willingly naïve disciples of lay Stalinism can doubt it) that many terrorist groups are almost always, if not created, at least taken over by foreign powers. Even the disciples of Stalinism once removed will admit as much, on condition of course that the Soviet Union, China and Cuba be crossed off the list of those foreign powers.

When the terrorist Ilitch Ramirez Sanchez, alias Carlos, evaded the French security services in July 1975, not without adding a few more corpses to his trophies, some newspapers hastened to write that he was surely not an agent of the KGB because he had been expelled from Moscow University for "misconduct." One would think no one ever read the abundant documentation on the classic stratagems practiced by the secret services of all nations, nor even John Le Carré's spy novels. As if the pretense that an agent is being dismissed when he is actually being put on assignment were not the most elementary of precautions! Nothing is certain in this affair, but after a few days' investigation the French government demanded the recall of three Cuban diplomats on the grounds that they were accomplices of Carlos; and the Cuban secret services do not take such actions without clearance from the KGB.[2] Do the armed groups that have been trying to foment chaos in Italy since 1970 receive no logistic support from the East? Those that call themselves fascist are more likely to be mentioned than the other groups, it might be noted. The Chinese Communists also practice terrorist

[2] As one would expect, *L'Humanité's* headline (July 7, 1975) read: "Havana: The expulsion of the three Cuban diplomats from France is part of a campaign against the socialist countries and détente." André Thirion, author of *Révolutionnaires sans révolution* (Paris: Robert Laffont, 1971), wrote me on this subject that the "expulsion" of Carlos from Moscow University seemed like a bad joke. He went on as follows: "When I pointed out the similarity between Communist actions in Portugal and Zinovievism to André Ferrat, he reminded me that Zinoviev was the theoretician of urban guerrilla war. It is hard to believe that all these little groups, which have plenty of money and are able to stage attacks and kidnappings all over Europe (and elsewhere), are not manipulated from outside. Those who attribute it to the Russians are probably right. In about 1934 Ferrat was a French Communist representative at the Comintern and an instructor in the Comintern school. One day someone with the rank of general asked him to give two lectures on the Communist International to students at a 'special' school. He was taken to a place in the suburbs where he met some fifteen French-speaking students, among them Tréand. This special school prepared its students for illegal work; in particular it provided excellent military instruction for the complete terrorist. One was graduated with the rank of major." Thirion concluded: "On that day [the day he was "expelled"] Carlos may have left the university for a special school." Thirion also observed that there is no truth to the legend that the Communists have always been hostile to terrorism and political assassination. He listed a long series of such actions by the Russians, including pre-war urban terrorism in China and the assassination of Leon Trotsky. As for André Ferrat, who taught at the Comintern school, he was later expelled from the party and joined Léon Blum's Socialists.

"destabilization." It is well known that for years China has been training and supplying guerrilla groups in the north of Thailand —but the Thais demonstrate against the American presence.

Thus the idea is implanted in non-totalitarian nations that after all there is no real democratic legitimacy, that in the final analysis the Netherlands of 1976 is the same as Nazi Germany of 1938, and both are to be combated by the same methods. Since everything is totalitarian, Stalinism is justified.

Its success in linking in the popular mind the elimination of human rights with that of social injustice, thereby legitimating totalitarianism, is one of Stalinism's great intellectual triumphs. It undermines resistance to the installation of authoritarian regimes, and it allows them to pass for progressive if they do no more than take the precaution to announce that progressive is what they intend to be. Democracy provides a legal mechanism whereby in the normal political process, without civil war or coup d'état, one administration can be replaced by another if the majority, right or wrong, so decides. Such a system is captivating to few if any of those who hold power. Once they are informed that their socialist conscience forbids them in the interest of the revolution to permit any provision for their own replacement in power, that conscience will also prevent them from allowing any criticism whatever of themselves—especially of their achievement of "socialism"—because criticism is a waste of time if it cannot be translated into a change of administration. If political pluralism is deemed anti-socialist, so also is free speech, for without diverse political opinion it serves no purpose. Once freedom of speech has disappeared, of what value is freedom of assembly, since people usually assemble to express themselves? Besides, such poor folk are likely to let themselves be deceived since they are not "ready for democracy." They must not be left to the mercy of news media manipulated by the money of "imperialist" "multi-national" corporations, for which must be substituted the pure independence of media which are conceived of as an extension of the state, which in turn is an extension of a single party or a military junta.

That kind of reasoning was used to justify the military junta's seizure of Peru's newspapers in August 1974—the seizure being naturally camouflaged as a "return to the people," specifically to the unions, of the papers. But the unions were under outside control and the only political party that was free to operate in Peru was the Communists, who derived from their association with the junta power they still could not obtain from the people: in the last regular elections, in 1962, the Communist party had received fewer than 100,000 of the 3 million votes cast.

In Venezuela, the only Latin nation in which the press is neither censored nor lives in constant danger of government reprisal, an association of journalists put out a statement approving what the Peruvian military had done! Since we cannot assume that all these journalists had suicidal tendencies, we must conclude that Stalinism, of either the unofficial or orthodox variety, prevailed among them—and this in the last nation in Latin America that enjoys a free press. Having commented unfavorably on the junta's measures in *L'Express,* I received several letters from Frenchmen taking me to task for putting the "right to do damage" of the press owned by "feudal capitalists" above the pursuit of the "progressive" Peruvian "experiment."

In fact, the military had suddenly become angry with the papers and expropriated them, not to put them in the service of the people and to perfect the Peruvian experiment further, but rather because the failure of that experiment was becoming ever more obvious to the people, and the junta found it distasteful that the press was reporting the difficulties caused by their administration. The need for silence was particularly urgent because in the fall of 1973 the junta had put down uprisings that certainly originated among the people, among the peasants. The number of bodies buried on that occasion had to be kept secret in the interests of socialism Peruvian-style. A year and a half later the people had the poor taste to riot this time, strangely enough, despite the total absence of a press enslaved by "money," and were again bloodily suppressed by the intransigently anti-imperialist junta. This time the bloodstains could not be concealed from world opinion, the uprising having taken place in the capital itself. But there had been many others that were discreetly shielded from multi-national malevolence. It will be said that Pinochet further to the south is just as barbaric, to which I answer that no one has any illusions about that, and that our ears are not assaulted daily on the topic of the "model society" and the "unique revolutionary experience" of Pinochet's Chile.

Peru's revolutionary model, the "Inca Plan"—conceived, by the way, by a Yugoslav theoretician—provided at that time, in 1975, for the total nationalization of the economy, as the first step toward installing worker management in all enterprises. The Inca Plan rests on what it has become fashionable to call the "parameters of the revolution." Peru's two parameters are nationalism and nationalization. But after six years of revolution the situation is worse than it was in 1969. The ban on foreign investment has had the effect of strangling production, exports have fallen (in an economy almost totally dependent on exports), inflation runs around 30 to 40 per cent a year and, worst of all, *half* the working-age population is unemployed. Nor did the military oligarchs prove impervious to the lures of prevarication and peculation: it was learned in the spring of 1975 that they had illegally sold a million dollars' worth of sugar abroad. It was easier to hush up this scandal at home, along with several others, because the press was no longer subject to the evil capitalist profit motive but was controlled by "the Peruvian people on the march." A journalist explains:

"I tried to ask the general who is in charge of the Ministry of Information how this 'authentic freedom of the press' is now working in practice. I asked him what would happen if the peasants organized in co-operatives used 'their' newspapers to demand an increase in the price they are paid for their products, and the government opposed them. The general did not answer me, but the expression on his face was one of surprise, as if such an eventuality was inconceivable in the progress of the revolution. After a long silence, he tried to salvage the situation with this formula: 'Each must consider the interests of all.' Certainly, but who assumes the responsibility of defining those interests?

The government, of course! 'Naturally, we are for total partici-

The Totalitarian Temptation

The government, of course! 'Naturally, we are for total participation, but it cannot be achieved in a day.'[3]

Confronted with the collapse of the economy, the military had
to admit, in confidence, that "The revolution has lost its spirit; it
has paralyzed its own parameters." What the Peruvian military
and their *caudillo*, General Velasco Alvarado (later ousted by
one of his comrades in arms, who promptly announced he would
follow the same policies—as if they had been such a success!),
were learning at their expense—or, rather, they learned nothing,
and it was at the expense of the people—was that it takes skill to
govern. It serves no purpose to nationalize a mine if no one
works it, nor to distribute land to the peasants if the government
is incapable of reorganizing agriculture, with the result that the
peasants lack the tools and seed and fertilizer needed to work
that land, the sound currency for which to exchange their products, the manufactured goods to buy with that money—so they
abandon the land and swell the growing tide of the urban un-
derclass. Victims of the slogan that everything would run by itself once the economy was nationalized, the Peruvian colonels
just wanted it not to be said that people lived even more misera-
bly after their revolution than before.

In 1975 Indira Gandhi joined the list of heads of state who had
decided that they could not govern unless people were prevented from learning how they were going about that governing.

After proclaiming a state of emergency, her first precaution
was to put her political opponents in jail and to impose censorship on the Indian and foreign press. The new censors explained
that not only would the dispatches filed by foreign correspondents from India be censored, but the correspondent would be
held responsible and punished for anything that appeared in his
paper, even under someone else's by-line. The Washington *Post*
correspondent was expelled four days after the state of emergency was proclaimed for an article reporting that support for
Mrs. Gandhi in the Indian army might be less than unanimous.

I am well aware that freedom of the press and the smooth run-

[3] Hans Heigert in *Resumen*, June 1, 1975. *Resumen* appears in Venezuela,
not, obviously, in Peru.

ning of a Western-style Parliament are not the most urgent problems in India or Peru. Two hundred and fifty million Indians (out of a total population of 600 million) live at the lower limit of physical survival and often fall below that limit. Hundreds of millions of villagers, almost all illiterate, are unaware of the existence of the *Times of India,* and, for the most part, have never even seen a newspaper.

But note that the case can be argued in reverse: if the press does not reach the great mass of Indians, it can have no subversive influence on them, and there is no valid reason to control the press. If the press is, like *República* in Portugal, a luxury for intellectuals, why attach so much importance to it? Mrs. Gandhi once announced a program of major agrarian reform and campaigns against corruption and waste. The press did not prevent her from implementing that program: she had been Prime Minister for almost ten years with an absolute majority in Parliament. Nor did the foreign press prevent her from applying the remedy, since it had regularly reported on that very corruption, that very social injustice, that very exploitation of poor Indians by the rich. Granted that the foreign press sometimes criticized Mrs. Gandhi, about her atomic bomb and her brutal annexation of Sikkim, about the funds squandered by her incorruptible son on his project for the manufacture of a national automobile, the Maruti, "Daughter of the Wind God" (which, faithful to her name, never materialized out of thin air into base metallurgical form). But, even admitting the existence of criticism, such pinpricks could hardly prevent the Prime Minister from implementing her socialist program. I have certainly not noticed that the villagers of Bihar or the fishermen of Kerala fight over copies of the Washington *Post* or that the human wreckage that "lives" on the sidewalks of Calcutta holds critical seminars to discuss the editorials in *La Stampa.*

In fact, Mrs. Gandhi's offensive against her opponents and the foreign and domestic press[4] was *in no way a consequence* of

---

[4] Foreign correspondents who refused to sign a promise to obey the directives of the Indian censorship were expelled, and their papers' bureaus were closed.

India's social and economic imperatives, or of the nation's need to be less badly governed, and can *in no way contribute* to solving those problems. Her actions had nothing to do with India's problems. But they had everything to do with Mrs. Gandhi's own problems, with her personal vanity, and with her recent conviction for electoral fraud by the Indian Supreme Court. Had she lost her seat in Parliament, Mrs. Gandhi under the Constitution of her country would have been forced to resign as Prime Minister. It was under those circumstances that Mrs. Gandhi realized that the struggle against corruption and misery was so urgent that she could not be so cowardly as to delay the suspension of constitutional rights by as much as a single hour.

It was surprising to see even serious-minded professors of political science argue the line that there was a causal relationship between India's need for reform and the establishment of the dictatorship. This linking of the two phenomena is particularly comfortable since under the dictatorship it can become difficult, if one is not an official guest and therefore future apologist for the regime, to gain entry to the nation in order to see how the government's proclaimed reforms are progressing. While awaiting the brilliant success of those reforms, a regime of lay Stalinism was installed, and is ripe to become a client of orthodox Stalinism. Can anyone explain just what the following measure has to do with India's misery? At the first session of Parliament about a month after the state of emergency was proclaimed, journalists were told they could report the ministers' speeches in as much detail as they chose, but they could not report a single word spoken in response to those speeches. Doubtless the starving illiterate masses of Uttar Pradesh and Maharashtra must have felt a great relief and sensed an immediate improvement in their lives in knowing that they had been rescued from the evils of formal democracy and offered the first fruits of people's democracy. (Mrs. Gandhi, by the way, refused to allow a delegation from the Socialist International to enter India, something neither Salazar nor Franco had dared to do a decade earlier.)

The true obstacles to reform in India are, besides the huge size of the nation, its technological and administrative backwardness, perpetuated by the great inertia caused by linguistic and religious divisions and the caste system, which weighs on daily life far more than national pride will admit. And also the incompetence and corruption of the bureaucracy. I do not see how the absence of press criticism will help solve these problems—quite the contrary. If the elimination of "formal" democracy in fact created conditions so stimulating to economic development, our planet should be overflowing with wealthy nations.

In reality, Mrs. Gandhi decreed the state of emergency to head off an Indian Watergate. We underestimate the vanity and ego of chiefs of state. In our view of modern politics we discount the psychological factors whose importance we recognize in history. But individual pride is just as important as it ever was, especially when we allow the reconstitution of monarchical situations with political star figures—like Mrs. Gandhi.

I happened to be in New Delhi on December 1, 1975, during Leonid Brezhnev's official visit to Mrs. Gandhi. Toward the end of Brezhnev's stay, a leader of the Indian opposition suddenly announced that it was inexcusable for Brezhnev not to have met one of its members so that the Soviet leader could add to his impressions of India at least one conversation with someone outside governmental circles.

Surprised, Brezhnev met the opposition leader at literally the last minute, at the New Delhi airport just before he took off for Moscow. During their conversation, Brezhnev asked the Indian to explain the exact nature of an opposition that was free to act and to speak out. The Russian leader ended with a remark whose humor, cynicism or perhaps monumental lack of sensitivity made it both laughable and appalling. This is how it was reported in *The Indian Express* (December 1, 1973):

"Mr. Limaye told Mr. Brezhnev that he was welcoming him on behalf of the Opposition. But Mr. Brezhnev asked him why there should be an Opposition at all. In the Soviet Union, the Central Committee of the Communist Party discussed various issues and implemented them. *An Opposition prevented the crea-*

tion of an emotional bond between the people and the Government." (Emphasis added.)

It seems, then, that eighteen months after that lesson in high political morality, Mrs. Gandhi decided to tighten the emotional bond between herself and her people by suppressing the opposition. She was backed in this by the Soviet Union and by the one of the two Indian Communist parties that is faithful to (and subsidized by) Moscow. Thus Mrs. Gandhi had brought her domestic policy into line with her foreign policy, which for some years had consisted of increasingly following the Soviet line in order to counterbalance American and Chinese influence in Asia. India was quite a recruit for Moscow's world strategy.

Stalinism is not always so fussy in its choice of clients—as long as they are dictators, that suffices. The Soviet Union has gone so far as to express great esteem and friendship for the tragicomic and bloody tyrant of Uganda, General (later Marshal) Idi Amin Dada, and has supplied him with arms. When other African heads of state expressed reservations about the demented butcher of Kampala's candidacy for president of the Organization of African Unity, the Soviet Union itself protested against this campaign of slander, which it said was due to "imperialist machinations." After this fine example of Soviet non-interference, Amin won the desired presidency of the OAU. Moscow's support of Amin had a foreign policy purpose: its African rivalry with China, quickened by America's indifference or even absence. In particular, China's penetration of Tanzania incited Moscow to seek a counterweight in neighboring Uganda. At the same time, the Soviet Union was stirring up a civil war in Angola, then on the verge of independence, by pushing into action its local organization, the Movement for the Liberation of Angola, which Moscow had lavishly supplied with arms, just as it had lavishly armed the Nigerians when they were exterminating the Biafrans in the late sixties. I do not deny that this is the kind of game the great powers have always played. I do say that if those actions had been taken by Western powers, the Americans and the CIA, we would still be hearing the din of protest and demonstration. But if it is a crime and a mistake for the Americans to support

Diem in Saigon and Park in Seoul—and I believe it is—why is it not the same when the Stalinists support similar dictators?

According to Stalinist logic, there is also a domestic policy reason for this support of dictators—a reason which wins the approval of those leftists who have been conditioned by the prejudices of unofficial Stalinism. The Russians and the Chinese find it easier to deal with authoritarian states than democracies because these states have social structures similar to their own. If they are not yet Communist they are much more likely to become so than is any democracy. "Third-world socialism" would serve the same purpose. Thus they must be aided to make themselves totalitarian, to isolate and arm themselves, to become economically independent—which is to say economically and militarily dependent on the Soviet Union.

Lay Stalinists greet such regimes with approval or at least uncritically because in their hearts they have become convinced that socialism and democracy are incompatible. Their consciences do not trouble them because as time goes on they are ever less able and ever less willing to see what is happening in the closed society of the authoritarian state, while they remain well aware and critically in full detail of the faults and failures of democratic states. Thus the socialists give their benediction to a pell-mell procession of new authoritative states, some of which are classical Communist regimes belonging to the International, while others are vaguely leftist military dictatorships, as in Peru and Ethiopia, which are granted a license to commit exploits as bloody as those of Pinochet in Chile while also enjoying the status of creators of a revolutionary "model." Pinochet kills, jails and oppresses people. They have simply progressed beyond "obsolete" democratic liberalism.

Unofficial Stalinism is far more prevalent and influential in the world than the docility toward Stalinism of those known since 1917 as "fellow travelers" has ever been. These non-party members in taking Stalin's side against Trotsky have always been a minority: willing and talented propagandists, yes, but still a minority. And for good reason: it is impossible to transport more than a few thousand "impartial" witnesses per year, and the special contribution of the fellow travelers—a great name for a travel agency, by the way—has always been the donation of political tourism, followed by the political bread-and-butter letter. David Caute has a chapter titled "Conducted Tours" in his book *The Fellow-Travelers*.[5] These are the people who depicted the Soviet Union of the 1930s as an Eden of feasting and freedom, where everyone ate his fill and the citizenry's relationships with those in power were characterized by that freedom from fear, sunny confidence, affection and frankness celebrated forty years later in India by Mr. Brezhnev. It was they who announced around 1950 that the Soviet Union would soon start exporting its food surpluses to the capitalist world, which was notoriously unable to maintain its own production. (The Soviet Union must in most years import millions of tons of wheat from the United States and Canada to avoid famine.) They are the ones who since 1956 have been describing the irresistible progress of universal de-Stalinization, without bothering to note that since the brief and timid paternalistic interlude under Khrushchev re-Stalinization has resumed its normal course of jailings and deportations, inherent to this kind regime, under the leadership of Brezhnev, who in domestic affairs is simply a buttoned-down Stalin without the old man's dementia. Meanwhile, the fellow travelers had discovered the road to Cuba, where it took them a decade to discover that Castro had perhaps committed some economic blunders that could not be blamed on the American embargo and had created a police state run by Soviet advisers, with "re-education" camps, televised brainwashing and state-encouraged informing on one's neighbors. They were a bit upset in 1971 when a writer, Herberto Padilla, was incarcerated: while

[5] New York: Macmillan, 1973. How edifying such tours can prove is suggested by Simon Leys' account (in *Ombres chinoises*, p. 13) of the journalist who wrote an excellent description of his voyage to China without actually going there. He just borrowed from other descriptions. Had he gone, he would have followed exactly the same itinerary, visited the same factories, attended the same banquets, heard the same speeches, in that never-never land, neither the West nor China, that is "China for foreign visitors." On his return he would have written the same account that he did write, probably not as good. The only surprise is that he was found out.

repression is revolutionary when it falls on peasants and workers, it can be totalitarian and intolerable if it strikes a colleague, an intellectual, though of course it is incidental and without roots in the system (a thoroughly scientific Marxist interpretation!).

Thanks to Mao, the fellow travelers could soon forget about the embarrassing Castro. Shipped in droves to China, they returned with books and articles that are faithful copies of those their forerunners wrote about the Soviet Union in the 1930s. The fellowship recruits non-Communists, of course, many of whom are sympathizers, but not all. Stolid members of the bourgeoisie, eminent professors, protean thinkers, all are in this category, with no obligation to profess Marxism-Leninism. The only ideology shared by all fellow travelers is that of the organized tour ending with a favorable, constructive report—the prospect of being denied a visa or not being invited back being among the greatest terrors that afflict mankind. André Gide, when he returned from a pre-war visit to the Soviet Union, made himself conspicuous by his courageous and clearheaded refusal to sing the usual rhapsody.

Today the fellow travelers in their role as propagandists continue to help to promote an atmosphere of indulgence toward the minor sins of Stalin-Maoism and receptivity toward official claims of Chinese and Soviet successes. (And even Albanian ones. In 1970 a Marxist Maoist journalist, Gilbert Mury, wrote a series of articles[6] under the title *Albanie, terre de l'homme nouveau,* which, as the title suggests, notified us that that nation, under the regime of Tirana, was the crucible of future human liberation.)

But unofficial Stalinism is not limited to the phenomenon of the fellow travelers. It has a much larger following and does not always draw its inspiration from the Soviet Union or China.

In 1974 President Ramanantsoa of Madagascar proclaimed that he was "setting the nation on the socialist path," like the many others whom we are more likely to find at the beginning rather than the end of that path. Nasser's Egypt, Boumediene's Algeria and al-Qaddafi's Libya are (or were) nations in which a

[6] In the now defunct newspaper *Combat,* January 9–16, 1970.

117

totalitarian or authoritarian state undertook in the name of socialism to collectivize the economy by means of nationalization and bureaucratic rule. Thus the state has become effectively Stalinist, even if it is ruled by practicing Moslems who are categorically anti-Marxist and in foreign policy anti-Soviet or anti-Chinese or at least, from a diplomatic point of view, "non-aligned." They are, however, recognized as "progressive" leaders. In any event, a good dialectician can always manage a synthesis between differing beliefs. Here for example is an episode related by an Algerian intellectual:

"One day we met Roger Garaudy. In a lecture given in Algiers, on March 11, 1965, in the Ibn Khaldoun hall jammed with students, Roger Garaudy, after a ringing defense of Islam, took on the famous line: 'Religion is the opiate of the people.'

"'The line dates from an 1843 text: in his *Critique of Hegel's Philosophy of Right*, Marx is only twenty-five; he is not yet a Marxist, he is only a Feuerbachian, not yet a dialectician.'

"And Roger Garaudy concluded with this fine rhetorical flourish:

"'We will reach socialism with the Koran in one hand, *Das Kapital* in the other.' Some Marxist students who had expected intellectual sustenance from the great French Marxist thinker were left stupefied."[7]

Promising beginnings are more willingly hailed than the gloomy morrows are described, and it is rare to see in black and white that, for example, "The Burmese way of socialism has slowly driven the country into misery" (Catherine Lamour in *Le Monde*, August 31, 1975).

The "non-aligned" socialist states still tend despite that label to line up on the side of one or the other of the two great Communist powers: on the Chinese side in Southeast Asia and a few parts of Africa, on the Soviet side almost everywhere else, as we can see from the diplomatic posture at one time or another of Nasser's Egypt, Syria, Somalia (where the Soviet Union has installed missile bases) and, more recently, India.

The Soviet Union with its vast military might openly supplies

[7] In *Elements* (1970).

help either to the nationalist ambitions of a state it wants to make a satellite or, in the case of armed conflict within a country, to the faction it wants to bring to power. Such maneuvers are denounced with much less vigilance even in the West when they are made by the Soviets than if the instigator is a Western power, especially the United States. Assuming that both sides are equally guilty, the resistance to their misdeeds is not equal, for there is in the Communist nations no group that is pro-Western or indulgent toward the West—at least none that is free to act and has access to the means of information and mass communication. There are in the Soviet Union or China no political parties that can serve to justify or minimize Western imperialism, as Soviet imperialism is served or minimized in the West.

For example, on July 20, 1975, during the news telecast of the first French television network, TF1, the network's special correspondent in Angola covered the local situation by taking his camera and microphone to the Luanda airport, flooded with Portuguese settlers who had been camping for days in the hopes of getting on a flight to Lisbon. These were only the comparatively small number who already had tickets: thousands of others had been on the waiting lists for weeks. The special TF1 correspondent explained that these Portuguese had been unduly panicked by "reactionary propaganda." This could only mean that independent Angola was about to become a peaceful nation in which the colonial settlers could work and prosper. The TF1 correspondent's comments amounted to dismissing as insignificant the civil war then raging in Angola, the thousands of lives lost in the battles among the various Angolan movements, fronts, parties and tribes, the very real insecurity that prevailed in the country. According to African sources at the OAU meeting then taking place in Kampala, Uganda, the combat among the rival liberation groups had already cost more lives than the war of liberation against Portugal. Truces and cease-fires were repeatedly proclaimed and immediately broken. Besides, one may be opposed to colonialism, as I have always been, and still not refuse to recognize that a country achieving independence—even without civil war—does not overnight become a terrestrial paradise of political wisdom and respect for the individual. In particular, xenophobia is a natural enough feeling among those who have long been dominated by foreigners and who are just emerging from a ferocious battle for independence. Xenophobia is in fact widespread, and this makes it rare and highly unlikely that a large number of former colonial settlers will be accepted as a lasting element in a new nation. One of those cowardly Portuguese who had swallowed that "reactionary propaganda" answered the TF1 correspondent's sarcastic questions with a question of his own: "Are there many of the French settlers left in Algeria?" Caught off guard, the French correspondent sputtered unconvincingly: "Oh yes, there are still some left!" The correspondent was misinforming that Portuguese settler about Algeria just as he was misinforming his French audience about Angola, for he was stammering to avoid admitting that the huge exodus of the Algerian French after the Évian accords of 1962 is a known historical fact. I believe the French settlers in Algeria were blind to reality after World War II when they tried stubbornly and, alas, all too successfully to force the French government to fight to the bitter end to save a stupidly repressive colonial order. One can plausibly argue that the settlers drove the Algerians to revolt, and thus destroyed any possibility that the two people's could live in harmony. But let us try to understand them: clairvoyance is more often found among isolated individuals than among imperiled social groups, and thus has little influence on collective behavior except perhaps in those rare civilizations where free access to accurate information occasionally gains the upper hand over propaganda and lies. Nor let us cast stones at the Algerians for not observing the Évian accords: the clauses offering guarantees to the French who stayed and compensation to those who left were economically and psychologically impossible to implement.

At the very least, Algeria was a historical precedent that might have been taken into consideration before preaching sermons to the Angolan Portuguese who wanted to go home.

Nor could the Angolan crisis be accurately summed up by the simplistic notion of a conflict between "reactionary" colonialists and Angolans determined to lead their country to a tolerant and harmonious independence. The rivalry among the various liberation movements (with their underlying tribal rivalries) had degenerated some weeks earlier into open warfare, after a compromise arranged by the president of Kenya had broken down. The best-armed of the rival groups, the MPLA, was openly supported by the Soviet Union, while Radio Moscow, during the week of July 14–20, when the fighting was particularly murderous, accused its principal rival, the FNLA, of getting arms from China via Zaire. In short, it was an arena in which competing imperialists energetically stirred up local passions. They supplied their Angolan agents, with the bill to be paid later, just as they were doing at the same time in Mozambique, and in both cases the Soviet clients were far better supplied than their rivals. But, as presented to the French television audience, the only big bad wolves in the Angolan affair were those still nostalgic for the colonial past and, above all, the capitalist oil companies, who, aided by the CIA, coveted the rich enclave of Cabinda. That was not necessarily false, but it was hardly the only factor in the situation.

Thus Stalinism is strengthened, under the attentive and benevolent gaze of those it wants to destroy, either by the actions of political parties and partisan groups supported by the Soviet Union or China, or by governments connected with Stalinism though without explicit affiliation, or, in the few functioning democracies, by an all-or-nothing ideology that holds capitalism to be an absolute evil and subordinates all other goals to the destruction of the "system," root of all evil.

Unofficial Stalinism benefits from the climate of reaction against the cold war and McCarthyism. Those who too frequently discern Communist intervention in a nation's domestic affairs are easily dismissed as obsessive, even when that intervention cannot be denied. The result is inequality in the denunciation or even the description of the different types of imperialism. When it becomes known that American agencies or unions subsidized European unions after the war, or that Exxon and Mobil secretly funded Italian parties, or that the CIA has "de-

stabilized" a Latin American government—facts that by the way
are always brought to light by American investigations—the
news is widely and repeatedly published. By contrast, it is not
considered in good taste to discuss Soviet subsidies to Western
Communist parties, or the often spectacular acts of "destabilization" by Soviet agencies, or the large-scale means employed by
them, for example in Portugal, to prevent the establishment of a
democratic regime, thanks to their collaborators within the
armed forces movement. It is not surprising that the Communists
deny, camouflage or minimize all these operations: that is their
game, and if I were Communist, I would play it the same way.
But when it is done by the non-Communist Left, by liberals, concerned about détente—that is the phenomenon of lay Stalinism.
The French Communists, for example, have never been sparing
in their violent attacks on Mario Soares, the Portuguese Socialist
leader, whom frequently they accuse of conspiring with the "reactionaries." But the French Socialists, while they asssured Soares
of their "friendship" and "confidence" (but how belatedly and
how timidly), never dared before August 1975 to point the finger
at the Portuguese Communist party and denounce the military-
Stalinist plot that was systematically subverting the construction
of democracy in Portugal. On the contrary, the French Socialists
denounced those who denounced the Communists, reproaching
them for "shedding crocodile tears" over freedom in Portugal.
There is a flagrant lack of symmetry between the French Communists' untiring attacks on Soares and the equally indefatigably
conciliatory posture of the French Socialists, desperately denying
that there was a conspiracy in Portugal and refusing to see the
problem until it was too late. Besides, while the Communists allied to the Socialists in France are unanimous in their support of
the armed forces movement in Portugal, the Socialists allied to
the Communists are far from unanimous in giving even nominal
support to Soares. Thus a teaching assistant at the University of
Paris who is a member of the Socialist party wrote in a letter
published by *Le Monde,* which *L'Humanité* delightedly reprinted the next day (July 23, 1975):

"At this moment no one can predict the turn that events will take in Portugal. But it is enough just to look at television to see in those 'socialist masses' howling their class hatred the faces of the assorted bourgeoisie of Petrograd . . .

"More seriously, the demonstrations orchestrated by Mario Soares are similar in all aspects—I base this on information shown on French television—to those organized by the Chilean Right against the government of the socialist Allende . . .

"Kerenski had uniforms. Soares has none. That's the difference between them. Otherwise, no platform; 'policy' made on impulse; an electoral strategy according to which the party accepts henchmen of Salazar along with workers."

L'Humanité's headline did not distort the writer's views: SOARES CHOOSES REACTION. We see once more that Stalinists and socialists are not equals in their alliance. Although a substantial number of socialists join the Communists in heaping the standard Stalinist accusations on Soares, no Communist breaks with the party line to attack Cunhal and defend Soares. A fine example of unofficial Stalinism.

As we have seen, lay Stalinism also appears in the form of nationalist authoritarian regimes which often are military and call themselves socialist. In one of the political books that is essential to an understanding of out times, *From the Good Savage to the Good Revolutionary*,[8] the Venezuelan writer Carlos Rangel describes how Latin America, through a mixture of nationalism, inability to govern, feelings of cultural failure, leftism and *caudillismo*, always manages to strangle in the crib the conditions that would lead to a stable civil order, then lapses into violence and chaos, so that it is hard to distinguish except by their rhetoric those on the Left from those on the Right. The spread of pidgin Marxism in Latin America has relegated to the ideological dustbin "obsolete democratic liberalism," more or less honest Western-style representative regimes, freedom of information and pluralism. As I noted, Venezuela is the only remaining free republic in South America. But that accomplishment does not make it a "model" worthy of consideration, in the eyes of its neighbors and Venezuelan "progressives," especially because

[8] Harcourt Brace.

since 1973 it has taken the supremely despicable form of social democracy. It doesn't function too badly, and the government has the wrongful habit of instituting reforms without recourse to civil war. This solution is so unfashionable that one finds, for example, in the report on Peru quoted earlier, the following sentence, offered as a banal, self-evident truth: "Since 1969, the revolutionary regime of the Peruvian generals has governed this country without Constitution or Parliament, and the fact that it has presented itself as a leftist force has won it the sympathy and the support of *all Latin American intellectuals.*" (Emphasis added.)[9]

The tragic fall and assassination of Salvador Allende in Chile has been attributed entirely to the intervention of the CIA and to the timidity of Allende himself, who, we are told, should have had the courage to adopt completely the "revolutionary way": i.e. abolish democracy. This false analysis is then used to justify violence and authoritarianism as the only socialist solutions.

Finally—this is the third visage of docility toward Stalinism—the belief is spreading even in the oldest free democracies of Western Europe and North America that no transformation or improvement of the system is possible within the limits of the social consensus—even though such changes are in fact constantly taking place. Even in Great Britain, with the *Tribune* faction of the Labour party and the Marxist wings of some unions, even in the Netherlands and the United States, despite the absence of any significant Communist party, we find groups of ever growing importance that hold to the theory that the destruction of the system is the only key to any improvement. In those countries the flavor of pidgin Marxism is a stock ingredient of most of the thinking and writing of students in economics and sociology. According to this well-learned lesson, democracy is nothing but a particularly refined form of repression, indeed totalitarianism in disguise. Such conditions provide ever more fertile soil for the spread of authentic totalitarianism.

[9] *Resumen*, June 1, 1975. It was on October 3, 1968, that the junta headed by General Velasco Alvarado took power. The junta was overthrown in late August 1975 by General Morales Bermudez.

If the abolition of democracy were all it takes to "make the revolution," the world would have been reveling since prehistoric times in the most enduring kind of socialism. If, even, one could make the revolution without simultaneously creating or strengthening democracy, there would have been no revolution betrayed, anywhere. Democracy and human freedom are not an optional extra added to decorate the revolution when it seems strong enough to bear such embellishment. They are the brain of the revolution, and they develop with it just as the brain grows with the organism it directs. Freedom in a society is simply the use each individual is allowed to make of his mind, and democracy is the application of the minds of each and all to the directing of the society. Thus these are not incidental, marginal factors that can perhaps be postponed to be added later on, but rather they are guiding principles inherent in any civilization that lives, changes and survives. Doubtless revolution can occur in a society that is not yet able to stand, or, better, to make use of, more than a small dose of democracy and freedom. But to that extent the revolution is not a revolution. It is like a mentally ill person who enjoys only a few lucid moments per day; it remains rudimentary, embryonic, sickly. Such a revolution very soon becomes the opposite of what its originators intended. How can the obscurantism of the old regime, against which people rebelled, now prove an asset in constructing the future? Democracy and freedom are not sufficient conditions for the transformation and the effective function of a society, but they are necessary conditions. For that matter, there is no sufficient condition for a successful revolution: only the combination of necessary conditions will suffice.

Of course, elections and freedom of the press alone will not eradicate poverty, hunger, disease and inequality. As we've been told often enough, the Indian peasant finds himself no worse off for the imposition of censorship, of which he is unaware, in New Delhi. But the French peasant of the eighteenth century was equally unaware of the struggle for cultural freedom carried on by the Encyclopedists. Whether or not those men of the Enlightenment were allowed to publish in no way affected the peasant's daily life. Or so it seemed. But in fact the work of the Enlightenment was undermining the power of those who oppressed that peasant. And the freeing of the human spirit, even if not everyone was able immediately to benefit from it, was a decisive factor in the creation of conditions that led to the emancipation of the peasantry. Would it have been farsighted and "revolutionary" to maintain at the time: we don't need freedom to publish in a country where most of the people cannot read? After all, literature and education are in large measure the result of the freedom to publish. A strange kind of logic: something is lacking, so let's perpetuate it!

The nature of orthodox Stalinism in its strictest sense is to present reactionary theories—and, alas, not just theories but actions also—as revolutionary and make those who disapprove of those theories and actions be considered as reactionaries.

The nature of lay Stalinists is to accept that upside-down logic and to act as propagandists and unpaid agents for the Communist counterrevolution. That counterrevolution consists in particular of discrediting and destroying social democratic and middle-of-the-road parties, with the result that in a multiplying number of conflicts around the world the only remaining choice is between the extreme Right and Stalinist totalitarianism.

8

THE EXCOMMUNICATION
OF SOCIAL DEMOCRACY

In the London of 1775, according to George Christopher Lichtenberg in his *Aphorisms and Letters,* two groups of condemned men met, one coming from New Prison, the other from Bridewell. They arranged a race and bet on which would be the first to get to the execution grounds at Newgate. The group that came in second won the bet.

Similarly, the two main groups of socialists today are racing to see who will have the pleasure of being the first to arrive in prison, by which I mean a totalitarian or authoritarian society. This society may be either Stalinist Communist or of the extreme Right, as in Franco's Spain or post-Allende Chile brought on by the breakdown of the economy and of the last vestiges of the political consensus.

Under the Leninist doctrine of democratic centralism (which would be better named "bureaucratic centralism"), the Communists have no objection to this sort of society, the oppressive character of which they deny. In their view whether a society can be defined as totalitarian depends not on its structure and how it operates but on the answer to this question: "Who holds absolute power?" If their adversaries do, the society is totalitarian. If they do, it is not, even though the society is, in both cases, governed in the same manner. But what about socialists?

Once and for all, to avoid misunderstanding due to ambiguous usages, I am using the word "Communist" (not "socialist," as they like to call themselves) to designate nations governed by a Communist party in which that party exercises all powers: economic, political, legislative, judicial, labor, police, military, imperial, and the power of information.

The Totalitarian Temptation

We can no longer restrict the list of state powers to Montesquieu's accurate but too summary executive, legislative and judicial. These three powers tend to separate into other kinds of power, which become first administratively and then politically autonomous, and which a totalitarian regime can subsequently recast into a single form of power, which is therefore far more overwhelming than that of the old-fashioned dictatorship.

These "nine powers" are themselves affected by the lesser or greater weight of one of them, military power. In other words, each of the nine powers (including the military itself, according to whether it is more or less autonomous or dominated by another power) is internally divided into civil and military power, the degree to which a political, judicial, cultural, police etc. power is civil being determined by the army's lesser or greater weight in the society. The nature of Communist regimes is to join the nine powers into one.[1]

I reserve the name "socialist" for those opponents of capitalism who want to reconcile socialism and political democracy, that is who are anti-Stalinist. As I argued in the first part of this book, as well as in an earlier book, *Without Marx or Jesus*,[2] communism has always been Stalinist, if one bears in mind that the term refers to a way of exercising power and not only to the intensity—which will vary according to needs and circumstances—with which it is exercised. Stalinism in turn is merely Leninism, for an examination of Lenin's own political career demolishes the pious myth that he was betrayed by Stalin.[3] Just as did the Portuguese Communists fifty-eight years later in conjunction with the military, Lenin turned to dictatorship when the elections went against the Bolsheviks. The Russian "dictatorship of the proletariat" was installed in a country in which proletarians made up no more than 5 per cent of the working population. It was therefore inevitable that the dictatorship ten years later had

[1] See Chapter 14 for a development of this analysis, or, rather, an explanation of this list.
[2] Doubleday, 1971. See also *Les Idées de notre temps*, R. Laffont, 1972.
[3] On the subject of Lenin, see the landmark study by Maximilien Rubel, cited earlier, *Marx critique du marxisme* (Paris: Payot, 1974), especially the essential *postface*.

to exterminate, deport or reduce to serfdom those who made up the great majority of the working population—the peasantry.

Those with a taste for the study of dialectics will sample with relish the millions of words produced by the Left the world over in an effort to explain and to justify in the name of socialism the fact that the Soviet Union reintroduced the institution of serfdom abolished by the tsars in 1861. Forced assignment to collective farms is often preceded, as it is today in Tanzania, by the relocation of entire villages which have been dismembered and their residents mixed into new social groupings, according to the whim of planners. Such methods come right from Lenin via Stalin and Mao. I would not go so far as to affirm categorically that totalitarianism is already included in Marx's own Marxism.[4] Rubel disagrees, and so does Papaïoannou, the distinguished scholar, with the help of many very convincing texts. But the writings of Marx on the state are too dispersed, contradictory and utopic for one to be able to derive a coherent theory.[5]

Nonetheless, the streams of Marxist thought since Marx have flowed in the direction of totalitarianism, and if one holds to Marx's own historical determinism, the responsibility must at least in part be his. In theory Lenin is also very fuzzy on the subject while by contrast his practical application was all too clear.[6]

[4] This is the point of view expressed by André Glucksmann in *La Cuisinière et le mangeur d'hommes* (Paris: Seuil, 1975). I am particularly pleased to report this, since the author had written an article violently hostile to my *Without Marx or Jesus* (the French edition appeared in 1970), in which I argued that same point of view. A human being who changes his mind after reflection is so rare a thing that a special prize should perhaps be created to compensate such an evolution in judgment following the perception of new arguments or facts. It is true that Glucksmann's final diagnosis and supreme anathema is that the Soviet Union is the last bastion of capitalism.

[5] Pierre Nora, a historian, sums up this contradiction in one sentence when he describes "the twofold idea that Marx develops, on the subject of the Commune, in *The Civil War in France*, where he states at one point that the dictatorship of the proletariat will lead to the destruction of the state, and at another that the reinforcement of state centralization is a necessary condition of the revolution itself." (Pierre Nora, Foreword to *Les Luttes de classes en France et le 18-brumaire de L.-N. Bonaparte*, Karl Marx, new edition, "Libertés" Collection. Paris: J.-J. Pauvert, 1964.)

[6] See K. Papaïoannou, "Marx et l'état moderne," in *Le Contrat social*, No. 4, Vol. IV, and "Le Dépérissement de l'état," in ibid., No. 5, Vol. V.

If free socialists or libertarian Marxists, advocates of the reconciliation of socialism and political democracy, reject totalitarianism, what do they believe in and what do they want? There is in fact a political-economic system that has rather effectively reconciled socialism, freedom and self-government; that has substantial achievements in both the economy and social justice to its credit; a system that offers the added advantage of existing. That system is social democracy. But—a supreme paradox—that system, which would seem to represent an appreciable first step toward "socialism with a human face" if there ever was one, is condemned vehemently by libertarian Marxists, who hold it to be a veritable betrayal of authentic socialism and reject it with profound contempt.

Indeed, from the orthodox Marxist point of view, social democracy is "collaboration between classes." Its goal is not to abolish capitalism but to distribute its fruits more equitably, not to "destroy the system" but to humanize it and make it more egalitarian. "Capitalism with a human face" disarms the working class by making it comfortable in its exploited situation. But the class struggle is and must always be the driving force of history. That struggle must not cease from want of combatants or because the welfare state or the progressive equalization of income and opportunity has eliminated the cause of conflict. Rather the struggle can end only in the victory of one class and the disappearance of the other, the elimination of the proprietary class, the expropriation of the bourgeoisie and the conquest of the governing apparatus of the state by the proletariat.

From that perspective, such policies as co-determination, as it is called in West Germany, or industrial democracy, the term used in Britian and Sweden, are both dangerous and anti-socialist. Under these policies, supervisors, employee representatives and in some cases union delegates who are not employees of the firm sit together on the firm's administrative board or on another more powerful body, the supervisory board. (German companies, unlike American firms, have a two-level management structure: a management board which conducts day-to-day business, and a supervisory board which appoints the management board and sets over-all policy.) Under industrial democracy, the employee and union representatives have access to the firm's confidential records, which is necessary if they are to fulfill their functions on either of the boards. It is well known that when, as in France, worker representatives sit on the board, both they and the directors tend to avoid touchy issues. Even the directors who represent the shareholders do not understand most of the reports concocted by the management and thus are in no position to ask hard questions. Workers and union representatives are at even more of a disadvantage if they lack the information to exercise oversight competently and to bargain effectively. The issue of disclosure of industrial secrecy was discussed at length in Britain when a new industrial democracy act was being drafted, because disclosure can be used for the purpose of industrial espionage.

The general idea of co-determination leads to a form of economy in which management is less accountable to the stockholders (among whom turnover will be high) than to the employees (who will tend to stay with the firm) for approval of past actions and future plans. The logical end of this road is an economy managed by the unions; it has already been proposed in Germany that the decisive vote in the supervisory board be cast by a president who is not only designated by the union but who is not an employee of the firm.

Thus, there is virtually direct management of the economy by the unions, but without the elimination of capitalism, at least not in theory; though it is inconceivable that the practice of capitalism will not be profoundly changed after a few years of co-determination. Private investment remains, as well as the need to earn a return on investment, and the state intervenes as seldom as possible to salvage firms that are operating at a loss. But if we consider that controlling the economy means controlling investment—the decision where and how much to invest—co-determination cannot help making employees participate more and more in true economic power, especially since it will apply in credit institutions as well as in industry.

But this social democratic school is nonetheless excommunicated by the Marxists on the grounds that it prolongs the days of history's most famous and enduring dying personality—capitalism. To be a social democrat is to be what Marxist socialists call, in the time-honored terminology, a "loyal agent of big capital" or of "the bourgeoisie." The label of social democrat is therefore a term of opprobrium, the supreme dishonor, an ignominious accusation which any Marxist socialist, at an opportune time in a meeting, will hurl in the face of a rival he wishes to eliminate by shoving him into the same tumbril as the rightists. He himself of course remains forever faithful to the "strategy of breaking with capitalism." A very long-term strategy, to be sure, for in the present this Marxist socialist will limit himself out of "realism" to proposing a few usually trite reforms, far more likely to harm production rather than capitalism itself, and pretty pallid compared to the measures long ago adopted, implemented, and assimilated in the social democratic nations.

Co-determination is considered anti-Marxist not only in terms of long-term strategy, but also in terms of immediate tactics, because it implies co-responsibility. But once labor is taking part in management it becomes hard to demand all of a sudden wage increases of 30 to 40 per cent, as the British unions did throughout 1974, without taking into account either the situation of the individual firm or the needs of the national economy. Simply being informed about current problems has the effect of cramping one's style: "I don't want to know about it, let them work it out; if the company goes bankrupt, nationalize it!" A union movement that limits itself to making demands has no desire to take part in decisions, and therefore in whatever mistakes the firm may make in its industrial, commercial and technological policies. Finally and above all, if the union movement is both demanding and politicized, it does not want to enter into those social democratic agreements with management and "capital" under which the employees, in return for specified benefits, agree to make no further demands during the term of the contract and to refrain from striking as long as management also observes the agreement. Far from permitting capital to count on a period of labor peace and assured production, a Marxist union movement wants to exploit capitalism's difficulties, to keep capital off balance whenever possible, particularly by the weapon of the strike, which must remain unpredictable (though the legal requirement of a strike notice may reduce somewhat the surprise factor). Agreements with management are not so much contracts as pauses in the struggle. The struggle must resume as soon as possible, and meanwhile the union leadership, if it is consistent, must emphasize that it is not satisfied and that management has "refused to negotiate."

A social democratic union movement is well aware that if it helps hold down the rate of inflation it is protecting its members' purchasing power, that reducing the cost of living is the equivalent of a wage increase and that such a union policy is healthier for the economy as a whole than wage increases that are promptly canceled out by rising prices. A politicized union movement, by contrast, naturally prefers the kind of wage increase that aggravates the critical condition of the capitalist economy. Its ultimate goal is less to improve the situation of the working class than to prevent capitalism from functioning, so that it can take control of the state and install uncompromising socialism.

This sort of reasoning is notable for its abstract nature, its indifference to everyday realities. That is because capitalism is viewed as essence or substance. In scholastic logic, "substance" as the essential and unchanging nature was distinguished from "accident" as transient and superficial events and characteristics that do not alter the substance. The substance of capital is therefore invariable, no matter what form its accidental manifestations may take. Conversely, in a society where private ownership of the means of production has been eliminated, the evil has been removed by its roots and the substance is intrinsically good, even though its accidents may be disappointing or even catastrophic. If there exists an absolute evil, which is big capital, with the domination of monopolies, that evil and that domination are the same in Rio, Paris, London, Johannesburg, Calcutta and Stockholm. They rest on a cornerstone of solidarity and complementarity. In this interpretation, the lot of a Dutch citizen differs only in insignificant detail from that of a Spaniard under

Franco or a Filipino under Marcos, the subjection of the Dutch to capital being merely masked by the hypocrisy of human rights, an egalitarian distribution of the national income and democratic control of public health, housing and education.

If social democracy is excommunicated as reactionary, and if free liberal socialists ("liberal" in the political, not the economic free enterprise, sense) reject Stalinist bureaucratic rule, then what is left? What is their path to socialism? Some have sought to find it in what is called worker management. But worker management exists in only two places in Yugoslavia, where it has proved to be a fraud and a myth, and on the drawing boards in theoretical plans that, though interesting and worthy of respect, are too confused and contradictory to constitute a political and economic option that a government could apply in the here and now. If a socialist government were to receive carte blanche from the electorate tomorrow morning and were to be told: "Go ahead, implement worker management," it would not be able to define what it was supposed to implement.

Albert Meister, a sociologist at the École Pratique des Hautes Études in Paris, has studied Yugoslav worker management with great sympathy as well as insight.[7] Meister found that providing on paper for worker management had not ended the rule of oligarchy in industry, but had on the other hand reduced both efficiency and the dynamism of growth. While worker participation in decision-making within the firm has become more formal than real and has fallen into disuse, the firm has resorted increasingly to outside intermediaries, agents, consultants working on commission, to find raw materials or markets or even to reorganize the firm and straighten out its management. Meister concluded that "twenty years of worker management have made Yugoslavia a cemetery of unimplemented rules."

I would add two further observations. First, worker management has not prevented the emigration of those hundreds of thousands of Yugoslav workers who, particularly since 1965,

[7] Albert Meister, *Où va l'autogestion yougoslave?* (Paris: Éditions Anthropos, 1971), and "Autogestion: les équivoques de cas yougoslave," *Le Monde*, July 1–2, 1974.

have voluntarily harnessed themselves to the capitalist yoke in Switzerland, France, Germany, Great Britain. Second, the Yugoslav political system, while it tolerates some individual rights, including the right to emigrate, remains in essence an autocratic police state. Prison is still the Yugoslav remedy for deviationists. A Marxist would have to concede that, according to historical materialism, it is impossible for an economic base founded on worker management to be matched with so different a political superstructure. Thus, either the economy is not really worker-managed, which is probably the case, or else the political system was handed down by God the Father. I would make the same observation about those rural economies that are supposedly peasant-managed, the Algerian collective farms for example.

The ambiguities of worker management in practice are reflected in the plans drawn by certain socialists in the developed capitalist nations. In practice, we see that nominal worker management does not prevent the stifling of employee initiative by a techno-bureaucratic minority nor the manipulation of the workers by the cops of the single union. In a planned and nationalized economy the domination of state and party officials becomes inevitable. Furthermore, economic and technological progress depends on decisions, notably budgetary decisions, that workers' councils cannot effectively control.

This basic contradiction casts a long shadow. If each worker-managed enterprise is truly independent, that amounts to introducing competition and the free market in a socialist economy. In that case, what becomes of the planned economy, which is essential to socialism? The answer that planning will be flexible amounts to calling it dry water, for the flexibility of a plan is inversely proportional to its value as planning. The concept of flexibility, familiar in capitalist planning, means that the individual firm is not bound by the plan but simply implements it when it suits the firm's interests. Then what happens to worker-managed enterprises that go bankrupt: will they be salvaged with state funds? In other words, will other citizens be called upon, voluntarily or not, to make a fiscal sacrifice for their incompetent or unlucky comrades? If so, who makes the decision? If it is the state bureaucracy, that is the beginning of the end of socialist worker management; just as under capitalism (more so to the extent that unemployment is banned) the result is to empower the state to hold for ransom some branches of industry and their employees, in order to perpetuate the inefficiency of others. Or, as the spirit of this sort of socialism would suggest, would the workers of each enterprise throughout the nation vote on whether they were to be taxed for the benefit of others? And suppose the vote is no? That is possible, and even likely, especially since in post-industrial societies the industrial workers are a diminishing minority, while employment in services increases and agricultural employment persists. Will the winegrowers of the South of France and Italy come under worker management, and will it be left to them alone to decide whether to continue to overproduce wine that is both undrinkable and unmarketable? If not, will other French and Italian workers have the right to deprive the winegrowers of the subsidy necessary to continue an activity that does not pay, since earning a return on investment is not a socialist criterion? It all comes down to deciding whether the workers are to owner-managers or simply managers.

Making them owner-managers would be a revolution similar to the French Revolution of 1789, when parceling out the estates of the nobility to the peasants created the agricultural smallholder. That would result in a mosaic of small independent units of production needing massive tariff protection in order to survive, protection similar to that required in France in the nineteenth century to keep the agricultural smallholder alive. It is no coincidence that the advocates of worker management are also the most extreme economic nationalists. An example is Anthony Wedgwood Benn, leader of the Labour party's left-wing, during his spectacular tenure as Harold Wilson's Secretary of State for Industry from February 1974 to May 1975. In his ferocious campaign against the referendum vote by which Britain joined the Common Market, Mr. Benn raised the specter of "the end of national independence" with a talent for demagogic vociferation and weeping accusation worthy of the old Gaullist school.

The same is true of the left-wing of the French Socialist party, which advocates worker management and at the same time wants France to refuse membership in a "Europe of the monopolies" subservient to capitalism. One of them, Michel Rocard, even argued at a conference of socialist economists that the construction of a socialist society would require that France retreat into virtually complete economic self-sufficiency and political isolation.[8] Note in passing that those socialists who claim to be the most libertarian and anti-bureaucratic are also those who, by their dogmatic opposition to European integration, serve best the foreign policy interests of the Communists.[9] This is not the only case—Portugal is another—in which the socialist ultra-leftists, in theory those the most opposed to Stalinism, find themselves in practice on the same side as the Stalinists, whose methods they also emulate in internal disputes.[10]

But in the other alternative, if the workers are to be managers but not owners, who then will own the enterprise? Not capital, which by definition is eliminated. The remaining candidate is the state, which brings us back to bureaucratic centralism, with all the political consequences we know about, not to mention the economic consequences, which we also know about.

None of the theoretical plans for worker management has avoided the absurdity of simultaneously envisaging the reinforcement of the state's central authority, necessary to assure the transition to socialism in spite of the opposition of powerful class enemies who will try to stop it, and the decentralization designed to put decision-making power back in the hands of workers and peasants. This contradiction shows up repeatedly in

[8] At Suresnes, June 5–7, 1975.
[9] At the Suresnes conference, the first secretary of the Socialist party, François Mitterrand, rebuked Rocard, reminding him of the "internationalist calling" of socialism.
[10] For example, the way in which a "moderate" (that is, social democratic) Labour Member of Parliament, Reginald Prentice, was denied in June 1975 his party's nomination for the next election illustrates the use of purely Stalinist methods of action. The party committee in his district was methodically stuffed with "pure socialists," many of them from outside the district, who, once they had a majority, then voted Prentice out during a meeting at which he was barely permitted to speak. This "majority" of the committee represented a faction which commands the support, in the district and in the nation, of less than 10 per cent of the electorate.

the reports of conferences and meetings of the French Socialists.[11] It appears also in the writings of the British Labour party's left-wing, for example in Stuart Holland's book *The Socialist Challenge*,[12] of which Peter Jenkins accurately observed in *The Guardian,* July 25, 1975: "The whole argument is pitched against Social Democracy . . . Mr. Holland relies on workers' control as his second panacea. At no point does he attempt seriously to reconcile the edifice of his planned socialized economy . . . with the preservation of an open, democratic society."

The theoreticians will protest that I am oversimplifying outrageously, that there will be stages: capitalist ownership will not be eliminated all at once in the "transition to socialism." But after observing the proliferation of conferences on, in Holland's words, "a strategy which makes possible a democratic transition toward socialism," I want to know what will happen *after* that transition. I am told it is too early to decide that, and meanwhile we'll pass the time by analyzing once again the crisis of capitalism. Socialism is on the march, it is in a state of constant self-renewal, it is necessary to save the world *from its doldrums.* Yet all it has to offer is still a transition toward itself.

All of this is so because Marxist socialists do not dare go to the end result of the line of thinking in which they are engaged, nor do they dare formulate explicitly the conclusion of the reasoning whose premises they drone on about interminably.

If on the one hand Marxist socialists do indeed reject social democracy as consisting of class collaboration, and if on the other hand they concede in general that worker management is still just a theory with no practical value and thus not a policy to be offered as a practical alternative to bureaucratic socialism, then indeed the only path open to socialists is nationalization under the aegis of the state, which means going back to bureaucratic centralism with Stalinism as the obligatory political super-structure.

To believe that if a leftist coalition came to power tomorrow it would have a choice between bureaucratic centralism founded

[11] Notably October 12–13, 1974 and June 21–22, 1975.
[12] London: Quarterly, 1975.

on nationalization of the economy and some version of socialism *other* than social democracy amounts to entrusting the future of the world to fortunetellers. Granted that socialist thought can be enriched in thousands of ways. But the issue is not ideas alone, it is action, for one cannot govern by conferences. Today in the real world of power and policy-making there exist as alternatives to capitalism at this stage in its history just two proven systems, each of which functions with its own limitations and defects: social democracy and communism. One is, in my view, the only viable starting point for socialism, the other is the Stalinist counterrevolution. The real struggle is between these two systems. Those dissatisfied with capitalism as it is who fail to choose one system are in effect choosing the other. And those who claim not to choose either while saving their harshest attacks for social democracy's "class collaboration" are in fact choosing Stalinism. All the more so because Stalinism uses such brutally efficient methods to gain power that neutrality in the face of them amounts to abdication.

Three

THE SUICIDE OF
THE SOCIALISTS OR
THE INDIRECT JUSTI-
FICATION OF TOTALI-
TARIAN SOLUTIONS

9

EXCESSES IN THE ECONOMIC CRITIQUE OF CAPITALISM

Industrial capitalism was pronounced incurable at its birth. No economic system has been so criticized for so long a time. Today it is indicted on two counts. One is economic: capitalism is not viable, it is in a permanent state of crisis, afflicted with "contradictions" that are either insurmountable or that can only be temporarily overcome by palliatives. The second count is moral: capitalism is the exploitation of man by man, the profit motive supreme, the rule of money, the inevitability of injustice.

Modern capitalism—associated with the industrial revolution and scientific and technological innovation, incarnated in the entrepreneur and taking the material form of the firm, a new unit of production organized and run according to new principles— dates from the end of the eighteenth century. By the middle of the next century, socialists were diagnosing it as being in a state of advanced putrefaction, portending an early collapse into horrible convulsions. The death rattle was, and still is, to occur because capitalism could only survive by satisfying demands that are incompatible—so it could not survive. Because of one of these demands, capitalism must increasingly impoverish its own employees, thus depriving itself both of its consumers and its labor force. Because of its doctrinal importance to Marxist theory, this thesis of absolute impoverishment was still quite recently being defended against all the evidence by the Communists. In 1953 Maurice Thorez, the secretary-general of the French Communist party, was describing "economic decline, disorder in public finance, misery, unemployment, the multiple

143

difficulties of workers in the cities and in the fields."[1] In 1953 Europe had just entered into the greatest economic expansion in its history; in France, the nation Thorez was describing, public finance had just been reorganized by Antoine Pinay (his budgetary orthodoxy and its class impact were subject to criticism but were certainly not "disorderly"); the "misery" caused by the 1929 crash and the Second World War was diminishing as signs of prosperity appeared.[2] Unemployment was diminishing and indeed disappearing, for industrial capitalism was entering, for the first time in its history, an unprecedented twenty years of full employment (which came to be so taken for granted that the developed nations panicked when full employment ebbed in the 1973 energy crisis, though earlier catastrophic depressions had caused much greater unemployment).

In 1955, a year in which France's growth rate was one of the highest in the world, Maurice Thorez sharpened his analysis still further with a description of "the stagnation of the nation's economy . . . the depression affecting many industries, many regions . . . the increase in the relative and absolute impoverishment of the proletariat." Having nonetheless dimly perceived in the said proletariat certain new consumer habits suggesting added financial resources, this spokesman for scientific socialism confidently concluded: "New service stations and a few thousand more motorbikes are not going to change anything."[3]

[1] Quoted by Philippe Robrieux, *Maurice Thorez,* p. 431.
[2] I was away from Europe, living in Mexico and intermittently in the United States, from December 1949 to October 1952. I still remember my astonishment when I returned to find a well-to-do nation instead of the threadbare France I had left less than three years earlier. All the instinctive reactions I had acquired during the forties were anachronistic. Inflation, which had reached 58 per cent during 1948, was down to 12 per cent in 1952, and below 10 per cent in 1953. Let me add a personal note, lest my impressions be misinterpreted. My view of a newly prosperous Europe did not result from my having unusual resources or belonging to a privileged minority: I was employed as a functionary by the Ministry of Education, married (my wife was not working), father of two children; my life was not easy. But a difficult life in a country mired in poverty is quite a different experience from the same life in a nation whose economy is expanding.
[3] Robrieux, op. cit., p. 446.

In the face of the rising standard of living of the masses during the fifties and sixties, the theory of absolute impoverishment was quietly dropped in the wastebasket. Or rather placed on the shelf: for, though it cannot be factually sustained, it remains the basic text of all the sermons on the "insoluble crisis" of capitalism. Even if it is not officially proclaimed in political debate, the theory of absolute impoverishment is implied whenever the problems of capitalism are discussed, not as ills which can be treated, but as a fatal illness leading inevitably to the ceasing of all economic functions, which cannot do other than cause absolute misery (still limiting ourselves to its economic critique). Capitalism is intrinsically not viable because it doesn't work. That is a tautology, but it reflects, in the last analysis, the rejection in principle of capitalism as a vicious system that impoverishes everyone, including the capitalists.

The conclusion that capitalism is bankrupt is, strictly speaking, more than a little contradictory. If one scans the socialist and Communist commentaries on the economic crisis touched off by the 1973 rise in oil prices and the attendant disorder in world currencies, one finds two main themes that are hard to reconcile: one, that the capitalist system itself has run out of tricks and is about to founder, precipitating exploiters and exploited alike into a common bankruptcy; two, that the cause of the crisis was an increase in profits, with its consequence the imposition of austerity on the workers.

The second thesis does not seem to imply that capitalism is a failure in the purely economic sense, since if profits increase the system must be working. It is simply a variation on the theme of relative impoverishment, according to which capitalist growth, while it may slightly increase living standards, does not avoid the growing gap between wages and the earnings of capital. The two arguments are different and even mutually exclusive: that capitalism is at the end of its rope as a productive system and there is too much inequality in capitalist societies are two affirmations that cannot be argued as part of the same case and do not lead to the same actions. Correcting inequality is a practical objective that has been undertaken, and not without success, by some social democratic or just plain democratic governments since the turn of the century, and especially since 1930. One may denounce its insufficiency and demand more energetic intervention,[4] but in so doing, one assumes there is buying power to distribute and goods to purchase—that is, that the system is not moribund. On the other hand, it is futile to demand more if one contends that the system is in the process of destroying itself—even for its beneficiaries. Nonetheless, the two themes meet and mingle according to the most irrational logic of the emotions. On the one hand, socialists and Communists periodically announce that purchasing power continues to diminish and the workers' living conditions are steadily getting worse—which, considering their standard of living at the dawn of the industrial revolution, means the workers must by now be existing in the most abysmal misery. But on the other hand, the same socialists and Communists rightly demand wage and social benefits, which means they are betting that the system can produce those benefits. But no sooner are these benefits won than they categorically deny their reality and even their existence in order to re-establish the principle that capitalism is incapable of improving itself, correcting inequities or even simply making the economy work. Socialist literature is full of books and articles on, for example, the history of social security, family allowances, labor legislation or the democratization of education, in which the author, after describing precisely and competently the tangible improvements, indeed the considerable reforms in these areas (dating from as much as two generations ago, or only a few years or months), after discussing their strengths and their inadequacies, will suddenly conclude that all this is illusory and uninteresting as long as the root of the evil has not been removed, as long as one has not "eliminated capitalism."

I repeat that I am at present examining only the economic, not the moral, critique of capitalism. A system can be immoral and

---

[4] See especially Jean-Claude Colli, *L'Inégalité par l'argent* (Paris, 1974, Gallimard) and Lionel Stoléru, *Vaincre la pauvreté dans les pays riches* (Paris: Flammarion, 1974), with the very complete bibliography in the latter book.

function well; it can be moral and function poorly; finally—and this is the prescription followed most conscientiously by the majority of ancient and modern societies—it can be both immoral and ineffectual.

Moreover, an effective economic system does not necessarily function at 100 per cent: rather it is a system that, all things considered over the long term, shows a favorable balance sheet, with more successes than failures and fewer disadvantages than advantages. Even if the score were only favorable by 51 to 49 the question would be how to improve the record by diagnosing the system's ills through economic analysis and remedying them through political action.

But the socialist critics have concluded that the global collapse of capitalism is already predestined. Logically they conclude that it is impossible either to revive or improve capitalism. Capitalism suffers from leukemia.[5] Recession, inflation, unemployment, confusion in the exchange rates: these are not, in their view, problems that one might try to resolve while seeking to minimize the human suffering they cause. Rather they are symptoms foretelling the end. Each fact presages death, and so for that matter does its opposite. Whether commodity prices are rising or falling, the dollar is too weak or too strong, credit too easy or too tight, exchange rates floating or fixed—the prognosis is still

---

[5] The term is from one of the authors of the joint platform of the Left, J.-P. Chevènement (*Le Quotidien de Paris*, October 25, 1974). In this article, devoted to the crisis of capitalism in France, Chevènement announced as inevitable the worsening of inflation, the foreign trade deficit, the foreign debt and unemployment. A year later the first two of these ills had been treated with some success, inflation having been reduced to 10 per cent a year and the balance of payments being restored. But socialist commentators went right on talking about the "total bankruptcy" of the system. Though they had predicted correctly in one case out of the three, that unemployment would get worse, they failed to add that a law voted in the interim, guaranteeing those laid off for economic reasons 90 per cent of their pay for one year, was hardly based on the principles of "savage capitalism." One may object that the law's implementation was not perfect, especially at the beginning, but *imperfect implementation* is not the same as *total deficiency*. To say that there is not enough penicillin in a hospital is not the same as saying that medicine is at the same stage as before the development of penicillin, or that penicillin does not exist, anywhere, and *cannot exist*.

death. Until 1973, after twenty years of expansion with full employment and moderate inflation, the mortal illness of capitalism
was—inevitably—growth. After that it became stagnation. Before, capitalism was burning up the planet's resources while
alienating humanity through overconsumption; after, it was fading into the doldrums while starving the third world. Not that
the diatribes of Western socialists changed from one period to
the next; the same severity of language was used to denounce all
types of error in all its forms. For their part, doctrinaire Communists in Moscow itself discerned the classical symptoms, familiar
to those trained in Marxism-Leninism, of the "crisis of capitalism" as described back in the nineteenth century. On the contrary, in the two decades preceding 1973, capitalism's era of
abundance had resisted their usual tools of analysis. Now, in
1974 and 1975, the Communist ideologues were able to restore to
its place of Marxist honor the theory that capitalism, undermined
by its internal contradictions, was about to collapse, while the
Soviet press and television demonstrated the truth of the theory
and the imminence of the collapse by presenting numerous
disgusting and pathetic pictures of the social traumas of the
West. At the same time, and doubtless because they saw that the
last hour of their old enemy was at hand, the Russian leaders
were hurrying to take advantage of the dying man's final spasms
of vitality. First, in 1972 and 1975, they bought tens of millions of
tons of wheat, with credits that virtually amounted to subsidies, from capitalism's moribund productive system, to make up
for the shortage of food in the Soviet Union. Then they hastily
entered into long-term contracts with all sorts of multi-national
corporations (a fine gesture, when you think about it, since the
Russians knew those firms were about to follow capitalism out
of this life) under which those worn-out corporate whores were
to supply the Soviet Union with technology, know-how, even
capital, and in return were guaranteed forever against any expropriation or nationalization.

One wonders sometimes what would become of socialism if
capitalism were not there to support it. That support unfortunately does nothing to alleviate the senile debility of the capital-

ist system, any more than it authorizes us to doubt the basically robust health of the socialist economy. One may even shed a tear at the sight of that decrepit old man rushing to the rescue of a husky red-blooded youth. Despite all his crimes, the old fool knows how to go out in style.

The most active department of socialist thought for the past century can be seen as an undertaking establishment that keeps itself occupied, indeed overemployed, fidgeting over the details of capitalism's funeral arrangements. All is ready for the imminent delivery of the mortal remains. A cloud of witnesses goes to and fro, bringing news from the bedside, where the patient is forever about to expire, to the public outside, where the socialist funeral procession awaits only the final signal to get under way.

Soviet experts differ more than Western socialists in their views of the crisis of capitalism. The hardliners, whose point of view was expressed in a resounding article by K. Zarodov (in *Pravda*, August 5, 1975), believe they must take advantage of the enemy's current troubles to finish him off. The more cautious faction think it would be premature to launch a general revolutionary offensive. The same debate took place in 1947–48, and the hardliners carried the day against Eugen Varga. The result was that Communist parties resigned from coalition governments in Western Europe, and the cold war began.

Imminent or not, the outcome is inevitable, according to both Soviet ideologues and doctrinaire Western experts whose orientation is socialist but not Marxist. For the capitalist system's faults and setbacks are not the result of historical solutions, but are symptoms of the irredeemably pathological substance of capitalism. That is the verdict and the synthesis.

However, on the same grounds of history and technique, that verdict is hardly sustained by the evidence, and the synthesis in no way derives from a balanced interpretation of the principal phenomena known to us.

Indeed the essential question in this debate is not just whether capitalism has faults, but whether it has more or fewer faults than other economic systems past and/or present, and whether its faults are more or less serious than theirs.

Already I can hear the socialist rejoinder: rather than a mere flat comparison among various aspects of the past and present, all equally subject to criticism on different grounds, we must think in terms of the "dynamics of the future." Socialism is the creation of the new, socialism is the future.

Bravo! And here is my reply: If you say you are judging capitalism in terms of another economic system which does not as yet exist, I grant you that its imperfections and incongruities may seem intolerable. But your comparison in that case is so speculative and experimental that it would behoove you to be more humble and intellectually prudent, less dogmatic and intolerant. For in practice you argue as confidently as if you were comparing two real systems, rather than comparing a real system with a plan. You say, on one side there *is* capitalism, on the other there *is* socialism: let us compare them. But not only *is* there no socialism, not only is socialism not an existing fact (except in Stalinist eyes), but socialism is not a certain or even contingent reality of the future, if one reasons with any rigor.

When I say that you are taking the easy way in comparing what exists to a system that does not "as yet" exist, I am being overly generous. The "as yet" presupposes that we just have to wait for a known event to occur, as if we were expecting the arrival of travelers separated from us only by an interval of time. But what we are discussing is not future fact, it is a hypothesis. Human thought would of course be lifeless if it never speculated on the possible. But even speculative thought dies when it becomes incapable of distinguishing between the hypothesis and the event, so that it bases itself on one as if it were the other. Satirists have often lampooned the old-fashioned literary figure who scorns all his contemporaries' books in favor of the masterpiece he has not written. Alas—what is outmoded in literature seems to be avant-garde in politics, and what is ridiculous in the first becomes heinous in the second, because it is dangerous to others besides the impotent megalomaniac.

It is in fact dangerous to tell the public that one is in possession of a "model" system so perfected as to justify the *complete destruction* of the existing economic system, in the short or the long run (though here "the long run" is only a figure of speech, for we are told it is an "irreversible process"). We know that the strategy of breaking with capitalism (and therefore with social democracy and reformism)—that is, the repudiation of "class collaboration"—is one of the basic traits by which one can recognize Marxists: Communists, organized socialists allied with Communists, the increasingly influential left wings of social democratic parties and, lastly, the unorganized socialists, those diffuse omnipresent schools of thought that impregnate the attitudes of contemporary non-parliamentary leftist groups raised on pidgin Marxism. They all agree that "nothing can be done" within the "existing system."

So do not claim—I would say to the socialists in conclusion—that you are starting with a rational critique of the capitalist economy on which you intend to graft a political program leading, in an inevitably foggy future, to its transformation. That kind of prudence isn't your style, and you despise those who profess it. You are not seeking the right to explore, to experiment. Rather you claim the right of total social surgery, like the quack physician who claims to know, as if it were a routine operation he has successfully performed a thousand times, how to replace all the patient's organs at a single stroke. You also make excuses, to the point of turning our stomachs, for all your friends' surgeons whose patients expired on the operating table. For years and years you go on maintaining that the operation was a complete success and that the patient will exhibit the flourishing state of his health as soon as certain unfavorable conditions and maleficent adversaries have been eliminated. Should the deceased insist by chance on remaining dead, the latter will bear responsibility for the crime—you political geniuses! You have invented a new art of government which, according to you yourselves, can only succeed when it meets no obstacles and faces no enemies.

Yes, you loftily claim to possess the *only* remedy, to offer the *only* possible choice. Every day we read titles of this sort: "Socialism: The Only Solution to the World Crisis." You talk as if you had in your hands a completely constructed society, a fully proven solution, with an obviously favorable balance sheet. Why don't you claim the rights of the researcher, the explorer, driven by the urgent need for change, of course, but who nonetheless remembers that he is venturing into unknown territory?

Since your objective remains the *total abolition* of the present system, which *you* will replace with "the" socialist society, of which you concede there is no satisfactory example, although to listen to you go on so endlessly about it one would think there were dozens, you must assume that capitalism in its essence has been a *total* failure as compared to the complete success of non-existent socialism. And your method remains, not a comparison between hypothesis and reality, which is legitimately creative and induces action, but a comparison of what exists with what does not. Unfortunately such a procedure provides no base from which we can evaluate the economic merits and flaws of capitalism. Thus I am on sound ground in holding to my original rule: to judge capitalism we must begin by comparing it to systems that exist or have existed in the past. Then it is legitimate to plan change and to undertake action to implement that change, providing we have not too greatly distorted the probable gains and losses. But how can one decide what could be if he does not understand what is and what has been? I repeat: the faults of capitalism are obvious, but we must know whether they are greater or lesser than the faults of other economic systems past or present, whether they are indeed peculiar to capitalism and whether they can or cannot be corrected.

With respect to production and living standards, the capitalist economies have known their ups and downs, but no serious economist would deny the long-term increase in both over-all production and average per-capita income. Between 1925 and 1975 the standard of living roughly doubled (or, in some countries, tripled) despite two depressions, the first of which was truly catastrophic, despite a devastating world war in Europe and Japan, and despite the loss of the colonial empires. To summarize roughly the statistics and give an idea of the magnitude of change, average purchasing power increased by one half just in the decade 1960–70. And despite the recession that began at the end of 1973, the standard of living remained well above what it had been ten or even five years earlier, which after all on a historical scale is only a brief interval. Thus progress continued over the middle term. Of course production and purchasing power sometimes fall below a previously achieved level. It took several years for some European countries after World War I to regain their 1914 level, and for the United States to regain its pre-1929 level. But though jagged, the graph of this century is a sharply rising line. In any event, the capitalist system's capacity to produce seems dazzling compared to that of pre- and semi-capitalist and pre-industrial systems before the eighteenth century.[6] These latter, though they occasionally produced a surplus (little or none of which was reinvested), were characterized over the long term by economic stagnation, which in turn led, also over the long term to stagnant population figures.

The total population dropped tragically at times when food production fell; then, when conditions, climatic and other, improved, both production and population recovered, but this recovery was nonetheless not the beginning of that phenomenon we call growth. Economic growth does not make its appearance until the beginning of the eighteenth century. In any event the industrial revolution was preceded by a revolution in agricultural production which, by putting an end to periodic famine, set

[6] Jean Baechler, in his highly original essay, "Les Origines du capitalisme" (*Archives européennes de sociologie,* 1968, reprinted in collection *Idées,* Gallimard, 1971), showed that the preconditions for the capitalist system and its first human agents appeared in Europe as early as the eleventh century. But here I am speaking of capitalism as it is understood today, a kind of economy born of the eighteenth-century encounter between scientific development and the capitalist system. Jean Gimpel, in his *Révolution industrielle du moyen âge* (Seuil, 1975), rightly emphasizes the flowering of technological innovation in the Middle Ages, considerably greater in many respects than in the sixteenth and seventeenth centuries. It remains no less true that the birth of experimental science in the seventeenth century, the progressive discovery of the laws of nature, with the support of basic rather than empirical research, together provided opportunities for technological applications—for both agricultural and industrial innovation infinitely greater than those available to even the most ingenious in the pre-scientific age.

off the demographic expansion that provided the labor force for the industrial revolution. As the historian Emmanuel Le Roy Ladurie observed, French rural society from the early fourteenth to the early eighteenth centuries was a "society without growth."[7]

All these facts are well known now, for the work of "quantitative history" has brought within our grasp the bedrock of historical reality: food production and population. The works of such "quantitative historians" as Marc Bloch, Le Roy Ladurie, Poitrineau, Meuvret, Peter Laslett and Pierre Goubert provide the means for those who so desire to cleanse their minds of all that rubbish about the "golden age" of rural societies before the industrial revolution. For our purposes, the realities described above should more than suffice to underline the inanity of that favored theme of vulgarized Marxism according to which the result of capitalism was to "organize misery" and impoverish the majority of people.

The socialists will reply that of course they do not deny the over-all increase in production, only the equity of its distribution. But by implication they do deny the increase, for when they refer at every opportunity to the "constant worsening" of the workers' situation, that amounts to denying that production has gone up. Is it possible, even with the worst intentions, even in the most iniquitous society, even with no corrective taxation or transfer of money from one class to the other, that production could have increased as much as it has during the last two centuries in the West without making a favorable impact on the standard of living of even the worst-off proletarians? Thus to claim that these latter are ever more impoverished amounts to denying that production has increased. The imagination soars at the thought of the shouts of triumph that we would hear every day if a single Communist nation could claim to have achieved in so short a time the advance in the people's prosperity, as measured in statistics but also, and especially, in daily life, that occurred in the Western nations after World War II. As we know, failure is never evidence in Marxist eyes that the Commu-

[7] *Le Territoire de l'historien* (Paris: Gallimard, 1973), p. 19.

nist system is inherently inefficient, nor is success evidence that any efficiency is inherent in the capitalist system. Capitalism only displays its essence when things begin to go badly; it is only its true self when production stagnates or unemployment becomes intolerable. No matter that over thirty or fifty years production and real income in capitalist nations doubled or tripled and full employment was achieved most of the time—capitalism must still be judged exclusively on the three or four years of the Great Depression of the thirties and on the recession that began in 1973. This despite the fact that real income in the "recession" of 1975, *though its rate of increase had slowed,* was half again larger than the similar figure in the "prosperity" of 1960.

Unless one chooses to disregard all the statistics and all the facts, one must conclude that capitalism has at least solved the problem of production, beginning with producing the minimum necessary amount of food, which has been mankind's goal since prehistoric times.

A goal that, alas, still is unattainable in the third world. But capitalism and all that accompanies it in the West—most notably scientific and technological development and universal elementary education—have not been practiced in most of the third world. Though invaded by capitalism in its colonial form, the third world never had the power, nor in general the desire, to make capitalism work for its benefit. However, it is not our purpose in this book to evaluate the chances of transplanting capitalism, nor to describe the political and cultural conditions under which it might take root in a civilization where it was not invented and did not develop in conjunction with other changes in the economy, in customs and in ways of thinking. That is another discussion, which cannot usefully be undertaken before the one which now occupies our attention.

In order to reproach capitalism for its failure to solve the problem of production in underdeveloped regions, a grievance which is often heard, one must concede that it has solved it in the developed capitalist nations—that is, that there *are* developed capitalist nations. Otherwise the reproach is absurd and contradictory: how could capitalism explain and apply to others what it has not found for itself, or aid others when it is itself in need of help?

This indictment of imperialism and of capitalism's impotence in the third world implies the acquittal of capitalism's productive performance at least in the home territory where it was born and grew up. It assumes that it has already been proved that, compared to the pre-capitalist systems it replaces and the non-capitalist systems that are its neighbors, capitalism is by far the most efficient producer—one is tempted to say the *only* efficient producer.

Only the stoniest of hearts would reproach the Soviet Union for not going to the aid of the world's hungry people when it does not have enough food for itself and when its consumer goods industries can only painfully and belatedly imitate those of the West.

This is so much the case that observers who want to describe advances in production and the standard of living in Communist nations always make the same type of comparision: the windows of a few stores that now brighten such and such an Eastern European capital *are almost as well* supplied as those of the West; the people on the street are so fashionably dressed that, my word, you'd think you were in Rochefort or Piombino. If this paroxysm of luxury goes on, in five or ten years traffic in Moscow will be as congested as it is in Gournay-en-Bray! Nonetheless, statistics, eyewitness reports and personal experience all agree: the supply of food and other consumer necessities remains scarce and chaotic. Of course the consumer's everyday living conditions have improved, by comparison with the still greater penury of the past, but even these improved conditions would be considered unbearable in Western nations.[8]

[8] Here, for example, is a description of shopping for food in Moscow as late as 1975 (by Gerard Nirascou in *Le Figaro*, August 9, 1975): "No Muscovite goes out for a walk, to work or simply to visit friends without taking a shopping bag. This is because you must always be ready to stop at a store or a sidewalk stand to buy the kilogram of apples or oranges that the luck of the distribution system has placed in your path. Residents have been broken in to this over the years. If you see a line of two hundred or three hundred people in front of a store window, it means only one thing: an unusual delivery (bananas, that extremely rare fruit, or lemons, not to be found in

Even the complementary descriptions of improvements in the standard of living in Eastern Europe given by sympathetic (or grateful) visitors are a bit condescending, for they sound the note of "pleasant surprise" on finding that things look pretty good after all. The implication: compared to the disaster we expected. The star role attributed to East Germany, for example, is an inadvertent admission of bankruptcy. People forget that this richest Communist economy is a former capitalist economy wrecked by socialism, in the continent's most industrially advanced nation, comparable in this sense to Czechoslovakia, and that these two nations had high levels of education and were reservoirs of technology, management and skilled labor. To measure their achievement, they must be seen in the context of the rich industrial capitalist nations, not the other Communist states; compared to the latter, the mere vestiges of their past excellence still cut a fine figure. Of course, Germany and Czechoslovakia were devastated by the war, but so was Japan. In 1948, before the first Prague coup and the Communist take-over, Czech industry had recovered to the point that the Skoda plants were already exporting automobiles to markets as distant as Latin America.

To be fair, one should also compare countries that were mainly agricultural in 1940, like Romania and Spain. Romania, still very backward, in 1975 had the lowest standard of living in Eastern Europe (except for Albania); Spain has become a modern industrial nation. Sad to say, the Conducator Mr. Ceauşescu, and the late Caudillo Franco (the two titles are synonymous)

winter, or lettuce, a miracle). Often the Soviet citizen joins the line without even knowing what is being sold. Obtaining food remains a problem in the Soviet Union. No one dies of hunger, of course. But no one can plan a menu in advance or express any preference for lunch or dinner. Production and distribution are completely anarchic; in the Soviet Union you do not eat what you want, you eat what you find. Every housewife knows that basic rule." That pretty much describes Western Europe during the war and immediately after it. Communists will deny the objectivity of the description because the author is a bourgeois journalist. I need hardly add that this is always the case, the bourgeois journalist being the only one free to write, and that this description is only one example picked at random from a host of similar eyewitness accounts.

proved to be equally gifted as dictators, but not as administrators. Besides, the whole policy of détente with the West promoted since 1970 by Leonid Brezhnev has as its main object what amounts to contracting out to the capitalist world the development of what is perhaps the planet's greatest reservoir of energy and raw materials—the Soviet Union. Certainly Soviet industry is advanced in some categories: weaponry, space, nuclear technology. But, adopting the distinction made by Alain Besançon, a nation may be an industrial *power* without being an industrial *society*, that is without having succeeded in establishing incentives linking industrial production to the consumer market. Or, if one prefers Alberto Ronchey's expression, it can be an "underdeveloped superpower."

Agriculture in the Soviet Union is even sicker than industry. It is disturbing to note that Russia exported wheat before 1914, but today is periodically forced to import it to meet her population's needs, and that the productivity of Soviet agriculture is about one sixth that of the West, while by contrast the productivity of the *dvor*, the small private plots tilled by peasants on their own time, is about three times that of the collective farms. These tiny *dvor* are responsible for nearly one quarter of Soviet agricultural production, and are the cities' only source of fresh vegetables, via a parallel market that substitutes for the failure of the network of state stores. The deficiencies of a planned economy are aggravated by the anarchy of planned distribution.

I grant that the system does not always fail. As I wrote earlier, a system that provided *nothing* but failure could not long survive, despite the extraordinary virtuosity of certain chiefs of state who have managed to make such systems last for a while. Also the objection raised to criticism of the Communist nations—"You know, it's not all disaster, you have to recognize their positive aspects"—is irrelevant. There are "positive aspects" to everything, including Nazism. The systems we are comparing have their assets and their liabilities. The issue is to draw up a balance sheet for each system and to determine which is the *more likely* starting point for the construction of a better society.

It would seem from the evidence now available that, in terms of efficiency and economic viability, the defects of the Communist system are more numerous, more harmful and more persistent than those of capitalism: if, that is, the purpose of an economy is to serve economic goals (which is not always the case), if it is to be judged on its ability to produce enough for its population and to distribute its products in such a way that some of them somehow, someday end up in the consumers' hands. Neither of those two ideals is fully realized anywhere, but the economies of Communist countries are certainly far more distant from them than those of capitalist nations.

If that point is not granted, the discussion cannot be usefully continued. If it is, then further economic objections to capitalism can be made. Now, having passed the stage of systematic delirium or peremptory denial of fact, the counts of the indictment are more plausible. They all derive from this central theme: capitalism, it must be recognized, has had a prodigiously stimulating effect on production, because it subordinates everything else to the profit motive; but, for that very reason, it secretes deadly poisons and frees destructive forces, whose sources it is unable to block, so that eventually capitalism destroys what it has created. Among its baneful consequences are inflation, unemployment, financial and commercial chaos linked to the inevitable anarchy of a market economy (ruled by profit, not by needs), the waste of natural resources, inability to lift the third world out of undevelopment, imperialism.

Jean Baechler, in his "Origines du capitalisme,"[9] warns against the mistaken tendency to attribute to capitalism economic phenomena, human behavior, social ills or political crimes which history has witnessed before the birth of the capitalist system. I would add: and which one finds today in other kinds of economies. The scientific mind (basic to socialism, we must remember), even in its least lofty state, should be up to the task of not identifying as the cause of a phenomenon something that did not exist when the phenomenon was already present or that is not necessarily present where the phenomenon is found.

Baechler reminds us, for example, how we go astray when we

[9] Gallimard, 1971, p. 60.

assume that the market economy or the profit motive is peculiar to capitalism: "Extensively developed markets were known in Mesopotamian, Greek, Hellenistic, Roman, Abbasside and Chinese society." Certainly the interplay of supply and demand which constitutes the market economy has never been entirely free. Every system is a mixture in varying proportions of planned economy and free trade. Probably the only example of a totally planned economy was the Inca economy, where supply and demand played no role, for the state collected everything that was produced and distributed all income. As for contemporary capitalism, it is far less pure a "market" economy than many preindustrial economies (that of the Mediterranean world between the eighth and eleventh centuries, for example,[10] for both labor and product markets are extensively regulated. Nor is the profit motive characteristic only of capitalism. Of course, I don't mean profit motive in the general sense of human greed, which would make the observation a truism, but in the sense of an effort that has as its clearly defined goal making capital produce a return and generating a margin of profit. As early as the twentieth century B.C. in Cappadocia[11] in Asia Minor, and in the Neo-Babylonian era in the sixth century B.C., and even more in the Abbasside period of the Middle Ages, we find importers and exporters, commercial networks and chambers of commerce, banks and entrepreneurs financed by those banks. That is capitalism, though not accompanied by the modern technological industrial development which is the truly novel element introduced at the end of the eighteenth century.

Just as Baechler and other historians have questioned whether certain types of economic enterprise are really native to our times, we must ask whether the "contradictions"—inflation, unemployment—are really those of capitalism and capitalism alone. Again, there are two questions: Did they exist before capitalism? Are they found in non-capitalist societies? It takes a great indifference to history to affirm that inflation or monetary disor-

[10] Maurice Lombard, *l'Islam dans sa première grandeur* (Paris: Flammarion, 1971).
[11] Baechler is referring here to P. Garelli, *Les Assyriens en Cappadoce* (Paris, 1963).

der is peculiar to the "global crisis of capitalism" of 1973, or those still more "global" (if we may be permitted that usage) crises that preceded or will follow it. Ever since money was invented there has been good and bad money, it has appreciated and depreciated, there have been strong currencies used in international trade, and other currencies (as attested by travelers from Marco Polo to Taine, including Dürer and Montaigne) that one had to take care to dispose of locally because they were so weak that they were known to be refused outside the borders of the authority that issued them. This situation is still common today. In 1963, in *Bucharest*, they laughed in my face when I wanted to exchange a bit of leftover Hungarian currency for Romanian money—the state bank only accepted capitalist currencies. As for inflation, Europe and the Mediterranean world have rarely known a worse one than that of the last two centuries of the Roman Empire. (That inflation and the endemic economic, financial and monetary crises of those centuries have been described and analyzed by the Italian historian Santo Mazzarino.[12])

Bankers in second millennium B.C. Cappadocia (studied by Garelli) made loans at interest of 33 per cent a year, which would suggest that the currency was eroding. The second half of the sixteenth century A.D. was in Western Europe a time of steep inflation which painfully slashed the purchasing power of people on fixed incomes, trustingly established in an earlier time of price stability. In the second half of the eighteenth century wheat in some harvest seasons sold for ten times or more its normal price. Whatever the price fluctuations attendant upon our own constant and insurmountable crisis of capitalism, it is rare (except when cataclysms brought on by two world wars have put a temporary halt to virtually all economic activity) to see the family steak or a dozen eggs suddenly shoot up to the price of Sevruga caviar—a caviar which, for one or more seasons, would be the only available food.

[12] Santo Mazzarino, *Aspetti sociali del tardo Impero; L'Impero romano; La Fine del mondo antico*. The last book (first Italian edition in 1959) has been translated into French: *La Fin du monde antique* (Paris: Gallimard, 1973).

Some varieties of inflation caused by demand may not, on the other hand, show up in the apparent prices, which are controlled, but such inflation is measured in another way: by the length of the lines at the stores. That is a form of inflation found in Communist nations. If a product is not available, its price by definition cannot rise, even if the public has the purchasing power to buy it: this is forced savings. But if the product is just scarce, and its price is fixed, we find the phenomenon of a triple market: the special stores for privileged people—bureaucrats and those who can pay in hard currency; the lines at the state stores available to the general public; and a free market, either tolerated (like the free market in food supplied by the peasants' private plots of land) or parallel or "black." The marginal (but essential) free market and the black market are found in all Communist countries, and are subject to inflation under the pressure of demand that always exceeds supply. Every serious study of economics of the Soviet Union and the people's democracies makes short shrift of the propaganda refrain that there is no inflation under socialism. "The situation that is produced," writes Pierre Kende, "is a classic one in Communist economies, all the more because it can occur for many reasons other than a worsening of the terms of trade. It consists of an excess of purchasing power distributed across the total value of goods sold in the state stores and on the parallel markets. This disequilibrium appears in the form of insufficient supply, that is local or national shortages which socialist planners have no scruple in prolonging for years or even decades (Soviet Union, China)."[13]

[13] Pierre Kende, "Socialisme et inflation," in *Contrepoint*, No. 17, 1975. Kende also notes that "the difference between official prices and kolkhoz (free market) prices has continued to grow. In 1972, the latter were on the average 60 per cent higher than those of the state." Kende is a researcher in economics at the Centre National de la Recherche Scientifique and holds a doctorate in sociology. See also his *Logique de l'économie centralisée*, Paris, 1964, SEDEIS. The New York *Times'* Moscow correspondent, Hedrick Smith, reported on October 7, 1974, that ". . . one high official asserted that the Soviet retail price index had actually gone down three-tenths of one per cent since 1970. But ordinary Soviet citizens scoff or laugh at the official explanations, and groan about higher prices on everything from food or clothing to cars, private housing, entertainment or tutoring their children

Besides, it is impossible to verify the statistics that go into official indexes that are manipulated and laundered; their bias, which has been proved many times over, should be denounced by Soviet labor unions. And, for the problem that concerns us now, we cannot measure the rise or fall of the standard of living, which is finally what really matters, by comparing a mass of useless numbers with the fixed prices of goods that either cannot be found or are available only thanks to unpaid overtime work at a loss to the economy that should be included in the nation's accounts—the millions of hours that Soviet citizens waste every year standing in line. As it happens, the authorities sometimes have to decree brutal increases in the official prices, like those that provoked the bloody Polish riots of 1970, or have recourse to a typically capitalist subterfuge: the launching of a "new" product, more expensive than the old product over which it is supposed to be an improvement, which in fact is only the same thing under a new label. According to Kende, these "underhanded price increases" are even more common in Communist than in capitalist economies. In the latter, I would add, at least in the last few years, consumer organizations have been on the watch and have ferreted out such abuses more and more effectively, thanks to stricter legislation.

Thus inflation cannot be considered as exclusively capitalist in its origins. "That inflation also exists in the socialist economy will surprise some Western disciples of the planned economy," writes Ota Sik, "but it does exist."[14] Furthermore, if it is only fair to concede that socialist economies have sometimes shown remarkable resistance to inflation, we should also remember that capitalist economies, along with their bursts of inflation, have also known periods, sometimes of several years, of relatively stable prices.

Finally, it would also be only fair not to continue passing over in silence, as is now the strange custom under the influence of a

---

for college-entrance examinations." Smith also observes that the basic issue in a Communist economy is not the level of prices in state stores, but the adequacy of their supplies, the scarcity of supply compared to demand and the concealed inflation that results on the parallel market.

[14] *Argumente für den dritten Weg* (Hoffman and Campe, 1973).

fixation not of prices but of minds, the fact that the Communist countries *export their inflation,* the accusation classically and repeatedly leveled at the United States. The famous "transatlantic grain drain" of 1972 and 1975 enabled the Russians to play a political trump—the desire of Nixon and then Ford for détente—to buy the wheat they lacked from America on favorable terms, thus stabilizing their domestic prices and supplying their market despite their own shortfall in production, while the corresponding reduction in supply in the West caused a rocketing in the price of grain products ranging from bread in the United States to pasta in Italy. As Marshall Goldman observed, "This means that we in the United States have to bear the cost of storing the grain until it is needed by the Soviet Union. Similarly, we also have to suffer the high prices set off when the episodic Soviet purchases deplete the normal reserves built up to satisfy our regular world and domestic needs."[15]

On top of that, the generous purchasers, who understandably had every reason to take the broad view of things since they had gotten what amounted to a gift, then proceeded to resell (in 1972), at a profit, their surplus manna in the third world, which thus had the pleasure of receiving via Moscow, at prices swollen by speculation, wheat that without the Russian deal would for the most part have gone to the third world free as food relief.

I do not excuse capitalist inflation, I am just observing that millions of readers and listeners are told every day that inflation was brought to this earth by capitalism, as were unemployment and the destruction of the environment. Consequently people are led to believe that "eliminating capitalism" is all it takes to guarantee eternal price stability, universal full employment—with

[15] In the New York *Times,* July 3, 1975 (reprinted in the *International Herald Tribune,* August 5, 1975). Goldman is professor of economics at Wellesley College and a member of the Russian Research Center at Harvard. According to Milton Friedman (in *Newsweek,* August 25, 1975), the 1975 grain sale was inflationary because the Russians paid the market price, while the 1972 sale cost the American taxpayer dearly, because he had to subsidize the difference between the low price paid by the Russians and the high price paid to the American farmers. It was almost a form of foreign aid.

constantly increasing wages (just abolishing profit will do that, won't it?)—and the ecological paradise.

But unemployment existed long before capitalism, or, more precisely, what chronically prevailed, sometimes acutely, sometimes less so, was a relatively sterile economy unable to provide a living for all those born within its nest. And that is surely the most basic question: can a society assure the physical survival of its people in time of crisis—or can it not?

A decent living is another question, which raises issues of justice, equality, humanity. But people must be alive for those issues to come up, that is enough must be produced to meet their minimum needs, to solve the strictly biological problem—and that has never been achieved except in the time and place where industrial capitalism developed. So unemployment is a modern concept, deriving from the concept of employment, which in turn grows out of the existence of a labor market. For forced idleness to be felt as *loss of employment,* there must first exist the conditions that bring together employers and employees, labor contracts and wage earners, hiring and firing: concepts that are largely foreign to the pre-industrial world. Yet unemployment exists any time there are more hands than there is work in the fields, more mouths to feed than there is food, either chronically or at a time of particular difficulty, or, as is usually the case, a combination of the two. It is true that this kind of unemployment does not appear in any statistics. Yet in one sense it does: the unemployment rate in a traditional society or in today's underdeveloped rural societies appears in the mortality tables. Our situation-wanted ad in the classified section is the death notice, and the unemployment agency is the cemetery. The jobless are in the tomb. Or else they are on the road; beggars, brigands, vagabonds, bands of orphaned or abandoned children, those who have at least survived infant mortality and the common practice of infanticide. When in Southeast Asia a peasant dies slowly of hunger, lying on the parched soil waiting for the monsoon, he will not be listed among the unemployed; but if he goes to add to the overpopulation of an urban shantytown he will be listed, because he has appeared on the labor market. But the distinction is purely semantic. It produces this paradox: a high-level employee who has been laid off during a "recession" in an industrial nation, drawing unemployment compensation, doubtless owning his apartment and possibly a vacation home, will show up in the statistics as unemployed because he has "lost his job." By contrast, the victims of the 1973 drought in the Sahel are not listed, though they were far more surely deprived of their means of existence; nor is that rural youth in Algeria, Turkey or Sicily who, in a time of industrial recession, can no longer go find work in France or Germany or the United States, immigration being suspended.

In fact, the employment problem in the industrial capitalist economies has ceased since at least the middle of this century to be that of survival, while for the majority of the non-capitalist world the difficulty of surviving has nothing to do with the much-discussed problem of "loss of employment." We can say of most people that they are not rich enough to be unemployed—that is, they are not members of an economy that is sufficiently developed, rationalized, reduced to statistics, for the idea of employment and its corollary, unemployment, even to be clearly conceived and experienced. Also, in the industrial capitalist societies, today's jobless person is not what he was a century ago, or even in 1930. He had not lost his means of existence, of feeding, housing and clothing himself; he has not been totally ejected from economic life. Joblessness has changed its nature, and though it is still an ordeal, it no longer endangers the biological existence of the individual and his family. And remember that this happened only yesterday! Unemployment is still painful to one's morale, but it is no longer the economic phenomenon it was in older or even recent phases of capitalism, still less the misery of pre-capitalist economies. The alternatives then were simple: live or die. Today's job seeker has become selective; he does not seek any kind of work, and will not go anywhere to get it. Thus he can no longer be considered a defenseless proletarian, a homeless soldier in capitalism's reserve labor force, reduced to accepting each day any kind of odd job to earn the minimum needed to fuel the energy of his muscles, forced to sell that energy dirt cheap to the capitalist.

The problem of employment has now become separated from the problem of survival. Yet, each time there are layoffs and the number of job seekers increases, Marxists invoke the picture of the millions of unemployed as if they were still people who at each sunrise have no idea how they are going to find a crust of bread to see them through the day.

The argument that there is no unemployment in Communist countries must be seen in the context of how those nations organize, distribute and regulate employment. In practice the mass of the working population is assigned to a place of residence and a place of employment, a factory or collective farm, without the right to go elsewhere, either temporarily or for good, since any movement within the country requires authorization. Thus the migration from field to city and the conversion of farm workers to industrial workers are slowed or prevented, but the peasants are forced to remain at a very low standard of living. The percentage of the Soviet population still engaged in agriculture is the highest of any industrial nation. Thanks to political and ideological surveillance and repression, millions, at times tens of millions of Soviet citizens are kept permanently in concentration camps, reducing by that amount the number of people available to work in more normal enterprises. The prisoners are bound to forced labor, and are unpaid or at best get a pittance. Note in passing that this strategy for reducing inflation without increasing unemployment is not available to capitalist economies. If one could at will put one fourth or one fifth of the active population to work without paying them, it would be a miraculous cure for "cost-push" and "demand-pull" inflation. Of course the prisoners' productivity is very low, but that is true of all sectors of the Soviet economy, not only in agriculture, as is well known, but also in industry. Pierre Kende, for example, calculates that productivity in construction in Czechoslovakia is one sixth what it is in Western Europe, where in turn it is half the United States' figure. It is not unusual for Communist factories to remain idle for ten or twelve days a month because they have not received their necessary raw materials. In fact, Communist industry and distribution live in a state of chronic underemployment which, added to low productivity, guarantees their people a much lower standard of living than that of the West. Most Communist workers earn less than the capitalist rate of unemployment compensation. One can choose this system of "artificial full employment," in Alberto Ronchey's phrase,[16] but only if one is willing to take the consequences: a capitalist enterprise experiencing difficulties would not lay off anyone if it could keep two employees where only one was needed by splitting one salary between the two. There would be no loss of jobs, but rather unemployment on the job. But, alas, excess manpower for the same production inevitably means lower real incomes. This phenomenon is far from unknown in the capitalist system, for there are many enterprises where some of the employees could clearly be let go without affecting production. But obviously the productive employees cannot recapture, in wage increases proportional to their greater output, the amounts paid to the idlers. One can argue that this sort of solidarity is socially necessary. But, were it to be generalized, people would have to accept both the negative effect of the system on their standard of living and the restrictions on freedom of choice without which the system of paid unemployment would completely strangle production. In other words, the system cannot work unless society is organized in military fashion with job and residence imposed on the individual by bureaucratic authority.

But would workers in capitalist countries resign themselves to the socialist solution of disguised unemployment, of full employment in poverty and passivity? Today the Western worker is seeing a constant increase in his real income, as well as secure employment, and freedom to choose his type and place of work, not to mention the issues of quality of work, working conditions and participation in decision-making. I doubt that any socialist economy comes close to being able to satisfy all these demands simultaneously, while the capitalist economies have the means to make those ideals at least less inaccessible. The purely economic

[16] *Corriere della Sera*, December 1974.

and practical obstacles no longer seem insurmountable in all cases, and in fact have been partially overcome in some social democratic nations.

Artificial full employment assures job security at the price of a low standard of living. No Western European peasant, even in the poorest regions, could tolerate the harsh living conditions and above all the administrative slavery to which collective farm workers are subjected, as is so astoundingly and terrifyingly described by Andrei Amalrik in his *Involuntary Journey to Siberia*. The standard of living of industrial workers is higher than that of peasants, but lower than that of Western workers. To raise those standards, Communist authorities are importing technology and organizational know-how, buying from capitalist firms entire "turn-key" factory operations, sometimes even including more productive Western workers for the first few years. In any event, the insecurity of capitalist employment (mitigated by law, by labor unions and by the growing force of public opinion) has not sufficed to dissuade the masses in Communist nations from wanting to emigrate toward the precarious but higher wages of the West. In fact, the Communist world has to devote a substantial part of its police and financial resources to the meter-by-meter surveillance of the frontier it has fortified, not, as the Romans once did, to prevent the infiltration into its territory by barbarians—in this case, Western workers, they evidently being too beaten down by misery, alienation and totalitarian control even to conceive the notion of emigrating to the East—but rather to contain the inexplicable and suicidal desire of socialist workers to slip over to the barbarian world. The term "suicidal" is no metaphor, for the border guards have the right of summary execution, or rather it is their duty to shoot on sight, when they catch them, those socialist lemmings possessed by a diabolic instinct driving them toward capitalism.

Thus socialist unemployment is a reality, and it manifests itself not by official loss of work followed by the search for a new job, but by chronic underemployment accompanied by a lowered or stagnant standard of living and its inevitable corollaries, absenteeism and illicit work. Polish humor has spawned some good stories illustrating the customs produced by such a system. Here is one: A productivity inspector visiting a factory notices that two men are pushing an empty handcart to the end of its track; then, after taking a few minutes' rest, they push it back to its starting point, and then they repeat the operation. Furious at this waste of labor, the inspector asks the director of the factory: "Are these scandalous practices common in your factory?" "Not at all! Not at all!" stammers the terrified director. "This is most unusual—you see, the third man on that team is out sick today!" One may conclude that this sort of invisible unemployment is not as hard on the individual as the loss of his job, even if the loss is cushioned by unemployment compensation. But one cannot affirm that the imbalance between the population available for work and the number of jobs that are really needed, nor the imbalance between total population and total resources, exists only within and because of the capitalist system.

It would be equally naïve or dishonest to attribute pollution to capitalism alone, as in fact do the authors of the joint platform of the French Communist and Socialist parties: "Water and air pollution, degradation of nature and of the cities, congestion and noise weigh ever more heavily on the people's living conditions. These phenomena are not inevitably linked to technological progress, industrial development or urbanization. *The capitalist system bears the responsibility for them.*"[17] Not only is pollution known to be a serious problem in the Soviet Union, where it is not only attested to but also denounced and combated by the authorities, but if the destruction of the environment dates only from capitalist times how are we to explain the massacre of the forests over the last two millennia and the transformation of vast stretches of the earth into infertile dust bowls by shepherds who know as little of capitalism as they do of sylvan ecology? Furthermore, the erosion of the land and the exhaustion of its fertility are often due to primitive agricultural techniques which, in their ignorance of basic precautions, are more damaging than modern industrialized agriculture.

Certainly capitalism, technology and consumption have in the

[17] *Programme commun* (Paris: Éditions Sociales, 1972). Emphasis added.

process of their development created dangerous forms of pollution and mutilation of the environment, but they have also diminished or eliminated others, notably pollution by microbe and bacteria. They have aroused a new kind of ecological vigilance since the advent of industrial pollution and the thoughtless exploitation of natural resources. Industrial society, by changing popular habits through a huge educational effort plus the providing of the practical means, has at least begun to banish preindustrial pollutants: the garbage and excrement which used to decompose where people lived, infecting the air and water which then carried contagious disease. In his *Asian Drama*, Gunnar Myrdal reports the pathological consequences of the Indian peasant's habit of defecating in the fields: during the dry season, decomposed fecal matter mingled with dust is carried by the wind into the air people breathe. It is understandable why Gandhi attached so much importance to latrines that he wanted them dug in every village he visited. This refusal to use latrines in place of open-air defecation, in addition to its sanitary consequences for mankind, also deprives agriculture of a reserve supply of fertilizer that could be used at the appropriate time of year, as does the ineradicable Indian custom of using dried cow dung for domestic fuel, while wood is used to burn the dead. These customs are not intrinsically barbaric or morally reprehensible. But two things are certain: first, their economic and hygienic effects are negative; and second, they cannot be attributed to the influence of "monopoly capitalists."

Those who point the finger at capitalism as history's only miscreant guilty of producing pollution make the same error we described earlier in the case of employment. It is a double error: first, they do not recognize that there are several forms of pollution and unemployment, depending on the social context and the level of economic and technological development; second, they do not bear in mind—though this is something a Marxist dialectician of all people should not forget—that a positive development always has its negative aspect. Over a century or two, depending on the place, the increase in production due to industrial capitalism has created many more jobs, for a rising population, than any other economic system past or present. Depressions occurring within that long stretch of time have reduced employment, though relatively rather than absolutely. Usually the reduction is in the *increase* in the number of jobs, a fall in the curve marking the *creation* of new jobs. Though relative, that fall is all the less acceptable because people have come to consider the present standard of living as a minimum and they have growing expectations of job security and protection if they are laid off. These ever more insistent demands for material security as well as personal dignity constitute progress, and they *assume* previous progress in the form of an economy vigorous enough so that it is even conceivable that their demands can be satisfied. Naturally, the unemployed will scoff at "previous progress" and professional groups whose jobs are threatened see only that threat and could not care less about comparative history and sociology. But that indifference is scarcely appropriate to a theoretician or a political leader.

What then are we seeking to find out? Whether certain evils—inflation and unemployment being those most frequently cited—are native to capitalism and so organically linked to it as to justify the rejection of the capitalist system. If Marxist critics would limit themselves to telling us that capitalism must be reformed, or even transformed into a system as yet unknown to us, I would agree wholeheartedly. But they tell us a lot more: that capitalism *cannot* be reformed, implying that it never has to any degree been reformed, and that thesis cannot be sustained in the face of the historical record. Thus the preamble to any improvement is the destruction of the system, including its social democratic variety. This verdict, which would leave us with totalitarian centralism as the only available exit, is not justified by the strictly economic evidence. But since that verdict generally is rendered not just by Communists but also by a democratic Left that tends to repudiate reformism while claiming to reject Stalinism—a noble if puzzling stance void of practical import—we must conclude that the total condemnation of capitalism emanates less from economic considerations, serious though these may be, than from disapproval on moral grounds.

10

EXCESSES IN THE MORAL
CRITIQUE OF CAPITALISM

It does not seem proved that capitalism is totally unfit for economic life, in a purely practical sense, because of some congenital flaw. Its economic indictment owes its heat and its intransigence to moral sources that generate an implacable and
never-ending execration of capitalism. Capitalist civilization,
with its political and cultural aspects, is abhorred by socialist
ideologues and all those who, without campaigning specifically
for the totalitarian version of socialism, take its main postulates
for granted. In the final analysis what they condemn is values,
not the practical failings of a system of production. A clue to this
moral origin lies in the fact that the system is just as virulently
condemned when it succeeds as when it fails: the years of abundance, the consumer society, the *embourgeoisement* of the
working class" are the object of the same skeptical derision, the
same disgusted reprobation, as the lean years of recession, crisis,
unemployment and inflation. Whether the fruit is ripe and heavy
with juice, or scarce and dry, it is in any case poisonous.

Practical and moral contentions mingle and in fact are insepa-
rable. For, in order to be valid, a moral argument, especially one
as sweeping and categorical as is usually the case here, must be
based on an irrefutable practical argument. For example, if the
practical contention that the industrial proletariat must always
be further impoverished is borne out by the facts, as Marx and
Engels conjectured it would be, this would validate the moral
contention that the essence of capitalism is the "exploitation of
man by man." Moral choices must also be influenced by the diagnosis of the gravity of practical problems. If capitalism's con-

173

tradictions and imperfections show it to be structurally flawed, so that the system is bound sooner or later for shipwreck, it would be criminal not to put an end to it before it can do more harm. If, on the other hand, economic analysis does not warrant the definitive conclusion that capitalism is congenitally incapable of providing a tolerable and honorable living for most of its citizens, then those who would treat the patient by standing him in front of a firing squad are taking on a very grave responsibility. Most of the time, however, the moral argument is not based on a practical contention, but the opposite is true: a moral choice pushes to extremes a practical argument that is rarely conclusive in its own right.

While awaiting proof that economic crisis, depression, underemployment, inflation and waste exist only with and because of capitalism, its critics condemn it for its profound immorality. Capitalism is always led on stage "sweating blood and mud from every pore," as Marx wrote in *Das Kapital*. It is the exploitation of man by man, the monopolizing of economic and political power by a minority, the subordination of every human activity to profit, to money. Profit and money are always portrayed as evil geniuses of whose malign contagion humanity is unaware. Capitalism takes hold of the popular will and perverts it. It is truly a case of possession by demons, and thus subject to treatment not so much by an economist as by an exorcist—and we have plenty of those available. All in all, capitalism is a blemish on humanity.

Thus, one of the leaders of the French school of history, Emmanuel Le Roy Ladurie,[1] has this to say about Jean Baechler's essay, "Les Origines du capitalisme," which I referred to earlier: "These medieval 'origins' are also seen by Baechler as a random occurrence acting on the known facts; as an accident or 'irregularity' taking place in the tenth—eleventh centuries in a society whose technology was fertile but whose social fabric had decomposed into petty anarchy. This exceptional situation at the end of the early Middle Ages provided an opportunity to the small units

[1] In *Le Territoire de l'historien* (Paris: Gallimard, 1973), pp. 185–86. Emmanuel Le Roy Ladurie is a professor at the Collège de France.

of the lords of the manor, but also and from the beginning, to the towns, to the merchants, in short, to those individuals outside the system—the burghers. Thus chance made possible the birth of a logical structure, capitalism, which from its advent was endowed with an irrepressible and cancerous dynamism. Among all the possibilities offered to mankind over two millennia, that dynamic structure was to sweep all before it; in the space of ten centuries to engulf and pollute the entire planet; in short, if we are to believe Jean Baechler, to grow and to flourish without serious opposition, like catfish colonizing a body of water."

Note that the author in those few lines has accumulated a number of adjectives and metaphors intended to communicate to the reader his own dread and repulsion. The catfish, with its quill-like whiskers, fascinates and disgusts us like some sort of aquatic vampire; it drives out other species and spreads in a nightmarish swarm. On top of that, the beast is colonialist, which is only natural considering its capitalist relatives. I would add that the catfish originated in America, which makes things still worse, though in all honesty I do not think the author had that fact in mind when he wrote the paragraph quoted above. The spread of capitalism is "cancerous," thus neither creative nor positive in any way, but rather morbid, lethal. The image of the proliferating cancer cell, like that of the catfish, evokes the most distressing primordial fantasies of suffocation and of a corrosive flooding of the earth. Finally, another metaphor for poisonous infiltration, for a subterranean invasion secretly sapping the health of the planet—pollution.

Those value judgments do not appear in Baechler's essay, nor do I believe they can legitimately be deduced from it. Nor is it accurate to say that capitalism has polluted "the *entire planet*." Unfortunately for the planet, I am tempted to add, for if capitalism had functioned in Africa and India as well as in Japan, those lands might be able to provide a living for their people. That provocative remark will draw the immediate answer that Japan was never colonized. Granted, but India and Africa were never utterly destroyed as Japan was in 1945. Ethiopia, Yemen and Afghanistan were never colonized and yet they are among the poorest and most backward nations on earth. The paltry achievement of development policies since World War II in areas where the "thirst for profit" is far from unknown is evidence that capitalism is not as easy to transplant as some may think.

From the beginning, socialist critics have tended to attribute a global reach to a system that is still geographically quite limited, to view it as so omnipresent that, having reached its high tide, indeed its time of decay and withdrawal must already have begun.

In his *Marx et les marxistes,* Kostas Papaïoannou observes: "At the time that Marx and Engels were writing in *The Communist Manifesto* their rather extravagant obituary of the bourgeoisie . . . nine tenths of the world's people remained outside the 'capitalist system of production' and the industrial revolution; England was the 'world's factory'—the only nation where capitalism encompassed the entire economy and population. By contrast, peasants and pre-capitalist petty bourgeoisie made up the great majority of the population of France and Germany. America was still in the pioneer stage: not till 1890 did its industrial production exceed its agricultrual production, not till 1920 did its urban exceed its rural population."[2]

One may have many reservations about capitalism on moral as well as economic grounds, but they cannot form the basis of a useful critique and a progressive policy unless the evils cited are really specific to capitalism and inherent in its essence. Here again we forever see attributed to capitalism powers of evil that are in fact not its own, as if its duty were to assume the sins of the world, including those of its predecessors and even its adversaries. When the inquisitor blames capitalism for war, as is commonly done, or genocide, or the subjection of weak societies by the strong, or coups d'état, or the oppression of women, or sexual repression, or racism, or even illiteracy, it becomes difficult to reply, because one must lower oneself to giving a summary of world history that is as tedious as it is pedantic, so elementary as to verge on insult.

Let us take for example child labor in nineteenth-century in-

[2] New edition, revised and enlarged. Paris: Flammarion, 1972, p. 233.

dustry, a topic that has rightly inspired much indignation. Without in the least discounting the legitimacy of that indignation, we must nonetheless remind ourselves that child labor has *always* existed—in field and stable, in shop and store, in mill and bakery. Anyone who knew rural France before 1939 will remember the difficulty teachers had enforcing, during certain seasons, compulsory primary education up to the age of twelve, though this was a developed nation where schooling had long enjoyed prestige and conferred obvious practical benefits. In underdeveloped regions the conflicting demands of school and the use of child labor produce a daily struggle between teachers and families. Even in Israel this problem exists among Oriental Jews, though the population is relatively small and has been heavily influenced by the cultural goals of Israeli society. Child labor in the nineteenth century in fact constituted the transfer to industry of an immemorial practice that was completely accepted. Like the length of the workday, it was more an inheritance from the past than an innovation of industrial capitalism. Of course, the living conditions of the urban proletariat made both child labor and the length of the workday particularly shocking and moving. But that is precisely why these evils were very early denounced and combated. During the second half of the nineteenth and the first half of the twentieth century there was a proliferation of laws reducing the workday and the work week, requiring paid holidays and then vacations, and finally forbidding the hiring of child labor. In the perspective of history, the period of exploitation did not last a long time. All in all, industrial capitalism, which for three or four decades exploited children more cruelly than they had been before, was the system that put an end to child labor, just as it progressively reduced the workday from twelve or fourteen hours to eight, the week from six or seven days to five and the year from twelve months to eleven or ten and one half, depending on the occupation. And at the same time the workers' purchasing power was rising.

Obviously these advances were won by the struggles of the workers' movement. But two conditions were necessary for those struggles to be both possible and productive. One was technological: an increase in productivity that made it possible simultaneously to reduce the hours of work, to increase production and to provide a rising standard of living. The other was political: the capitalist system had to be compatible with a state that could be compelled to tolerate and then to recognize the workers' struggle, allow them to organize and lay their hands on the legislator's pen and the weapon of law. And these conditions, I would suggest, were not universally known before the advent of industrial capitalism and the free society, nor are they necessarily very noticeable today in other kinds of societies.

The capitalist system of production is socially neutral. Its calling is purely economic. That, indeed, is what its critics complain about. If we peel away all the non-essentials, we find that capitalism's goal is not to improve the conditions of the working class. But neither is it to make those conditions worse. On this point the Marxist explanation is mistaken, or at least (for I do not want to be dogmatic in my criticism of dogmatism) it is based on postulates that are assumed to be proved when they are not. It has not been demonstrated that capitalism can only achieve its economic goals through an ever increasing "exploitation" of the working class. While that interpretation may have seemed to express the fundamental law of the system in the nineteenth century, since that time it has been less and less in accord with the facts, most of which in practice contradict the theory of absolute impoverishment. The goals of the capitalist firm are production, profit and investment. Accordingly, the entrepreneur resists demands for higher wages. But that is not the *only* means by which he achieves a profit. Other factors are far more important—scientific research and its technological applications, higher productivity, better management. If keeping labor in a state bordering on want were sufficient to enrich individuals and societies, one wonders why the resistance to wage demands, *a principle scrupulously observed by all owners of the means of production in all times,* did not until the nineteenth century bring about that gigantic increase in production that far surpassed the achievement of the three preceding millennia. If we assume that the "exploitation of man by man" remained constant, other factors must have come into play. Those who maintain that exploitation has become worse under capitalism must determine whether that worsening equals the factor by which production has multiplied; they must also explain the increase in the workers' purchasing power which we have witnessed despite that supposed worsened exploitation—witnessed, let us say, during the two centuries 1775 to 1975 as compared to any two centuries in the pre-industrial era.

Marx had predicted the lengthening of the workday and greater exploitation of the workers, these being necessary to the profiteers of an ever more technologically backward capitalism as they engaged in the final fratricidal struggle in which they would destroy each other.

But on the contrary real incomes have risen steadily over the last one hundred years. Since 1870 average real per-capita income in the United States has risen by more than 2 per cent a year.[3] What caused this increase? If we assume that labor and the number of hours worked remained constant, the classical economists would say that increased productivity could only be explained by greater capital investment. They calculate that a 3 per cent increase in capital results in a 1 per cent increase in productivity.[4] Between 1909 and 1949, capital investment in the private non-agricultural sector of the American economy increased by 31.5 per cent per hour of work. Thus per-capita production should have increased by about 10 per cent. In fact, it increased by 104.6 per cent. The Neo-Marxist explanation of this phenomenon is that, granted that enormous difference is due to greater productivity, but that productivity was achieved only by harsher exploitation of labor, notably by means of the "infernal" speedup. But that is not the case, for the productivity of manual labor is not the essential factor. The role of technological progress has been carefully measured and is known to be by far the most important factor in the rise in productivity.[5]

[3] Daniel Bell, *The Coming of Post-Industrial Society* (Basic Books, 1973).
[4] This is known as the Cobb-Douglas function. See Bell, op. cit., Chapter III.
[5] Bell is referring in particular to the now classic study by Robert M. Solow, "Technical Change and the Aggregate Production Function," *Review of Economics and Statistics*, Vol. 39 (August 1975).

The history of capitalism, though recent and still brief, suggests that while in the short run the entrepreneur does indeed resist wage demands, in the long run that resistance is not characteristic of the capitalist economy. There has been a constant increase through ups and downs not only of nominal wages but of purchasing power, which rises both in direct wages and in the steady increase of a variety of fringe benefits.

Furthermore, to be completely accurate, it cannot be said that the entrepreneur even in the short run ceaselessly opposes direct or indirect wage increases. In times of economic expansion, it is the entrepreneur who raises the bid, offering higher pay to attract the most skilled labor and the most talented management, to the point that the state often feels obliged to take measures to brake what it considers the inflationary prodigality of some employers. One may say that in such cases the capitalist is only serving his own interests or those of his firm. I do not deny that. A policy of paying employees more so they can do you harm does not appear, unless I am mistaken, on the record of any society, past or present, as having been practiced by any entity, public or private. But the motivation of the capitalist or his manager does not detract from the observed fact of the long-term rise in purchasing power and living standards.

Thus, if capitalism as a purely economic system has no social purpose, neither does it have an anti-social purpose. There can be systems conceived in the light of social goals that have no economic or even anti-economic purposes. Any system can be judged on two criteria: production and justice, but no system can subsist in the complete absence of one or the other. Providing justice in a way that is incompatible with production, or production in a way that is incompatible with justice, is possible only through recourse to dictatorship or fraud, or both, simultaneously or in succession.

Production is the breath of the capitalist system. As an economic system, that is all we can expect of it. While responding to economic impulses that intrinsically are morally neutral, capitalism also may or may not produce more or less injustice. But one cannot say it has been shown that it can *only* function by creating *ever more* injustice—a belief that is at the very heart of the Marxist philosophy of history.

It is important to follow the same method in the moral as we did in the economic critique of capitalism, or we will be talking in a vacuum. If capitalism is viewed in a vacuum, that is by disregarding all other past and present economic systems, it is natural to underscore its flaws so heavily that attenuating them no longer seems a sufficient goal and total destruction becomes the only way to put an end to the ills of this or that sickly part of the system. And that brings us back to the question: what system will replace capitalism, or to what system shall we revert?

According to the fuzzy but unforgettably repetitive letter of pidgin Marxism, the exploitation of man by man is the original sin of capitalism and it can never be removed, because it is the spring, the very carburetor of the capitalist economic engine. This makes three assumptions that must be considered enormities if one has even a superficial acquaintance with history. First, that exploitation, or paying the laborer less than the value of his work, was created or at least aggravated by capitalism. Second, that capitalist profit and the expansion of production over the past two centuries were due exclusively to intensified exploitation, thus denying any role to progress in science and productivity. Finally, that exploitation can take no other form than that of producing profit for a capitalist enterprise, which leads to the conclusion that economic exploitation of man by man does not exist in Communist systems.

The English working class described by Engels in the mid-nineteenth century, or its French brothers depicted a little later by Zola in *L'Assommoir* and *Germinal,* are considered to be the most dreadfully exploited proletariat of all time, and this exploitation is the only cause of the enrichment of "the" bourgeoisie (as if there were only a *single* bourgeoisie!). This assumes that no group of human beings ever in all of previous history was as mistreated as the European urban proletariat of the nineteenth century. If anyone believes that, it would seem useless to try to alter his verdict by offering him elementary information about earlier civilizations, for the evidence indicates he has enclosed himself within the impregnable fortress of his innermost convictions.

According to this thesis, the position of the working class has gotten worse since the nineteenth century in direct proportion to the considerably increased wealth of "the" bourgeoisie. By now we should have a society in which the barriers between classes, the inequalities among classes, are much greater than a century ago, and the poorest classes are even poorer than they were fifty years ago. Communists still express this theory frequently when they define as characteristic of contemporary capitalism "the seizure of power by a *greatly* privileged *minority*,"[6] the "domination of a *handful* of capitalist corporations" that are "the cause of *all* the troubles that plague us."[7] There are several handfuls, it seems, for in the same article we find a reference to the "handful of *stateless* financial groups—the so-called multi-nationals—that have secured for themselves among us a place in the sun of imperialist competition." This "sun of competition," which is stateless besides, is neither very bright nor very orthodox. I had thought that, according to the Stalinist economic dogma, we were being crushed by "state monopoly capitalism." Be that as it may, the result is the same: "For millions of workers, this means *destitution.* The words I have italicized all evoke the fatalistic dialectic of absolute impoverishment for the benefit of an ever smaller minority, to which is added by the anathema called down upon the "stateless" (a term formerly used only by the extreme Right) a note of reactionary chauvinism, thus revealing the profound bond that quite logically unites communism and the cult of the nation-state.

The Italian liberal socialists and "Neo-Communists"[8] are more delicate in private conversation (always carefully off the record) than the ideological shock troops of *Pravda* and *L'Humanité.* But in their propaganda aimed at the masses and in their usual rhet-

[6] *L'Humanité,* July 22, 1974, "Les Mini-Réformes de Françoise Giroud," by Louisette Blanquart.
[7] *L'Humanité,* August 11, 1975, "La Question," by Jack Dion.
[8] We owe the term to the Italian political commentator Arrigo Levi, director of *La Stampa* in Turin. Levi described the consequences of Neo-Communism in *Newsweek,* July 14, 1975.

oric—the primary arena of ideology—they stick to the fundamental thesis that it is impossible to improve the standard and quality of life and to correct inequity as long as the basis of the system remains capitalist. The practical conclusion to be drawn from this thesis cannot be other than that of Stalinism.

Inequity in a society can be measured at a moment in time or over the long term. Two different questions are at issue. First, is there inequity in wealth and power in the society? Second, is it true that over the long run the system benefits only a minority?

In the case of capitalism, the answer is yes to the first question, no to the second. In the case of communism, the answer is yes to both questions.

Communist societies resemble pre-capitalist societies, which were egalitarian in the sense that the generally low standard of living caused virtually the entire population to live at about the same level, or rather to vegetate in about the same misery. In the *ancien régime* on the eve of the French Revolution of 1789, privileged people made up about 1 per cent of the French population. The greater the privileges and the fewer those who enjoy them, the greater the degree of equality among the masses. This is the archaic social structure of the Communist nations. Any society can achieve that structure—and many do not deny themselves the opportunity—by means of a general economic collapse. The capitalist economy, by contrast, has created a wide variety of social classes, of standards and styles of living. Thus it has both aggravated and reduced inequality. Capitalism has subdivided inequality and put it on display from the top to the bottom of society, so that it is everywhere present and everywhere felt. Thus differentiated and made relative rather than absolute, inequality in income, in wealth, in power, in opportunity, in access to favoritism and fraud becomes less clear-cut, more diluted, but at the same time more irritating. Because of the demands and conflicts caused by this gradation of inequality, capitalism will only survive if it reduces inequality and justifies it by equalizing opportunity. As for eliminating inequality entirely, the idea scarcely makes sense and has no practical meaning, now and no doubt for a long time to come. Inequality by meritocracy, as we know, raises as many objections and as much resentment as inequality by plutocracy. Even in the social democratic countries, where inequality has been most effectively reduced, we see the beginnings of conflict between equity in the distribution of the fruits of production and the differing abilities of those responsible for that production. In any event, justice does not consist of going back to equality in penury under the control of a dictatorship. Tearing up the definition of a problem does not solve it.

Besides, some capitalist societies are far from having liberated themselves from pre-capitalist attitudes. One persisting pre-capitalist custom is unjust taxation, in the form either of legal inequity or tolerated fraud. In nations like France and Italy, those practices, so difficult to extirpate, indicate a continuing acceptance of anti-economic aristocratic privilege, rather than the capitalist attitudes, which came late and are still poorly assimilated. The nations where capitalist attitudes were first and most completely adopted are those where the tax system is most fair and where fraud is most vigorously combated. The truly capitalist societies are those that tax wealth, an idea dismaying to societies based on landholding and hoarding.

A common error consists of attributing to capitalism that which is merely its defective application. When a poorly managed firm goes bankrupt, it is seen as a consequence of capitalism, when it would more accurately be described as a negation of capitalism. One must choose: either capitalism consists of making profits or of going bankrupt. It can hardly be guilty of both faults at once. If it is the essence of capitalism to refuse to tax capital gains, why was that tax first instituted in the United States and not in France?

Without a doubt, the creation of inequality is as congenital to capitalism as to other economic systems past and present, but may be that capitalism also does more to correct that inequality. Correction may occur in two ways: through increases in productivity and the standard of living; or through the influence of non-economic forces: political will, labor union action, a press free to inform public opinion about social inequities, etc. This correction of inequalities can take place over the long run even as new inequalities are being created that cut across different lines. Long-run correction appears in two forms: a reduction in the disparity among social groups, and a leveling of class differences over time. Leveling over time would exist if we could show that, for example, an industrial worker today has the same standard of living as the owner of a medium-size business did in 1910, or a stenographer today the same standard of living as an office manager then.

Jean Fourastié has conducted a great deal of research on changing purchasing power in capitalist societies.[9] In order to calculate the increase or decrease of the standard of living, he determines how many hours a laborer receiving base pay must work in order to earn enough to buy a given product. For example, a 2 CV Citroën car cost 3,456 hours of work in 1957 and 2,747 hours in 1967. In 1906 the cheapest French car, a Clément-Bayard two-seater, cost 10,000 wage-hours. In the mid-1970s the cheapest cars cost from 1,500 to 2,000 wage-hours, and they are much more comfortable, faster, more capacious and more reliable. According to Fourastié, here is what has happened to the price in wage-hours of a ten-trip book of tickets for the Paris Métro:

1900: 5 hours
1913: 4 hours and 20 minutes
1925: 2 hours and 10 minutes
1935: 2 hours and 15 minutes
1939: 2 hours and 15 minutes
1950: 1 hour and 30 minutes
1960: 1 hour and 36 minutes
1971: 1 hour and 40 minutes

Despite an occasional small rise, the general curve is strongly downward. One can also calculate earnings in kilograms of bread: in 1850 the miner at base pay earned in a month the

[9] See his *Économie et société* (Paris: Donoël, 1972), especially Part Two: "Problèmes économiques et sociaux" (pp. 217–62). Also his *Quarante Mille Heures* (Paris: Robert Laffont, 1966). Also his articles "L'O.S. et le conseiller d'état" (*Le Figaro*, April 3, 1973), and "Inflations, salaires et prix" (ibid., May 11–12, 1974).

equivalent of 80 kilograms of bread; in 1939 the laborer earned 300; and at the Renault plant in 1973 he earned 1,600 kilograms of bread. Of course, the numbers of hours worked was much less in 1973 than in 1850. Today, we must also add to the direct wages used in that calculation some 40 per cent more for fringe and social benefits. Purchasing power has increased the most in those sectors where rising productivity has most reduced the cost of production: in wage-hours, a radio in 1975 cost one thirtieth of its 1925 price. Thus capitalist profit does not derive only from the exploitation of labor, but primarily from investment, research and innovation. *Labor is most exploited in the societies that have the lowest productivity.*

Since the purchasing power of the lowest-paid workers has risen by the amounts shown in these examples, equalization over time has in fact taken place. Fourastié has calculated that a young laborer starting work now will earn more purchasing power by the time he is sixty than that earned during the career of a high-level government official who is now at retirement age. He adds (writing in 1973):

"In 1953, the chief engineer of the Department of Post, Telephone and Telegraph earned almost exactly, 1,100,000 old francs during the year. To transpose that amount into current francs, we must correct it for the change in the cost of living index from 1954 to 1973. We find that 1,100,000 francs in 1953 had a purchasing power equal to 24,000 francs in 1973. Thus the Renault laborer today has the same purchasing power that the chief engineer had in 1953 (with his Paris cost of living differential).

"Anyone by referring to salary schedules and cost of living indexes can make a list of standards of living equaled by today's laborer at Renault. Thus for example I found that he has the purchasing power of a government bureau chief in 1940 and . . . that of professors at the Collège de France in 1860. The cost of living today is almost four times what it was in 1860: 6,000 francs equals 24,000 francs. Six thousand francs was the amount earned by Jean-Baptiste Dumas, Ernest Renan, Marcelin Berthelot, Claude Bernard . . . As for Louis Pasteur, born in 1822, he was then only the 'director of studies' at the École Normale."

Nor must it be thought that the "alienating" cure for poverty, usually blamed on the "mass consumption society," only began with the pernicious exploits of the economic "miracle" after World War II. Even that good old all-purpose villain, the "savage" capitalism of the nineteenth century, was not afraid to make a few spurts of its own in the direction of that cure. This can be shown by examining the most basic factor in the standard of living: nutrition and changes in food consumption among the working class. John Burnett, a dietary historian, has demonstrated that the diet of the British working class improved in quality and quantity starting in 1850. Burnett writes in his *Plenty and Want, A Social History of Diet in England from 1815 to the Present Day:* "Industrialization was still far from a completed process in 1850, but the extensions of the revolution which were now taking place were proceeding under more adequate safeguards with respect to the health and comfort of the worker, his wife and children. Factory Acts and Trade Unions were beginning to give him a new protection and a new status; industrial towns were ceasing to be the unorganized barracks of slum populations; above all, a brisk demand for labour was providing employment, a rising standard of life, and—what was new for the majority of wage-earners—some margin of income over necessary expenditure . . . Another socially favourable circumstance was that food prices rose less than most others, resulting in marked increases in the use of tea, sugar and other 'luxuries.' Beer consumption reached an all-time maximum in 1876 at thirty-four gallons a head, though it is also noticeable that investments in Savings Banks and Friendly Societies, as well as subscriptions to Trade Unions, were mounting appreciably . . . Some of the rich were getting richer, but the important feature of this period was that, contrary to Karl Marx's prognostication, the working classes were taking the great stride out of that poverty which had been their lot for a century past. This improvement was maintained between 1873 and 1896, a period of very different character which contemporaries designated the Great Depression."[10]

[10] London: Nelson, 1966, pp. 91–92.

In short, capitalism is indeed saddled with injustices, but one cannot maintain that it functions to the exclusive benefit of a "handful of privileged people," nor that it is more resistant (rather it is less so) than other systems to the correction of inequality *if this goal is pursued in conjunction with an increase in production and average purchasing power.* It is after all very easy to increase equality by making production fall. But while this widely practiced and warmly praised policy may achieve uniformity in destitution, it cannot be said that it puts an end to exploitation. Entrepreneurial profit in the context of the firm is not the only form of exploitation of man by man or, to stick to Marxist terminology, of extraction of surplus value. The entrepreneur is watched over by the state, labor unions, the press. The whole history of labor legislation shows that management's arbitrary power has been steadily reduced. But the workers have no way of combating totalitarian exploitation. It is indeed another form of exploitation of man by man when a dictator inflicts chronic food shortages on an entire people by the violent imposition of a purported "agrarian reform," decided upon in bureaucratic abstraction, in the application of unverified and unverifiable theories, which is what happened not only under Stalin but also under Khrushchev. Let us apply a rigorously Marxist interpretation to the following facts. On the one hand, one third of the working population of the Soviet Union is employed in agriculture and produces considerably less food than its population of about 242 million needs. On the other hand, the 4 per cent of the American working population employed in agriculture produces so much more food than its population of 210 million needs that the surplus is exported to the entire world. It is clear according to socialist logic that of these two groups of agricultural workers, the second is exploited with unimaginable harshness—just think of the speedup!—while the first is essentially free of exploitation. I suppose anyone who goes to see for himself the respective living conditions of those workers, provided, that is, he can get permission to visit one of the two nations in question, will consider the theory verified. And let no one tell us about the American "head start." That shoe is on the other foot: in 1900 Russian agriculture was more productive than American agriculture.

If the exploitation of man by man is the *only* or even the *principal* cause of the accumulation of capitalist wealth, the above reasoning is correct, and American agricultural workers must be wretched subhumans toiling eighteen hours a day for a few pennies, while the Russian collective farmer, well rested, in flourishing health and freed from alienation, will certainly find time, as Marx advised in a famous passage in his *The German Ideology*, to devote several hours a day to painting and literary criticism. If contrary to all expectations, the apparently less exploited workers should appear more wretched than the others, this might perhaps prove that capitalist accumulation is also, indeed principally, due to the application of the science of agronomy (the real kind, not the Lysenko version that Stalin and Khrushchev imposed on millions of dismayed and helpless peasants), to organization and to increased productivity. What is true of agriculture doubtless also applies to industry and services. (In the case of services, where increasing productivity is more difficult and sometimes impossible, the Soviets have nonetheless called on two multi-national corporations, ITT and IBM, as well as Pan American Airways, to create in the Soviet Union a network of hotels and an electronic flight and hotel reservation system.

Once more, I do not deny that capitalist exploitation exists, nor that capitalist societies have many immoral characteristics. I am merely asking why injustice should be attributed exclusively to those societies, when we can observe as much and more injustice in other societies past and present, which offer to far less degree the compensation of a total increase in well-being, even though inequitably distributed. I am convinced that economic relationships are going to have to be organized on new principles, and in fact those relationships have already greatly changed since the early days of capitalism. But I fear that this transformation will end in tyranny accompanied by economic regression if, instead of being anchored in capitalism, change consists of destroying capitalism from top to bottom in order to substitute systems which to date have had nothing original to offer except state control of the economy and its inevitable corollary, totalitarian control of the state. But perhaps after all humanity really does aspire to return to poverty under dictatorship, and a political program based on that nostalgia is bound to succeed—indeed, it is already amply crowned with success. And perhaps the indictment brought against capitalism is aimed less at its economy than at its politics and culture, less at its disadvantages than at its advantages, less at the stomach than at the mind; for what is indicted, even more severely than the capitalist society, is its evil and ingratiating alter ego, that false friend, that Judas too slick to be honest—the free society.

11

THE MYTH THAT
DEMOCRATIC LIBERALISM
IS UTTERLY BANKRUPT

Yes, capitalism is in deep trouble, no doubt about it. By the end of 1973 its medical report was looking more like a death notice. Since 1973 recession had aggravated its economic difficulties and its social injustices. Bankruptcy was common among businesses whether small, medium or large, private or nationalized. The battle against inflation, partially victorious in such nations as West Germany, Japan, the United States and France, in others was stuck in a quagmire. In Britain, the Labour government that summer had a great deal of trouble convincing the Trade Union Congress to accept a ceiling on wage increases of 6 pounds a week (amounting to 312 pounds a year, plus midyear and end-of-the-year bonuses). But prices behaved as if they had not heard of that agreement, which in any event remained fragile. Throughout spring and summer Italy successfully defended its title of world strike champion, and managed even to beat its own record: half and sometimes all the public services, including of course hotels and restaurants during the tourist season, were in a state of paralysis, and this had become so customary that the foreign press no longer bothered to report work stoppages. Just as during the early Middle Ages, you had to go there in person to find out what was and what wasn't functioning. In Canada postal strikes occurred so often that the delivery of mail, when it happened because of a bizarre combination of circumstances, came to seem abnormal. Contrary to the received wisdom, the recession made "reformist" unions more militant than their "revolutionary" brothers. In September 1975 the installation of a new blast furnace, the largest and most modern in Britain, in the

Welsh town of Llanwern was enough to set off a conflict that soon paralyzed the entire steel industry of Wales and Britain. The eight men who were supposed to operate the blast furnace refused to do so, on the grounds that it was hazardous, unless they were granted a wage increase of 40 pounds a week, bringing their pay to 124 pounds, the equivalent of $1,000 a month. There was talk of dismissing them. Sympathy strikes were promptly called throughout the industry, threatening to bring the British Steel Corporation to its knees; that nationalized company, which had long since renounced any notion of turning a profit, was now prevented from modernizing its plant and increasing that well-known British productivity, now the lowest in the Western world. In that same September an international organization announced that 20 million people were unemployed in the industrial nations, and that things were bound to get worse in the next twelve months. Finally, the recession had made even more miserable the lives of that part of humanity now known as the "fourth world": the residents of those underdeveloped nations that lack raw materials, especially the most important of these, oil; from half a billion to a billion marginal people who do not produce, do not consume and do not long survive.

Thus it has seemed proper since the recession began to ask: "Can capitalism pull it off this time?" Pollsters and the organizers of discussion groups, public or private, put the question to the metaphysicians of our times: the golden age of the conference is also that of the economist. The economists had replaced the theologians and the philosophers in the social role of satisfying man's desire, in a rationalist culture, for gratuitous statements and unverifiable theories, for arcane terminology and futile debate. A meeting of economists, or the comparison of statements made by the best-known economists, could easily be mistaken for those seventeenth-century controversies on the nature of sin, grace and predestination. Taken as an individual, each economist is skillful in his presentation, categoric in his conclusion, persuasive in his prescription. But taken as a group the theses advanced by the economists prove to be mutually incompatible. Just as in metaphysics, doubt, if absent when listening to

the soliloquy, appears when doctrines are compared. Though trained in the same schools, imbued with the same authors, informed by the same statistics and using the same mathematical methods, some economists had become Stalinists, others monetarists or neo-liberals, still others advocates of socialist worker management. Still the public did not mind that day after day the economists showed themselves to be as contradictory in their explanations and muddled in their Gnostic assertions of revealed truth as they were peremptory in their recommendations. On the contrary: their popularity grew with their readers' confusion, their authority with the number of their mistakes, and the more their predictions were disproved by events, the more they were urged to prophesy anew. But then does not the charm of the prelogical sciences lie precisely in the jovial heedlessness with which their practitioners lay claim to healing illnesses and auguring phenomena of whose causes they are so manifestly ignorant? Less lamented than the crisis of the economy, that of the economists was no less lamentable.

Both the economy and the economists tended to make us forget that how bad or good we consider a situation depends on its context and what happened before. The frightening figure of 20 million unemployed in the industrial capitalist nations[1] should have been compared to a total working population of some 300 million. Granted, it was expected to rise even more. But the essential innovation in present-day capitalist societies, in contrast to all previous depressions, is that being out of work no longer means being without any resources. That improvement does not exonerate capitalism—that was out of the question—but it could hardly be used to heap further blame on its head. But in general that change was passed over in silence. Also overlooked as being part of the normal order of things was the fact that in most capitalist nations each worker and his family are guaranteed medical care no matter how slim their financial resources.

In the new spasms that will mark the final phase of its death

[1] The nine nations of the European Economic Community, Sweden, Finland, Norway, Austria, Switzerland, the United States, Canada and Japan.

struggle, capitalism will doubtless tend to make a distinction between the right to a living and the right to a job. That is already the case in practice, for in industrial and even more in post-industrial societies, two workers support three non-workers. The ratio of productive workers to non-producers, whom the former must directly or indirectly support, can only decrease still further, for the trend of social demands is toward lengthening the years of schooling, generalizing continuing education and lowering the retirement age. It is hard to see how those demands can be compatible with the rejection of increased productivity, whether due to technological progress, improved organization of work or greater skill on the part of the employees. Unions tend to oppose any innovation that will reduce the need for labor on the job at hand, though it has long been known that higher productivity has a multiplier effect that, by raising incomes and thereby generating economic activity, will create more jobs than it destroys. The example of the underdeveloped and Communist nations is an ample demonstration that putting twenty people on a job that one can do only leads to impoverishment. It means that one salary is being split twenty ways, not that twenty jobs are being created, for people can share only what has in fact been produced. Resources therefore diminish, and though the economy may accumulate what seem to be jobs, it is less and less able to supply the needs of its whole population. But starvation and the destitute condition of a substantial part of the human species demand that productivity be given priority. According to a Club of Rome report,[2] if under the most optimistic assumptions world population in the year 2000 does not exceed 2 billion 600 million people, it will be necessary by that time to have created a minimum of 1 billion jobs. Under a pessimistic assumption, those billion new job seekers will be here before the year 1990. Similarly, the International Labor Office calculated in a 1974 study that in twenty-five years there will be between 1.5 billion and 2 billion 600 million new job seekers. Thus the causes of unemployment do not seem to me to lie in the "crisis of capital-

[2] Mihajlo Mesarovic and Maurice Guernier, *Unemployment, a Creeping World Crisis,* June 1975.

ism," disorder in the international monetary system or the quadrupling of the price of hydrocarbons. As for the solution, it begins with raising the gross world product, not creating fictitious jobs. What good does it do for a society to claim, as do the Soviets, that it provides "work for all its citizens" if it cannot feed them, as is the case of the Soviet Union? It shows a strange lack of awareness to boast of a triumph of socialism that consists of making people work for a pittance.

During that same summer of 1975, the average wage in Hungary was between 2,000 and 2,500 forints a month, or $90 or 500 francs, which is one third the minimum wage in France, one quarter or one fifth most rates of unemployment compensation in capitalist nations, less than needy old people receive in France, and much less than the "American "poverty line" income below which one is entitled to public assistance. It will be said that many services are free in socialist nations. This is also true of capitalist countries, since direct wages must be increased by almost half to take into account employer payments for various social services. Even in Franco's Spain, patients have not been paying a penny for drugs for a long time. What is distinctive in socialist nations is that, while medical care may be free, it is hard to get treatment unless you slip the doctor something under the table—also true of every Communist official in a position to be of service to his fellow human beings. The rule of baksheesh is as inherent under communism as it is in any bureaucratic society. Along with the black market, it makes life less unbearable where one cannot get along on what is officially provided. At first glance, one would think that paid holidays, one of the most precious gains for the "quality of life" and the workers' happiness, would be more generous in the Communist economy, liberated as it is from the profit motive. Not at all: the paid annual vacation in the Soviet Union is about twenty days, and only a quarter of Russians take any sort of vacation trip. In short, by the criteria of the capital working class, Communist life is one of harsh austerity.

If the peoples of the two worlds had been able to change

The Totalitarian Temptation

places in that summer of 1975, the Western workers, including the unemployed, would have felt trapped in a sinister sort of misery, while the crippled and roundly condemned capitalism of the West despite its piteous state would have seemed like the height of luxury to the Communist workers. The Poles are aware that there is much they can learn, and especially obtain, from capitalism even during a recession. They have gone heavily into debt to the West to import consumer goods. At the end of 1975, their trade deficit was about $3 billion, thanks to which the Poles live better under Gierek than under Gomulka, despite a rate of inflation officially put at 6 per cent, unofficially at 15 per cent, which is higher, sometimes much higher, than inflation in the major capitalist nations, except Britain, but including Italy, where at this writing inflation is down to 12–13 per cent.

These are industrialized Communist nations. On the apparent theory that a still more primitive economy would hold the secret to curing the ills of the complex industrial capitalist eonomy, that is would have solved problems that it has yet to confront, Lionel Stoleru, economic counselor to the president of France, commissioned to draft the "revaluation of manual labor" in France, went to China, like so many before him, to observe the status of the workers. He brought back a cautiously worded account[3] from which one learns with relief that no Chinese solution can be transplanted to France. Curiously enough, his most crushing passages are written in the brisk and laudatory style that one expects in a communiqué proclaiming victory:

"The Chinese worker's purchasing power is infinitely lower than that of the French worker, his working conditions are harder, he works longer hours, with only one day off a week and no paid holidays, his housing conditions are far inferior (one family to a room, in many cases). Furthermore, his purchasing power has not changed for fifteen years, for most wages have not risen in that time, and few prices have dropped, while during that same period the purchasing power of the Western worker almost doubled . . . But the real lesson is not in absolute com-

[3] *L'Expansion*, September 1975, No. 88.

196

parisons: it is relative. Relative to other members of society, the place of the manual laborer in China is infinitely superior to the place he occupies in France and in the Western democracies. This is true of salaries, for an experienced, skilled worker earns as much or more than a doctor, a teacher or a rather high-level official." There is no more elegant way of saying that capitalism tends to raise the worker's standard of living toward that of the doctor or official, at least those of preceding generations, as noted in the preceding chapter, while communism on the other hand guarantees that the doctor and the official will earn as little and live as poorly as the worker. This latter concept of social reform has the advantage of being infinitely easier to implement than the former. Granted that China is an underdeveloped country and that any comparison with Western Europe would be unfair and without scientific import, but note that according to M. Stoleru, who is a careful and informed observer, the purchasing power of the Chinese worker, even measured in terms of underdevelopment, has been stagnant or worse for fifteen years. The Chinese "solution" for the economic take-off seems less miraculous in the light of that reality than it does in Maoist rhetoric. It is alarmingly similar to the gigantic "progress" of the Stalinist economy between 1927 and 1932, which pretty much irreversibly destroyed Russian agriculture, and several million peasants besides. Permit me this opportunity to observe that the suffering endured by workers in the capitalist world during those years, great as it may have been, did not begin to compare with the ordeals deliberately inflicted on the Soviet people.

We may conclude from this overview of some aspects of the world economy toward the end of 1975 that the results of capitalism after all are somewhat less dreadful than those of other systems, though in the capitalist world they are commonly depicted as still more dreadful.

If capitalism always seems ill, sometimes because it is in recession and sometimes in feverish boom, sometimes because it cannot meet our needs and sometimes because it satisfies them to the point of waste, anticipates or even perfidiously incites needs, if capitalism always seems to be in "crisis"—perhaps this is because it has always been linked to a critical society.

First of all, it really is in crisis. Secondly, its illnesses are assiduously reported. What economic system has ever enjoyed constant good health? But what economic system other than capitalism has been so carefully watched by its own society? Like it or not, we must face the fact that modern democracy was born in conjunction with industrial capitalism. ("Modern" as distinguished from the democracies of certain ancient and medieval cities or towns, which, either juridically or in practice, included only a tiny fraction of the population.) I do not know which of the two caused the other, but this coincidence between the growth of the free society, resting on political democracy, and the flowering of the capitalist economy is an undeniable if disturbing historical fact. It is characteristic of the free civilization that criticism becomes a necessity, the society seems unable to function without it, while other societies by contrast seem unable to function with criticism. They destroy it in self-protection, making criticism marginal, clandestine or impossible.

The principal target of criticism in a free society is the economic system itself. Economics emerged as a separate discipline at the time that capitalism and democracy were becoming the dominant systems of production and government on both sides of the Atlantic. Even if that supposed science is merely an ideological justification of capitalist exploitation, at least it had to exist for the impostor to be unmasked, there had to be political economy so there could be a "critique of political economy," Adam Smith and Ricardo had to write before Marx could refute them. Ideological or not, economic theory starting in the eighteenth century made economic life, till then unconsciously experienced, a topic of observation, analysis and discussion. The variety of economic interpretations coming in rapid succession is evidence that calling the "system" into question is now a habit, perhaps a necessity. This question extends to the primacy of economics itself, a contention that began with romanticism and is found today in demands concerning the "quality of life," reflecting awareness, in the words of John Kenneth Galbraith, that "the test of economic achievement is not how much we produce but what we do to make life tolerable or pleasant."[4] The adoption of such a criterion presupposes that production has already reached a level that in fact has been attained by capitalism and capitalism alone.

The critique of economic life is unknown in pre-industrial societies, except from the moral point of view, because they have not learned to isolate it from other aspects of life nor to see it in its entirety, and it is forbidden in Communist regimes because to criticize the basis of the economy is to undermine the foundations of political power.

Besides, the belief that a social organism either changes completely or not at all, that the only choices are immobility or revolution, arises from a mistaken application to all societies of a rule that is valid only for totalitarian collectivities. Only in those societies are the parts so interdependent that a modification in one endangers the stability of the entire edifice. The ruling class is indistinguishable from the holders of political power, and there is no power other than the political, in the economy, in custom, in the arts and sciences. The Council of Trent vigilantly regulated aesthetic creation in minute detail, even banning theater in Italy, just as it is forbidden today in China, other than the two or three operas composed by the party. Thanks be to heaven, the cardinals and bishops of the sixteenth century were better connoisseurs than today's Soviet and Maoist leaders, and Christiantiy was spared, at least in the plastic arts, the total artistic disaster that has befallen the Communist world.

By contrast to totalitarian societies, free societies are not made up of a block whose parts are so rigidly soldered together that the slightest indiscretion on any point, by a single member of the group, is viewed as a rebellion aimed at the existence of the entire system. The free society is characterized by the autonomy (not absolute, of course, but relative to what existed before) of

[4] In the preface to *A Contemporary Guide to Economics, Peace and Laughter* (Houghton Mifflin, 1971). It was probably Galbraith, in 1963, who launched the expression "quality of life." The first chapter in the above book is titled "Economics and the Quality of Life," and is adapted from a 1963 lecture.

its various spheres of activity. The very fact that the Marxist theory of "ideological superstructures" was invented in the mid-nineteenth century is in a way indirect proof that by then the bonds joining the domains of production and political opinion had been loosened. To assert that literature, painting, philosophy express the aspirations of the ruling class, that they justify power and are addressed to those who hold it, to erect these ideas into a *theory*, did not seem necessary until they were no longer entirely true. His subordination was evident to an artist living in the time of Louis XIV, and its proof would have seemed superfluous, if not ludicrous.

The free society first introduced the method of choosing its rulers known as political democracy, along with a rough but often satisfactory approximation of Montesquieu's advice on the separation of powers. It then introduced diversity, therefore choice, in the fields of culture, philosophy, morality, religion, education, information, personal life-styles, art and taste—including bad taste, and political options—including the option that aims at destroying the society in which it exists (which is a remarkable innovation in the history of social systems). I prefer to call it *diversity* rather than *freedom*, whether it is cultural, ideological or political. The word "freedom" has metaphysical overtones, and there is already enough metaphysics in politics and politics in metaphysics. Any potential despot knows the obvious artifice of saying that nobody has been able to make an exact definition of freedom of the press or the freedom of labor to organize. So let us leave this unfathomable mystery to the vision of the Stalinists, and merely observe that everyone in practice knows the meaning of having a *choice* among several newspapers, several television or radio stations, several workingmen's organizations. The choice obviously cannot be merely a numerical one (Soviet citizens have a "choice" between Pravda and Izvestia) but must include diversity in content, origins and leadership. The fact that capitalism gave rise to the labor union movement would seem to indicate that its functioning is linked to liberalism. True, the unions' achievements were not the gift of management but won by the workers' struggles, produced not by the system but against it. But that only strengthens the case, for it shows that the free society has this remarkable property: actions undertaken *against* the dominant class and power give rise to accepted *institutions* that dilute and share in that domination. Not a very common occurrence in man's history. It is important of course to distinguish what is accomplished by from what is accomplished against the system, but still bearing in mind that both kinds of results are obtained *within* the system, up to and including those that substantially change that system. This is because the term "liberalism" designates less a pre-determined set of social norms than an attitude of permitting those norms to grow out of the interplay of classes, groups and individuals. All other civilizations propound and impose on the individual a single truth, a single morality, a single goal. Only the free civilization does not exempt the individual from that responsibility, and it could not do so without denying its own basic principle of diversity and choice.

Perhaps that is an omission, but it must be realized that it can be remedied only at the price of returning to a state religion, as in France before the revolution, or a state philosophy, as in the Soviet Union, or both at once, as in China, where the cult of Mao has merged with dialectical materialism. If you consider that extremely rare and only recently tolerated phenomenon, *the co-existence of several systems of morality,*[5] as one of the rights of man (which is increasingly the case in the free societies of Western Europe and North America), you cannot at the same time ask society to choose your morals for you. Nonetheless, torrents of rhetoric flow daily from that inconsistency, and the same preachers who lament that our society offers no "values" to youth also wax indignant when society does so, apparently on the grounds that proposing one set of values amounts to censuring other values and limiting individual choice. On the one hand they blame society for not defining our values for us, and on the other they accuse it of being repressive when it limits the field of our sexual or intellectual experience; even teaching must be non-

[5] This is what Marc Ullmann emphasized about the United States in "La Révolution silencieuse," *Informations et documents,* No. 301, December 1, 1970.

directive or it is viewed as the harmful abuse of the power of knowledge.

The goal of the free state, as defined by Locke and Montesquieu, is to grant the members of society as much autonomy as is compatible with the effective management of public affairs. Today that aspiration is thwarted by the growing demands of groups and individuals that the state intervene to protect and rescue them from all manner of difficulties. Owners of winter sports resorts ask the state to compensate them if the snow falls too late for them to enjoy a full season; small shopkeepers ask to be saved from bankruptcy; the employees of a failing business ask that the state protect their jobs too by subsidizing the business (though without meddling in management). Hostages captured at home or abroad by political rebels or by thugs count on the state to buy their freedom at no matter what financial cost, just as theater companies and symphony orchestras count on its subsidies. By contrast, no group or individual will tolerate any regulation of its activities by the state, especially in the rare cases when the state is not being asked for aid. Now, these two sets of demands are contradictory, since any state action in favor of one individual or group has an adverse effect on other individuals and groups. For example, when the state intervenes in *favor* of French wine producers by taxing Italian wine, it is intervening *against* French consumers of Italian wine by forcing them either to pay more or to switch to French wine. At its extremes, this means every group of citizens in the free society demands that the state exercise tyranny on its behalf against all other citizens. Under these conditions, the contemporary free state is called upon ever more aggressively at once to intervene and to keep hands off. That is why wielding power subject to that conflict is so trying on those in public office. The strain is bound to shatter the mind of anyone who is not unconquerably stolid, or already demented.

Nonetheless, free societies have been able, particularly since 1960, to extend quite far the satisfaction of these two conflicting demands: the increased responsibility of the state for each of its members, and the widening of the area in which the creativity of individuals, minorities and subgroups can flourish without hindrance.

But the polemics of Stalinism and its servants depict free societies as essentially totalitarian, when in fact they have become fragmented societies, whose bits and pieces are increasingly hard to fit into an over-all design.

The description of free and democratic societies as totalitarian rests on several lines of reasoning that have in common under their apparent diversity making the exception appear to be the rule, the marginal appear to be the basic phenomenon. Or else, a procedure we observed in the case of economic realities, repressive practices are said to have been invented by the free society, to express its very essence, when in fact those practices were inherited and have often been mitigated by the free society.

For example, Michel Foucault, in his *Surveiller et punir*,[6] argues that Western civilization since the beginning of the nineteenth century has resorted to all sorts of "confinement": children in schools, the sick and the insane in hospitals, convicts in prisons. Thus the entire society and every individual in it are subject to constant surveillance. Furthermore, according to Foucault, that is when and why the individual makes his historic appearance. The idea of individuality is a product of that surveillance civilization, which transforms each person into an individual case to be pinned down and recorded in the files. Thus Foucault outlines what is literally a police state, in which power watches over and dominates each individual twenty-four hours a day—but that totalitarian society is not that of the Soviet Union or China or Nazi Germany or Orwell's *1984*, it is present-day France or Holland or the United States.

Foucault's thesis rests on two key notions: first, he considers the situation of the pupil, the mentally ill and the convict to be identical; second, he assumes as proved that those three catego-

[6] Foucault is a professor at the Collège de France. I note that fact, as I did earlier in the case of Professor Le Roy Ladurie, not for the sheer joy of listing the titles, credentials and chairs held by the authors I am quoting, but to emphasize the significance of the opinions I am reporting; these are not the fantasies of provocative eccentrics, but the thoughts of eminent members of the most official sector of the French intellectual establishment.

ries represent the entire society. But not only do those three kinds of confinement differ considerably among themselves, they are far from making up the entire population. Besides, as barbaric as prison conditions were, and as dismal as nineteenth-century school and university life may seem, both were the results of efforts to humanize the penal and educational systems. Far from appearing under the free society, the repressive confinement of schoolchildren began in the fifteenth century and by the nineteenth was giving way to the now universal practice of nonresident study without "surveillance."

Philippe Ariès, one of the historians whose research has contributed the most to our understanding of pre-liberal societies, tells the history of schooling in his *L'Enfant et la vie familiale sous l'ancien régime.*[7] After reminding us that teachers in the early medieval school took no interest in their students' behavior outside of class—an indifference that has reappeared today—Ariès writes: "The authoritarian and hierarchical administration of the secondary schools beginning in the fifteenth century made possible the establishment and development of an ever more rigorous disciplinary system . . . In defining that system, we see that it had three principal characteristics: constant surveillance; informing institutionalized as a principle of administration; the extensive application of corporal punishment . . . The preoccupation with humiliating childhood, for its own good and to differentiate it, was to diminish in the course of the eighteenth century, and the history of school discipline shows how public opinion changed . . . In France, public aversion to the system of medieval discipline resulted in its elimination, especially after 1763, when the expulsion of the Jesuits from France was used as an opportunity to reorganize the school system." Thus the author of *Surveiller et punir* finds that the enslavement of schoolchildren began at the very time when in fact it was losing its hold.

I want to emphasize that I am in sympathy with many of Michel Foucault's pertinent observations about penal and psychiatric conditions. I am just trying to show how, first by invert-

7 Paris: Plon, 1960. New edition: Seuil, 1973.

ing the historical process, and secondly by extending the experience of certain sectors to the whole society, this philosopher manages to suggest the image of a totalitarian society where we thought we were seeing a free society—with of course some repressive features, which is not at all the same thing.

What matters, in defining and characterizing a society, are its predominant features. There are portions of freedom in totalitarian societies, and fascist behavior in free societies. But what historian would be believed if he wrote that Britain is a Catholic country because there are Catholics in Britain? Or that the practice of the Protestant faith is forbidden in twentieth-century France because there is no Protestant church in such-and-such a Breton or Basque village, and a Protestant child has to endure the jeers of his classmates?

But that is another of the currently fashionable intellectual processes by which free societies are transformed into totalitarian societies. Forgive me for using an episode in which I was involved as an example, but the facts that stare us in the face are not unconvincing:

The French translation of Noam Chomsky's *Bloodbath*, in which the noted linguist once more denounces the crimes of American imperialism, especially in Vietnam, was published in March of 1975. The French edition, *Bains de sang*,[8] included a preface by the talented writer and philosopher Jean-Pierre Faye titled "Bloodbath Archipelago." The title seemed obviously intended to invite comparison with *The Gulag Archipelago*, a comparison that was not overlooked, notably by the socialist weekly *Le Nouvel Observateur*,[9] which added the news that Chomsky's book had been "censored" in the United States. Thus—we learned in the conclusion of that review—the symmetry between the Soviet Union and the United States was complete. The Bloodbath Archipelago found its exact equivalent in Gulag, and Solzhenitsyn's book was banned in the Soviet Union as was Chomsky's in the United States. But—and this is what was so outrageous—everyone was talking about Gulag and not about

[8] Robert Laffont.
[9] March 29, 1975.

America's crimes, about Solzhenitsyn's exile and not about the repression that stifled Chomsky's voice.

I took note of this with interest, since I was scheduled to take part that same week in a television program about the United States during which *Bloodbath* and other books were to be discussed. The statement that America's crimes in Vietnam had "never" been denounced struck me as a bit of hyperbole bearing only a remote relationship to reality. But that after all is a value judgment: those crimes are never sufficiently condemned. By contrast, the assertion that *Bloodbath* was "censored" in America was a venture into the area of provable fact. The word "censor" has a specific meaning: the action of an official body that has the power, before or after the fact, to suppress all or part of a written work or a film. Of course there are hidden forms of censorship, like the failure of French television to discuss President Georges Pompidou's health before his death, but that could only be effective on a nationalized network. If there is no direct control, avowed or secret, pressures may be exerted, but that is no longer censorship in the strict sense of the word.

Disagreeable as it may be to most Europeans, the fact is that censorship has never existed in the United States, even in wartime, even when the American press in 1942 published military information useful to the Japanese, even when in 1971 it published secret state documents filched from the Department of Defense, the famous Pentagon Papers. In the latter case, not only was there no censorship or seizure but the system of justice, from the humble court of first instance to the Supreme Court, dismissed the government's case and exonerated the newspapers.

Thus Chomsky's book could not have been censored as the term is understood in Europe, that is by an official process contrary to the United States Constitution, which as I said has never been violated on this point. It also seemed improbable that the government would suddenly set out, two years after the fighting had ended in Vietnam, to silence by surreptitious machinations an author who had been free during the war itself to write and speak like an avenging angel. Besides, Chomsky is too illustrious not to be able to publish what he wants when he wants. The whole thing was implausible.

So I telephoned a friend in the United States and asked him to inquire about the facts.

This is what had happened: Chomsky had signed a contract with a publishing house which shortly thereafter had merged with another house. The new editor in chief who took over as a result of the merger decided to cancel the contract and not to continue distributing the work. He did this, it is true, for political reasons; he had rightist views, and Chomsky's book displeased him.

But that refusal to publish has nothing to do with censorship. If the editor of *Le Nouvel Observateur*, for example, rejects an article critical of the Socialist party, he is not committing an act of censorship, he is simply exercising his right not to propagate an opinion contrary to his own. This right is not contrary to freedom of opinion in a pluralist society where the right to publish political articles is not restricted to one person, or one party. Unlike the Soviet state, a capitalist publisher does not hold a monopoly on publication and therefore the absolute power to prevent ideas contrary to his from appearing in printed form, nor does he have at his command legions of policemen to arrest and deport those of his fellow citizens who do not share his views. That the recalcitrant publisher in the Chomsky affair was a reactionary does not make his legal or practical powers any different from those of the editor of *Le Nouvel Observateur*. A democratic society is not one in which nobody holds rightist views; it is one in which nobody holds a monopoly on opinion or on power. To consider a theater owner's refusal to show a given film the equivalent of a state monopoly on film production is irresponsible, to say the least. Besides, long excerpts from *Bloodbath* had already appeared in *The New York Review of Books*. In any case, one thing was certain: government officials had played no role at all, direct or indirect, in this story.

That is what I said on television (the program being shown on April 4). But that was hardly sufficient to change the minds of those who believe that American "censorship" is the equivalent of the Soviet variety. Of course—they replied the following week —it would be silly to deny the existence in the United States of "formal" freedoms (there we go again!). But what must be understood, and what happened to Chomsky provided the most striking kind of proof, is that in so highly perfected a system of censorship the government *does not even need* to intervene directly in order to obtain the banning of a book whose contents it wants to suppress.

That reasoning is not at all unusual. Indeed, it is so commonplace that we may consider it a summary of the position of lay Stalinism once removed, a position held by all Marxified speakers of pidgin Leninism, at least in its Western European and Latin American dialects. If it is true, as many people believe, then it follows there is only a negligible difference between a society where censorhsip is exercised by the power of "money" and one where it is exercised by the state's police. The latter is even somewhat more moral than free capitalist society, because, while both are basically totalitarian, Communist society is at least not subject to the tyranny of "profit." In the words of one of France's best economic journalists, a man for whom I have great respect and who is not at all fanatical, which makes his opinion all the more typical of a mood that is average, normal and general: "Our society has nothing other to offer youth except unemployment, inflation, the tyranny of money, bloodshed on television and bare asses at the movies." *Nothing* other—that's what he said. So is not any change bound to be for the good, since nothing could be worse than our tragically wretched situation?

Without being so rude as to dwell on the continuing "tyranny of money" in Communist nations, as evidenced by corruption and the black market, it should be noted that the citizens of totalitarian nations are well aware of the fundamental difference between the surveillance and repression to which they are subjected and the "repressive" free society, no matter how rotten it may be. They excel at describing their fate with a wealth of detail indicating their ever watchful intelligence and keen powers of observation. One sometimes reads in the Soviet press descriptions of the impact of a totalitarian regime on daily life that are enough to make one's blood run cold. It is true that the spotlight shines only on distant phenomena, foreign nations and false friends:

"For me China is an immense barracks living in a permanent state of tension and fear," writes David Karpil in the Soviet weekly *Literatournaya Gazeta*. "The Maoist way of life is based on surveillance of the citizenry. Several houses make up a cell whose members are required to report their thoughts and actions to each other . . . Each week the head of the family reports on the ideological situation in the family to the neighborhood revolutionary committee, which is nothing less than a system of informing. In practice everyone is required to do the same, including schoolchildren who at the end of the week write essays on the class struggle in their families and among their classmates. The individual has no right to a personal life: each of his actions is subject to rigorous surveillance. Everything he does at home . . . where he goes, what he talks about, what he eats, what he reads, what he listens to on the radio, all this is immediately learned by those around him and reported to the neighborhood revolutionary committee!"[10]

It is rare to find so bleak a picture of the workings of the Maoist police state in the Western press. Those who shape public opinion in the West tend to condemn repression by fascist regimes more severely than its Stalinist counterpart. The latter cannot excuse the former, but neither should fascist repression serve to excuse or minimize Stalinist repression, which is often the case, as Solzhenitsyn complained when he was still living in the Soviet Union. The late dictatorship of the Greek colonels, General Pinochet's crimes in Chile since 1973, Franco's garrote, South Africa's apartheid: all these must not serve to diminish the horrors of psychiatric murder and the hell of the concentration camps (or vice versa). Yet we often hear it said that it is not the time to denounce Communist totalitarian methods while repression flourishes in Rio and Santiago, and fascist atrocities are

[10] Quoted in *Le Monde*, August 10–11, 1975.

more likely than Communist ones to provoke protests and demonstrations. Totalitarianism should concern us and be considered dangerous wherever it exists, all the more if it is making converts and spreading around the world. But you would think from their behavior that Western defenders of democracy were endowed with only a fixed amount of moral indignation which ceases to be available for Stalinism at the slightest alert on the fascist front, and in fact is hardly ever available to be directed against Stalinism. Pinochet and Park and the bloody tyrants of Indonesia are odious enough, but at least their regimes are not held up to us as "model societies," as has long been the case with Stalinist or Maoist terrorism.

This differential treatment implies, of course, that because of its goals totalitarian Communist repression is not as intrinsically vicious as the other kind, and besides it is in the process of relaxing its grip. Thus we find once more the myth of innate goodness under the unfortunate surface, of the inevitable liberalization of communism, a myth that is tenacious—it is in the nature of myths to be tenacious—even though always contradicted by the facts. Amnesty International, the London-based organization that investigates repression throughout the world, lists in its 1975 report the following nations where the violation of human rights occurred on a "disturbing" scale: the Soviet Union, Indonesia, Iran, Iraq, Guatemala, Morocco, Spain and Brazil. The authors of the report stress living conditions in Soviet prisons and work camps, *conditions that have become harsher during the last five years,* especially for political prisoners. They state that "discipline has become more rigorous and punishments more arbitrary," that "the life of individuals is characterized by chronic malnutrition and excessive labor."

Paradoxically, fascist regimes seem more inclined than Communist states to loosen the stranglehold on their people as they grow old. Despite the dreadful death sentences imposed on Basque dissidents in September 1975, it must be acknowledged that Franco's Spain had for ten or twelve years permitted the growth of "free circulation of ideas and people," which we are still awaiting in Communist nations despite their promises at the

Helsinki Conference.[11] The dictatorship of the Greek colonels, which during the 1972–73 polemic against Solzhenitsyn was often thrown up to the critics of Soviet dictatorship as a case of sin "on our side" that absolved the sin of Gulag, collapsed in the

[11] This was almost explicitly recognized by leftists who cannot be considered soft on Francoism. On September 22, 1975, a "commando" of French intellectuals went to Madrid to hold a press conference designed to draw the attention of international opinion to the atrocious verdict on Basque militants accused of terrorist crimes and sentenced to death after an expeditious trial contrary to all civilized judicial norms. This is how one of them, Jean Lacouture, described the journey, in *Le Quotidien de Paris* for September 24, 1975:

"Our gesture must be seen above all as an act of solidarity with the Spanish opposition. An act with no risk, it is true. But a protest and a call for justice that satisfied the opponents of the Franco regime, as we later learned. The only risk we ran at the beginning was that of simply being denied entry when we got off the plane, since numerous contacts with Madrid journalists had been made. But apparently the phone taps were not working well. It was one more proof of the technological spluttering that prevails south of the Pyrenees. The fact that we who went there as protesters got to Madrid was in itself evidence of the contradictions of the deliquescent regime. We contribute a bit more to exposing the criminal imbecility of Franco. We can also testify to the crime against the press of the police who handcuffed the journalists who came for our press conference. Insofar as our colleagues have been freed—and we must salute their courage—we believe that we did well. Monday morning, on arriving at the Barrajas airport, we feared the worst. But, and it was almost humiliating, nothing happened; we might as well have been in Switzerland. We went through as ordinary tourists, even Régis Debray, as if there was nothing to it. There were two colleagues—one French and the other Swedish—to greet us, and that was all! The group then went to the Hotel Torre de Madrid, in the center of the capital, where a suite had been reserved. Montand asked the hotel management to set aside space at six o'clock, to hold a press conference. They immediately offered him the bar on the fifteenth floor, without even asking about the nature of the statements he was going to make. It must be about a film, they thought.

"Then finally things began to go wrong. The police intervened during the press conference. That evening the protesters returned to the airport and, after an identity check that delayed the Air France flight for an hour, they took off for Paris. We can only pay tribute to these demonstrators, who were determined to dissuade the Spanish government from executing the Basque separatists. But one must agree that in a *totalitarian* nation worthy of the name, not merely *authoritarian*, it would have been impossible to make this impromptu trip because visas would have had to be obtained in advance; nor, on arrival, to meet for hours nothing but indifference on the part of the police, an indifference preceded by that of the eavesdropping services; nor, finally, to leave without suffering any more reprisal than a rather extended passport check."

following year. It had lasted all of seven years, which is seven years too long, but not much compared to the longevity of the Communist branch of totalitarianism. We have seen a lot of varieties of fascism disappear in the twentieth century, but as yet not a single Communist regime.

It is true that the democratic powers, as a result of a perhaps inevitable misunderstanding of their own best interests, have repeatedly committed the error in their foreign policies of supporting authoritarian regimes. This "external fascism," in Maurice Duverger's expression, is doubtless a necessary consequence of the intrinsically imperialist nature of the state and will only disappear along with the nation-state and what is now called "foreign policy." But it is also true that the existing democracies energetically combat totalitarian fascist threats at home, while the interests of democracy are not defended with the same vigor when it consists of fighting against a totalitarian undertaking calling itself Communist. In such cases, it is all too easily conceded that democratic liberalism is obsolete and that democracy is harmful or an accessory to the derailing of revolutions. Why have the socialists yet to learn that, on the contrary, the absence of democracy is the reason all their revolutions have failed?

12

THE REFUSAL TO ANALYZE
THE CAUSES OF FAILURE

During the weeks when Communist influence in the Portuguese armed forces movement appeared to be diminishing, I had a conversation with a French Socialist who was very close to his party's first secretary. He told me that, like his party leader, he expected that the Socialists would soon be in the Lisbon government and that the process of democratization would resume. "Unfortunately," I said, "the economy is in such a state of chaos that, after the Stalinist plot, democracy is in danger of being undermined by bankruptcy." He made the inevitable reply: "Bankruptcy existed before the revolution for the majority of the Portuguese people, who lived in misery." "Yes," I said, "which is all the more reason for not making their situation even worse. That's what the military revolutionaries should have kept in mind."

A look of amazement crossed his face. Then he told me his basic belief: a leftist government is not required in the short run to do better than a rightist one. It is in any event superior because it is a *good* government, while the rightist regime is a *bad* government. The future belongs to socialism, and if that future never arrives, it is not because it was made impossible by what was done in the present, not because we went about it the wrong way, it is because socialism was strangled in the crib by the Right.

That is exactly how General de Gaulle reasoned: he had set his country on the right path, and that was enough. To quibble over the results was almost dishonest. I have no doubt that the regime of Salazar and Caetano was detestable; I myself condemned it to the extent that its torpid mediocrity required any attention at all. But does the praiseworthy aim of providing the opposite to that regime endow anyone with infallibility? Alas, the Left's critical faculty seems to end at the point where its power begins. The Left does not recognize failure, or rather it never takes responsibility for it. The Left is often defeated by a rightist counteroffensive, never by its own mistakes. Incompetence, lying and intrigue are unknown in its ranks. Its analysis is always correct, and when its policies lead to disaster, it would be an act of bad faith to use that fact against the Left. The explanation for the unfortunate outcome rests elsewhere than in the poor design of the plan or the ineptitude of the actors.

Let us pass over the fact that my Socialist friend was confusing two situations that, while they may occur at the same time, spring from different causes: an unjust society and a bankrupt economy. The refusal to face the consequences of one's own mistakes is more disturbing. Everyone makes mistakes. But if to err is human, it would seem dangerous to entrust power to those who consider themselves exempt from that rule and are convinced they have never blundered either in conception or execution. Before, during and after the disasters they inflict on others and themselves, it is their invariable custom to attribute exclusively to fascist and capitalist machinations the warnings they receive, the objections that are raised and the accounting that is demanded of them.

Thus it becomes harder and harder to discuss progressive regimes that would like to become democracies and to ask what would make them viable. The intolerance of their friends digs their grave and whitewashes the headstone after the funeral. When such a regime is in its infancy it is forbidden under pain of being classified with the Right to detect the slightest smudge on its image. If things turn sour, it is sacrilegious to go back and try to reconstitute the sequence of events that led to disaster. In effect, trying to determine what methods one should employ to avoid another Pinochet is deemed tantamount to approving Pinochet.

The result is a form of censorship whose principal weapon consists in knowingly confusing those who analyze the weaknesses of a policy with those who want it to fail, those who want to understand the causes of a failure with those who rejoice over it.

For years it was impossible, without being relegated to the "fascist" camp, to observe that Fidel Castro was committing blunders in his domestic administration and that his regime was drifting into an ever more police-ridden authoritarianism. Not till 1970 did the work of previously warm advocates of Cuban socialism, notably K.-S. Karol and René Dumont, paint a bleak picture of the Castro economy, showing that the American embargo was not the only cause of its underdevelopment.

Similarly, during the first two years of Allende in Chile, his foreign sympathizers frequently denied the obvious facts of economic dislocation, social tensions and political contradictions inherent in a minority presidency. Any reporting of such information was dismissed as pure calumny, bound to discredit Allende, if not deliberately intended to damage him. But would not the leftist politicians who made the pilgrimage to Santiago have been doing their duty had they emphasized, even to the point of exaggeration, the seriousness of the growing list of problems faced by the Chilean president? And how long must we wait, how many more eye-opening events must be endured, before people stop complacently justifying the increasingly dictatorial Peruvian regime?

The suicidal myth that is so desperately propagated in such cases is that no leftist regime, be it defunct or degenerate, has ever been in error. Its collapse or decay is always attributed to the villainy of other forces: foreign imperialism and domestic fascism.

But it is hardly realistic to maintain that all the causes of failure are external, nor is it—must I say it?—at all Marxist. It amounts to saying that a society's structure, its culture and the state of its economy have no effect on political events.

This reasoning is particularly harmful because it spares the Left any critical evaluation of its strategies. Should, for example, a government like Allende's give the acceleration of social reforms priority over the need to maintain production? Should it allow wage increases of 50–60 per cent when inflation is already running at 100 per cent a year? Or should it quickly launch an ambitious agrarian reform, indispensable it is true, but bound in the short run to reduce agricultural production, when the nation already has to import food? Should the press be censored when it reports the government's errors and should political rights be suspended or postponed in times of great unrest? Or does the fact of censorship tend to exacerbate existing problems? When everything that happens is attributed to foreign or domestic enemies, who supposedly assassinated a government that was in the best of health, the Left is excused from asking, and therefore answering, such questions.

Furthermore, no statesman worthy of the name should be surprised that he has enemies. Threatening some interests is inevitably part of politics. So when a responsible leader plans his actions he should anticipate how those interests will react. I have already referred to surprisingly indignant statements along the lines of: "What did you want me to do? My adversaries did me wrong! Those whom I wanted to destroy did not support me!" Thus the French high command could have shed responsibility for its 1940 collapse by attributing it to the infamous hostility of the German army—and then accused those who found that defense somewhat wanting of siding with the Vichy government.

The Portuguese situation in the year that followed the April 1974 revolution could certainly not be blamed on the new regime. Salazar and Caetano had bequeathed it an inflation rate of 30–40 per cent, one of the poorest, least industrialized and least educated nations in Europe, and a working population shrunken by colonial wars and massive emigration. But after 1974 the situation got worse: emigrant workers stopped sending their savings home, foreign capital stopped investing, summertime tourists grew scarce. That wasn't entirely the fault of the new regime, but it was still a fact. Other mistakes could clearly be attributed to military incompetence and Communist sabotage. The question is whether the Portuguese leaders will try to put the economy back on its feet and initiate democracy, or whether they will go looking for scapegoats and impose censorship, in order to provide an excuse for the crisis and to prevent people from talking about it.

Having overthrown an unjust regime does not guarantee that everything the successors do will be just. And being themselves overthrown by a fascist junta does not retroactively make them innocent of responsibility for the catastrophes they have caused, including the advent of fascism. The problems evident in Chile yesterday next appeared in Portugal and Greece, in Spain and, in a different context, in Italy and Yugoslavia.

Socialist governments, other than the social democratic regimes of northern Europe, have until now been unable to reconcile socialism and a high standard of living. And they have either been overthrown by dictatorships or have themselves become dictatorial. That is historical fact. Should we pass it over in silence—or ponder it?

The Left's duty is not merely to rail against fascist dictators—it is to keep them from gaining power. Forty years of worldwide protest and demonstration against Franco would have been unnecessary if the Communists during the civil war had not devoted their primary attention to eliminating the Socialists so they could gain a monopoly of the Republican cause, instead of seeking above all to save the Republic even though they did not have and could not count on winning a majority. That Pinochet is a disgrace does not suggest that Allende's policies can be viewed in retrospect as a success.

The Portuguese people, on April 25, 1975, gave the lie to their helmeted mentors who thought them "too backward to vote." Their civic behavior disproved the self-serving doctrine that a people "emerging from fifty years of dictatorship" should be plunged right back into it. The "putsch" of March 11 was a complete fabrication[1] designed to permit the military to create their High Council of the Revolution and to impose on the political parties a "pact" annulling before the fact the expression of the people's will in the forthcoming elections. Major Jesuino, the

[1] The television cameras (government only, of course) were already on location in front of the notorious barracks supposedly attacked by the "putschists" about an hour before the assault began. The film of the operation was shown on the evening news.

Minister of "Social/Popular Communications"—i.e. propaganda—had let it be known that the armed forces movement had "made a mistake in authorizing the formation of political parties after April 24, 1974." At the same time, in a speech delivered in Évora, Alvaro Cunhal, the Communist leader, stamped on Mario Soares' forehead the brand of ultimate infamy—the Socialist leader had conspired with General Spínola, leader of the supposed putsch! General Costa Gomes, the president, rescued Soares by generously adding his name to the list of revolutionary personages that Spínola was going to arrest on March 11, according to the official fairy tale of the attempted coup d'état, exposed in the nick of time, forty-eight hours before the elections. The president then said in his last address that "all legitimate power comes from the people." This was totally contrary to the doctrines of modern constitutional law espoused by then Prime Minister Vasco Gonçalves, Alvaro Cunhal and General Carvalho, the head of the paratroopers. According to their doctrine, all legitimate power came from the armed forces movement, and legitimacy was inversely proportional to the number of votes won at the ballot box.

Thus honest elections could be allowed to take place, but Portugal had not yet achieved the basic minimum of democracy. The military oligarchy, by forcing the parties before the elections to subscribe to a single platform, had deprived the electorate of its natural function, its reason for existence, which is to choose among various policies. The junta had achieved the second result, the logical corollary of the first, that opposition in practice was henceforth forbidden. For if all the authorized parties had signed the pact, that amounted to a de facto government if not of a single party at least of a single platform (with a single source of news and opinion), which is almost the same thing. Threats began raining down on the heads of the people's choices right after the election. The army would be implacable (said Jesuino) if the parties were to question the pact or seek the slightest change in it. The Socialists would be committing a fatal error if they "exploited their electoral success"—what a strange notion—to try to influence the administration of the country. That would be "suicide," Captain Vasco Lourenço warned in the name of the High Council of the Revolution. A real "hara-kiri," was how Otelo de Carvalho put it, speaking for himself and going on to say that the parties had "discredited" themselves during the campaign and that their deplorable debate had "traumatized" the people. Although the trauma was not particularly noticeable, who was going to raise his voice against the general who commanded the shock troops?

It is not easy to challenge the army in a nation that has the highest percentage of its population under arms in the world (after Israel, for different reasons), an army that moreover had just been cut to the quick by the voters' refusal to legitimize its omnipotence. Despite what it later claimed in an effort to save face, the armed forces had in fact asked the voters to cast blank ballots. Jesuino himself admitted that a "secret" poll had led to the hope that 40 per cent would cast blank ballots, but the effort had been a tactical and psychological error, for it had offended the voters—did the military think them backward?

Not only the military, but also the Communists, emerged from electoral failure with their powers enhanced. Despite its disaster at the polls, the Communist party kept its position in the news media, the single labor movement, the army—and the police, where the party now controlled the files of Pide, Salazar's political police. Everything was done to prevent the new situation created by the election results from initiating a new political process. Soares had repeatedly warned the French Socialists in the most urgent terms: "We are heading toward 'people's democracy.' The news media are completely in the hands of the Communists. We have to negotiate with typesetters who belong to the single union for the publication of every article in the only paper still available to us."[2] That paper was *República*, closed down for good by the Communists *after* the elections.

[2] Quoted in a confidential report made in March 1975 to François Mitterrand by a French Socialist party member named Antoine Branda. The text of the report was published in *Corriere della Sera*, where I found it, and was the subject of no denials by the French Socialists, neither when it was published in Italy nor when I quoted it in *L'Express*. In any event there is need to have recourse to "secret" reports to find dozens of similar statements by Portuguese Socialists and their leader between January and June of 1975.

But in the face of situations that had long been both visible and predictable, the French Socialists, with a skill in evading questions that would have made Pontius Pilate turn green with envy, kept shelling out the same two or three platitudes: "The situation is evolving," "It is too early to take a position" and, the best one, "Portugal is not France." Now, any novice knows that Portugal differs from France. The question was not that difference but rather the position of the Portuguese Communists: had they devoted their efforts to creating a pluralist democracy, or to joining the military in the creation of an authoritarian regime? The question of political *will* is entirely separate from the specific problems inherent in the Portuguese situation. And there is not the slightest doubt as to the direction in which the Communists' political will impelled them, nor is there any doubt that the French Communists lavishly encouraged them to take that direction. And if those planispheric geniuses come solemnly to enlighten us with their cartographic insight that France is neither Portugal nor Chile, we must ask them, if that is indeed the case, why they so long and so stubbornly refused to see or acknowledge what was happening in the latter two nations?

The Portuguese situation in 1974 and 1975 was characterized by, first, the disastrous economic consequences of the military's mentally defective administration and, second, by a brilliantly conceived and steadfastly executed Communist plot to conquer the state, encouraged by the Stalinist faction of the armed forces movement.

The economic situation did not in fact have much in common with the French situation. In that regard, the authors of that unforgettable maxim, "Portugal is not France," were partly right. But only partly. For, despite the differences between the two countries, the actions of the Portuguese military and the platform of the French Left have in common the panacea of nationalization. Admitting that the Portuguese economy was bleeding to death would therefore have opened the door to doubts that might undermine faith in nationalization and, more generally, so-

cialism. It must never be said that an economic administration
that calls itself socialist is in a poor state of health.

Because socialism is intrinsically benevolent, is it thereby exempt from such boring obligations as professional experience,
awareness of reality, managerial skill? We know that capitalism
can be well or poorly managed, that there are good and bad
finance ministers, conscientious and clownish administrators.
These differences in skills disappear in the case of socialism, as if
socialism acted by itself rather than through human agents. Thus
one cannot admit it is having economic difficulties without casting doubt on its very principles. Hence the prolonged censorship
of reality, the repeated assurances that the ship is in perfect condition, when the passengers are already standing up to their
waists in water.

As for the political plot, it bore some resemblance to a potential French situation. As in Germany in 1932 and Spain during its
civil war, the main objective of the Communists in Portugal in
1974 was to rid themselves of the Socialists and centrists and to
prevent the creation of a pluralist system, *which typically leads
to a situation in which the extreme Right also gains strength and
eventually the only alternatives are likely to be Communist dictatorship or fascist dictatorship.*

No matter what they say, that is the situation the Stalinists
prefer. They choose the risk of fascist reaction, which as a bonus
supplies them with a valid propaganda theme good for several
decades, over a parliamentary republic in which they remain a
minority. That latter prospect is hardly promising, for it seems to
doom them to a gloomy political poverty. No doubt the world
Left was happier with Franco to hate from 1939 to 1975 than it
would have been had the Spanish Republic survived, imperfect
as it would necessarily have been, and necessarily not very
socialist with its conservative peasantry, anarchist workers and
bourgeois reformers. On top of that, the Communists can always
hope that fascism will end in an uprising during which, though
in the minority, they can seize the levers of power thanks to their
tried and true methods.

In Portugal that strategy, pursued with a somewhat too visible cynicism, backfired on the Communists. As a result of their abusiveness, it was their turn to be repressed as violently as they had tried to repress others. At that critical moment, Georges Marchais, the French Communist leader, began calling on the French Socialists to come to the rescue of the Portuguese Communists, seemingly indicating that Portugal had suddenly become France, which it had not been when it was a matter of helping the Portuguese Socialists against the Communists. Marchais summoned Mitterrand to point an accusing finger at Soares, who according to Marchais was the "fascist" instigator of "anti-Communist hysteria." Once more we saw that the needs of the two great leftist families are not entirely mutual, for Mitterrand had never demanded that Marchais publicly condemn Cunhal's "anti-Socialist hysteria."

After a year and a half of revolution in Portugal, the danger of Stalinist dictatorship had been warded off—though at the cost of re-creating the conditions for a possible return to dictatorship of the Right. But the disintegration of the economy was so advanced that the line ran right off the bottom of the chart. The social democrats of northern Europe had been clear-sighted about both the political plot and the economic crisis. By contrast, Mediterranean socialism and the diffuse Marxism of unofficial Stalinism in Europe and throughout the world continued to dictate the classic analysis, according to which the failure to institute democracy, or, rather, its delay, was due to the ghost of Salazar and to a "structural" revolutionary law: socialism comes before democracy. Often disproved in practice, that law had in fact just been tested in Portugal, demonstrating once again that trying to impose socialism without democracy ends in the simultaneous downfall of both. Perhaps if there had been more democracy from the start, if that is as many Portuguese as possible had been involved in the decision-making process, rather than leaving everything to the incoherent whims of limited military minds, such gross blunders would not have been made and the economic base of a viable socialism would not have been wrecked in the space of a single year.

By the middle of 1975 production had come to a virtual standstill. Employees in nationalized enterprises were paid directly by the state, that is by the printing press, with the usual inflationary results produced by such fiscal sleight of hand. Though a million emigrants were in Europe and Brazil, unemployment at home was running over 10 per cent of the remaining working-age population of 3 million, a figure swollen each day by one thousand to fifteen hundred settlers returning from Angola and looking for jobs.

The foreign trade deficit reached $2 billion in 1975—on a gross national product of $13 billion. Bankruptcy was only staved off thanks to the last remains of the gold reserves piled up by Salazar, and the new provisional government, formed in September after the interminable expulsion of Vasco Gonçalves, frantically negotiated an emergency loan from the European Economic Community, an idea that the Portuguese "revolutionaries" had scorned, for the sake of their socialist and third-world purity, when it was advanced at the beginning of the year.[3] While the economy collapsed around it, that soap-operatic government went on grinding out its daily ration of mock-heroic adventures.

I must admit that I am unable to see what this buffoonery and its consequences has to do with socialism. The belief that the legitimacy of the struggle for the oppressed miraculously endows one with clairvoyance is a very costly illusion. Unlike capitalism, it is true, socialism does not enjoy the asset of being forever in "crisis," because first it would have to exist. Not having been

[3] I wrote in *L'Express* on February 10, 1975: "All hope is not lost of sparing Portugal economic ruin and military-Communist dictatorship or a dictatorship of the Right due to a counter-coup à la Pinochet or else civil war. But in order to banish those dangers, an *immediate and total European economic solidarity must be organized for Portugal,* with respect for democracy and in the interest of permitting it to survive. Why should not the act of financial aid that temporarily saved Italy be repeated for the Portuguese people, who deserve it more? Why should not Mssrs. Helmut Schmidt and Giscard d'Estaing take the initiative in creating a *veritable Marshall Plan* of the European Economic Community for the development of a democratic Portugal, which at the same time could join that Community. A little political imagination, in this relatively simple case, could save this little neighbor of 10 million people—and with it many things in Europe."
That article appeared under my name, but the proposal advanced in it was not exclusively mine; it reflected the point of view of the magazine and ideas exchanged in editorial conference.

born, how can it sin? Until now the only crisis socialism has experienced is the crisis of non-existence. The blame for its impotence is always laid on capitalism so that the capitalist system is guilty of its own crises and those of socialism. Naturally I do not hold socialism responsible for the difficulties of Communist economies, for they are its antithesis. I am referring to the alarming series of failures the Left has experienced in its attempts to build socialism in freedom.

These failures are, as I noted, usually blamed on betrayal by hostile capitalism. That felony appears in its most perfidious incarnation in the notorious "flight of capital." Assuming the socialists ever managed—doubtless after many late nights over the books—to comprehend that attracting that which one expressly announces one wants to destroy is a difficult ambition to achieve, then we can ask under what conditions investors will stay rather than flee. To answer that question, one must first clearly set forth the goal: complete state ownership of the economy, or will there be a transitory phase of social democracy, and if so, for how long and with what guarantees to investors? Will industry be nationalized or left under regulated private ownership? If the former, it is worth remembering that *nationalization has always made production fall,* at least at first, that is *the most critical period,* and sometimes permanently, as is the case with agricultural production when the land is collectivized or put into co-operatives. The replies of most socialists to these questions are confused and contradictory, and so are their actions when they come to power. When their policies are clear, as in Venezuela, they work out very well. Incoherent policies produce the worst of all results: anarchy. Anarchy was rife in Portugal, and it caused the flight not only of capital but also of many Portuguese, both blue- and white-collar, who were not Salazar henchmen but rather terrified by the absurd chaos around them.

Portugal fell victim to the presumptuous nonsense that it was too good for "Western-style" democracy and social democracy. It was above and beyond such capitalist toys, which are obviously just excess baggage on the ascent to socialism. That doctrine—it might better be called a revelation—has never been confirmed in practice. To put it simply, not once has experience even suggested its plausibility. Yet socialists continue to treat it as an axiom whose universal truth has been so abundantly demonstrated by history as to be beyond any possible doubt. It was to be expected that revolutionary Peeping Toms all over the world would adopt this Portuguese version of the fairy tale that once upon a time there was socialism without pre-existing democracy —which is the tale of the adult that was never a baby, the baby that was never a fetus, and the fetus that was never an egg. It was equally logical for the Communists to enrich the legend with their classical Leninist thoughts. One can hardly blame Stalinists for trying to establish a Stalinist state. They at least make sense. What is far more disturbing is that serious-minded people with reputations for integrity went on for months spreading fanciful interpretations of facts that were staring them in the face, in the name of socialism and "true" democracy. They provided a cover of impartiality for a picture of Portugal that had been whitewashed with propaganda.

Those who fear or deny the truth—polite ways of saying "liars"—undertook an opposite sort of task when they rewrote the history of Allende's Chile. Portugal started from a rightist dictatorship in its effort to create a socialist democracy. Chile, at the time Salvador Allende became its president, was a democracy in good working order that *already* had a socialist bent; three years later it came under a fascist dictatorship. Thus history offers us demonstrations of both the theorem and its reciprocal. In the first case, the Marxist leadership was incapable of constructing democracy, and therefore socialism also. In the second case, an existing democracy was destroyed and with it any hope of socialism. In both cases, the economy disintegrated so rapidly that the substratum of society, the object of their reforms, vanished in the revolutionaries' hands. Now, you cannot socialize an economy by first making it disappear. Of course, international socialist opinion blamed these fiascoes almost exclusively on foreign enemies and rightist plots.

The version of the three years of the Chilean Popular Union or Unity generally accepted in leftist circles throughout the world can, I believe, be summarized as follows. Allende was a democratic chief of state, brought to power by popular suffrage, who respected the Chilean Constitution but who from the start ran into the opposition of the Right, the army and American interests. From abroad, the big American corporations he had nationalized, aided by the CIA, instigated the social and economic difficulties that propelled Chile into inflation, want and chaos. At home, fascist elements in the army and the congress, far less representative of the people's true aspirations than the elected president, used these artificially provoked troubles as a pretext to drown in blood a leftist experiment that they had never accepted, and to abolish democracy. Thus it is impossible to make a revolution by legal means, for neither the Right nor the imperialists will play the game by those rules.

Granted, some of Allende's sympathizers who have studied the subject in some depth do not restrict themselves to that version of history. But that summary is generally accepted when the Chilean experience is discussed by leftists in conversation, in articles and even in serious-minded books.

Now, how does this credo hold up when we test it against the most clearly established facts?

First: It is untrue that Allende was borne into office on an irresistible tide of popular opinion. The election of 1970 was a three-way one. The Christian Democratic party, whose candidate, Eduardo Frei, had been elected president in 1964 with 55.6 per cent of the vote, had since split with its conservative allies, who now put up their own candidate. The result was that Allende, the candidate of a popular front coalition, came in first with 36.2 per cent of the vote, while the conservative got 34.9 per cent and the Christian Democrat 27.8 per cent. The process of addition informs us that 62.7 per cent of the Chilean electorate voted against Allende.

Second: It is untrue that the competing parties did not forgive Allende his victory and were bent on his overthrow from the beginning. On the contrary, Allende owed his office to those parties and their constitutional legalism as much as he did to his own supporters. When, as happened in 1970, no candidate receives an absolute majority, Chilean law provides that the president is elected by congress, which may choose *either* of the top two candidates. In this case, nothing in the letter of the Constitution nor in its spirit (since more than half the Christian Democratic vote could be considered closer to the conservative candidate than to Allende) would have prevented the Congress from choosing the candidate who, though he got 1.3 per cent fewer votes than the leader of the Marxist-Leninist Left, was more likely to be able to bring together a coherent governing majority than Allende, whose heterogeneous following ranged from the ultra-Left to the socialists by way of the Stalinists. Yet the centrist and conservative leaders, *though they held a large majority in Congress,* the most recent legislative elections having strengthened the Right not the Left, decided to make Allende president *in order to give the Left a chance at holding power.* It is difficult then to say they were implacably hostile to Allende at that date, and indeed the Christian Democratic leaders supported his coalition for the next two years. The first intervention attributed to the CIA occurred before that 1970 congressional vote, when the multi-national corporation ITT offered to provide the agency with funds to bribe members of Congress to vote against the leftist candidate. But according to later investigations by American congressional committees, the U. S. Government appears to have told the CIA to refuse the ITT offer. In any event the plot failed, and Allende got the votes he needed; also a failure was a sordid plot that involved assassinating a general in the hopes of provoking an army uprising against the new president. This latter provocation failed because of the strong tradition of political neutrality in the Chilean military. It must be emphasized that the military did not begin to think of taking illegal action *until the spring of 1973,* by when the disintegration of the economy and the state was sufficiently advanced to explain, if not to justify, a certain weakening in the military's commitment to neutrality. All in all, it is idle to claim that Allende's political adversaries tried at the beginning to deprive him of his relative electoral victory, since they had no reason to resort to plots had they wanted to prevent him from taking power: the Constitution gave them the right to do so in complete legality.

Third: It is not true that Allende could honestly have considered himself to have received a mandate to revolutionize Chilean society, and that his fall proves the impossibility of transforming a society by legal and democratic means. It merely shows that it is impossible to do so by legal and democratic means *when one is in the minority,* and that is no great news. Everyone who dreams of a coup d'état knows as much. But Allende acted as if he had received a total mandate, from, say, 80 or 90 per cent of the voters. In contrast to Léon Blum, also a minority leader in France in the 1930s, Allende did not understand that his technical victory allowed him to *exercise* power but not to undertake the *conquest* of the state. Why did Allende so lose his head as to treat 62 per cent of his fellow citizens as class enemies of the 36 per cent who voted for him, and to govern as if those 36 per cent were the entire population, when they did not even agree among themselves? (Allende's coalition included no less than six parties and factions.) I shall leave the answer to that question to Carlos Rangel, whose basic work on Latin America, published in France under the title *Du Bon Sauvage au bon révolutionnaire* (Robert Laffont, 1976), naturally deals with Chile at length.[4] Among other explanations for Allende's suicidal policy of maximalism, Rangel envisages this one: "The emotional (and ideological) upheaval caused in Latin America by the Cuban Revolution was undoubtedly one of the fundamental causes of the failure (or, in any event, of the violent end) of the Chilean experiment with the Popular Front. If he had not felt obliged to show that he was 'equal' to Fidel and Che, and above all if he had not had the pressure on his left of the Fidelists and Guevarists, it is probable that Allende would still be alive, would be president of Chile, and that he would hand over the presidency to a regularly elected successor in 1976."

Rangel then emphasizes the many common positions that appear in Allende's platform and that of the Christian Democratic

[4] American translation, *From the Good Savage to the Good Revolutionary,* Harcourt Brace.

candidate, Radomiro Tomic; the latter, in addition, was an active propagandist for Allende's cause in the troubled period in 1970 between the popular and the parliamentary votes. A coalition platform between the two would doubtless have included *hardly any less* nationalizations than were ultimately undertaken. "This," Rangel continues, "would have provoked desertions from the extreme left of the Allende coalition (but also from the right of the Christian Democrats). Furthermore, Allende would certainly not have been hailed the world over as a 'revolutionary.' On the contrary, he would have been abused and taxed with 'treason to the cause of the proletariat' and 'submitting to imperialism.' But Salvador Allende would still be alive, and with him Chilean democracy; and the world would never have heard of General Pinochet."

When one mentions Allende's minority status (of course, many democratic governments are based on a minority of the popular vote, but they do not believe themselves either mandated or entitled to remake society from top to bottom, not just for ethical reasons, but because *it wouldn't work,* not without imposing totalitarianism), when one describes the weakness of his popular base as shown by the 1970 election, Allende's apologists usually hasten to change the subject and proceed directly to the 1973 legislative elections, when Allende's supporters won 43 per cent of the vote. But Allende had been in office two and a half years when those elections took place, and he had already abused his mandate. Besides, he was still in the minority, for having 43 per cent of the voters for him means under current mathematical practice having 57 per cent against him; that vote was far from the triumphant retroactive plebiscite that perhaps might have legitimized the preceding thirty months. Finally, that 43 per cent vote was unexpected, better than anticipated, and international opinion, whether opposed or favorable, was greatly surprised to see Allende strengthen his position in Congress, when the economic debacle was no longer denied by anyone and the nation had been in a state of constant protest for a year. An astonishing outcome. Indeed it was, and this is why.

Fourth: it is not true that Allende scrupulously observed the spirit of democracy in general and the rules of the Chilean Constitution in particular. Marxist-Leninist thinkers can rest easy: he wasn't overthrown because he obeyed the law—let us clear his name of that vile slander. The leaders of Allende's coalition made no secret of the fact that their respect for the letter of the Constitution, such as it was, was only a tactical concession.[5] Thus, each time the coalition's candidates lost an election in labor unions or student or peasant organizations, the government promptly created another, obedient organization, gave it official backing and funds, and refused to recognize the authentic, representative organizations. They also took a grip on the news media by methods similar to those the Communists were to employ in Portugal four years later—this should be borne in mind in connection with the CIA's subsidies to some Chilean newspapers: the foreign secret services followed the trail of illegal practices already blazed by the government itself. Add a planned educational reform that was intended to make Marxism-Leninism required doctrine in the schools, and the influx of tens of thousands of heavily armed foreign guerrillas from all over Latin America, who constituted a government-tolerated militia—and it becomes easier to understand why the six Chileans out of ten who had not voted for Allende felt themselves imperiled. The clandestine stocking of weapons was the decisive factor that caused the high command to abandon its well-known and long-standing tradition of neutrality in politics.

No one knows better than the Stalinists how to make human rights and legal guarantees "formal" by emptying them of all content. Nowhere but in the Communist nations does one find such superb constitutional edifices that are total shams. In free societies, the law in practice suffers a certain amount of leakage; in Communist states, that leakage is on the same order as the percentage of the vote won by the single party at election time—99.9 per cent.

Allende's governing coalition not only tried to reduce to a formality the rights of the majority that opposed its policies, it vio-

[5] See especially Regis Debray, *Entretiens avec Allende* (Paris: Maspero, 1971).

lated the letter of the law itself, in particular during that famous election of 1973, which contrary to all expectations resulted in a gain for Allende's supporters, an electoral miracle made possible only thanks to revolutionary irregularities. Two months after Pinochet's putsch, former president Eduardo Frei, Allende's predecessor, wrote a letter to the Christian Democrat world union in which he attempted to trace the origins of the putsch. On the subject of the most recent legislative elections, we read in this document that the Allende coalition, in March 1973, was still in the minority with 43 per cent of the vote, "although [the government] had intervened as never before in the history of Chile, made use of the whole administrative machinery of the state, used enormous financial means and exercised pressure . . . which went as far as violence, [not to mention] fraud, attested to after the fact, involving at least 4 to 5 per cent of the votes, for the public services, among other [fraudulent practices] falsified thousands of identity cards."[6]

One might think that there must have been a means of invalidating irregular elections in a nation with such a long-standing British-style tradition of political life. There was, at least in theory—but by then Allende had for two years been disregarding the decisions and opinions of the courts and other bodies charged with the oversight of the executive branch. The Chilean Constitution was not the parliamentary variety, so the legislature could not oust the executive, but it could take recourse to judicial arbitration if it believed the executive had violated the Constitution. In hundreds of cases in which the Congress charged the executive with abuse of power, the courts had found against the president, and Allende had taken no heed of their judgments. The conflict went as high as the Supreme Court, which found against the president by a *unanimous* vote— but this did not motivate Allende to obey the law. Thus, in the spring of 1973, Allende was accused of the same violations of his country's institutions that Nixon was to be charged with a year later. But Nixon was forced to resign though he had been re-elected two years earlier with a large majority, while Allende

[6] Quoted in Rangel, op. cit.

continued to govern in defiance of the legislative and judicial powers and in spite of his minority base among the public.

Fifth: It is not true that the crumbling of the Chilean economy was due *primarily* to an "invisible blockade" organized by American capitalism and internal subversion organized by the CIA as reprisals for Allende's nationalization of American companies. The nationalization was not the work of Allende alone. During the six previous years, from 1964 to 1970, under the Christian Democratic administration of Eduardo Frei, *the Chilean state had acquired a 51 per cent interest* in the copper mines, Chile's greatest mineral wealth. A timetable providing for the gradual transfer to the Chilean state of the remaining 49 per cent interest had been agreed upon with the American mining companies. This event had not caused the cutting off of foreign loans, and though Allende's sources of new loans gradually dried up, he continued to benefit from those negotiated by his predecessor.

But why did Allende find that the sources of loans were drying up especially after the beginning of 1972? It is difficult here to distinguish what can be attributed to a concerted desire to starve out the Chilean economy and what was simply the result of growing and quite legitimate doubts about Chile's solvency. From detailed studies of the evolution of Chile's foreign debt it would seem that the lending organizations and investors generally, which included the World Bank, the International Monetary Fund and European and American banks, private as well as national, were too diverse and too dispersed to make it likely that they could have carried out such a conspiracy.[7] Some of them wanted to strike back after the new government had decreed the expropriation *without compensation* of foreign properties, others may have been responding to ideological considerations, but not all: thus the World Bank subsequently, in 1974, made a major loan to Tanzania to finance a most radical venture in socialization of the land, under the guidance of Chinese advisers. (Not the only time socialism has been subsidized by capitalism.) Besides, because of its difficulties, Allende's Chile not only obtained

[7] See in particular "The Invisible Blockade and the Overthrow of Allende," by Paul E. Sigmund, in *Foreign Affairs*, January 1974.

new lines of credit in January 1972 to replace the former ones, but in April it was granted an exceptionally generous moratorium on its repayment of debt. The agreement reached at that time between Chile and its creditors joined in what was called the Club of Paris (the United States, Canada, Japan and Western Europe) provided for the postponement to 1975 of payments on which Chile had defaulted in November 1971 as well as the payments due at the end of 1972. Those concessions were so decisive, that on August 30, 1973, a few days before he was overthrown, Allende had more short-term credits on the international financial market than he had when he took office in 1970 ($574 million compared to $310 million). Thus, if there was indeed a plan by some to create a financial crisis in Chile, it was far from systematically applied and certainly not crowned with success: it is ridiculous to look in that direction for the basic causes of the deterioration of the Chilean economy.

Finally, was that deterioration primarily fomented by the American secret services? The actions of the CIA were exposed by American investigations and were strongly condemned by public opinion, as witnessed by polls, by columnists like James Reston and David Broder and by political scientists.[8] In fact, American protests against clandestine intervention in Chilean interal politics set off the general onslaught on the CIA; the notorious agency is watched over to the point that some doubt whether it is capable of coping with its Communist competitors in espionage and subversion. Certainly the CIA's activities tend to be more harshly and more frequently condemned than those of its counterparts, for the Communist secret services are never exposed and criticized at home, and other sources of information, being foreign, are naturally suspected of bias or paranoia. Yet we are entitled to less one-eyed vision from supposedly impartial spectators: to notice, for example, that after one year of Allende, the Cuban Embassy in Santiago *had more staff members than Chile's own foreign ministry*. Fidel Castro himself made an astounding month-long "official visit" to Chile, during

[8] See especially Richard B. Fagen, "The United States and Chile, Roots and Branches," *Foreign Affairs*, January 1975. Fagen is a professor at Stanford.

which he toured city and country, dispensing speeches, admonitions and intrusions into purely domestic matters, with such aplomb on his part and such inertia on the part of the Chilean government that one would have thought he was about to seize the reins of power in his own hands. Of course, one person's incursion does not excuse the other's, and the immorality of the CIA's operations is not diminished by the cynical exhibitionism of an agent of the Communist International who made no effort to conceal his desire to push the Chileans into liquidating bourgeois democracy. But do the CIA's efforts at "destabilization" suffice to explain Chile's economic collapse, or must we attribute primarily to domestic causes the crisis that in three years destroyed the nation's democracy?

It has been claimed that the chronic and innumerable strikes and demonstrations against the high cost of living, an inflation that soon reached 100, then 200 per cent a year, against shortages of many staples, were secretly organized and subsidized by the United States. It has even been proved that some unions, the truckers for example, received CIA funding. But the truckers' discontent, most of them being owners of one or two rigs, did not begin with CIA money but rather with the government's intention of "nationalizing," i.e. requisitioning, the implements with which they earned their living. Then, too, if you consider that work stoppages and demonstrations mobilized, sometimes for weeks or even months at a time, miners, bus drivers, nurses, housewives, shopkeepers, taxi drivers, dentists, airline pilots and many other categories of workers and consumers, it becomes hard to imagine that the secret agents of imperialism could have been both so extraordinarily effective and so munificently generous: they really would have had to pay off a lot of people.

But those who refuse to recognize the cause of disaster are willing to attribute the most improbable talents to clandestine agitators—the causes in this case being the excessive speed of the nationalization of industry, a savage agrarian reform, the catastrophic decline in food production and therefore in its export, and the general paralysis due to the proliferation of an incompetent bureaucracy. As an example of the aberrations into which one can be led by the conspiracy theory that interprets all history by secret-service actions, one of Allende's zealous American partisans wrote about school uniforms that "mysteriously disappeared from the market" at the beginning of the 1972 school year, and that this suspect shortage could only be the work of some obscure machination by the Right and its imperialist allies.[9] On this point the author was better equipped with outrage than with information, for on the same topic Allende's Finance Minister, the Communist Orlando Millas, had on March 15, 1972, with a worthy capacity for self-criticism denounced "cronyism, political patronage quotas, sectarian proselytization, waste and inefficiency" in newly nationalized factories run by "bureaucratic organisms like the Textile Sector Committee, whose incapacity was once again evident in its failure to program a timely supply of school uniforms."[10]

Schoolchildren's uniforms have often been missing in the history of socialism. That is why they are so often replaced by generals' uniforms.

[9] Dale L. Johnson (Editor), "Chile and the Forces of Counterrevolution," in *The Chilean Road to Socialism* (Garden City: Doubleday/Anchor, 1973).
[10] Quoted by Norman Gall in "Chile: Hard Times," New York *Times Book Review*, July 1, 1973.

Four

STATE AND REACTION

13

THE STATE AS NARCISSUS

The division of the world into sovereign nation-states is fundamentally contradictory to the nature of the decision-making centers and methods of operation that alone could eventually resolve the problems now facing humanity.

The nation-state with its national territory is still, perhaps even more in this last quarter of the twentieth century, the only instrument of decision and implementation that can in practice be applied to world problems. Other sources of influence have arisen, from the most official, like international organizations and labor unions, to the most informal, like groups of pacifists mobilizing public opinion against nuclear testing, or consumer organizations, or even terrorist commandos. But influence and terror are not action; in order to be effective, they must exert pressure on nation-states and force them to act.

In groups of states, like the European Economic Community, the Organization of Oil Exporting Countries or the Andean Pact, each nation makes its own decisions, and if one is in disaccord with the rest, they cannot oblige it to accept their decision, unlike a democratic society in which the minority bows to the will of the majority. Thus the sovereign state remains the ultimate political reality in those treaty organizations. When recalcitrant minorities are whipped into line, as in the Warsaw Pact, it is not because the member states have willingly agreed to submit to supra-national authority, it is because one nation-state in the alliance is in fact the master of the others.

Only the state has the power to take actions, or make gestures, that have an immediate impact on international affairs. This is due less to actual power than to political anatomy. The smallest state as well as the largest, the poorest as well as the richest, can close its borders to a given type of goods, expel a group of residents, noisily withdraw from a military alliance, extend the ocean limits of its territory or announce itself threatened by some other state near or far (which of course is also a way of threatening that other state). In so doing, it introduces a new element, corrective or disturbing according to one's point of view, into the general balance of forces, which other states must then take into account. Even if that action is presumptuous, even if the state has neither the means nor the ability to back it up, even if the nations it disturbs succeed in checkmating it, if necessary by war, invasion and destruction, yet it is still universally recognized and treated as *action.* Yes, the myriad hopes and fears of humanity, the birth and decline of religions, the appearance of geniuses and monsters, the advance of knowledge and the stubborn fidelity to aberration, new popular mystiques and the disappearance of once sacred causes, the wealth and poverty of peoples, medical discoveries and the progress of agronomy, technological innovation and stagnation—these are indeed the true raw material of history, of life itself. These great forces weigh forever and everywhere on all nations, they raise up and support nations, destroy them or impel them down the road of the centuries; their power is greater beyond measure than that of politicians. Yet, that being said, it remains true that man does not live in the long run, that in daily practice, whether at the local or global level, in the brief interval that alone has meaning within the individual's life span, only the nation-state has the power to change reality in what we misname the international community.

For the nation-state rests on the one principle that today is generally recognized and more or less respected—sovereignty. Other principles, notably those on which treaties and human rights are based, are only abstractions, their application in practice being dependent on the good will of the sovereign states. The sovereign state is the machinery through which action must necessarily occur.

The State as Narcissus

To say that the sovereignty of the state is the only principle recognized in daily international practice does not mean that each state refrains from trying to destroy, subvert or dominate other states. Far from denying the idea of sovereignty, that will to dominate confirms it, just as struggles among rival companies, each trying to undermine, acquire or eliminate the others, do not deny but rather confirm the idea of property. The only available means to deny sovereignty is the refusal to recognize a government, which in any event usually means challenging the legitimacy of a particular regime rather than the sovereignty of the state in general. Besides, the absence of diplomatic relations with any de facto power is so inconvenient that the gap is typically soon filled by roundabout means—proving once more the state's indispensable role as interlocutor.

From the moment a state exists, within any territorial unit on which the accident of history and the indolence of diplomacy have conferred the status of nationhood, it is thenceforth inviolate. Whether it be democracy or dictatorship, republic based on law or police state based on concentration camps, governed by regularly elected leaders or by a junta, or even a madman, the state is respected. The "conscience of mankind" may well disapprove the barbaric practices to which a state occasionally or habitually subjects its people, but another state, even a more powerful one, has neither the means nor the grounds to bring other than moral pressure on the offending state to make it abandon those practices. Besides, such moral pressures usually come not from other states but from political parties whose selective sense of outrage is determined by their orientation, or from groups of people scattered around the world, to which the state need pay no heed. If disapproval is expressed by another government, everyone knows that this "humanitarian" position was probably taken for political reasons—that the government is seeking to increase its own power. This is promptly rejected as "interference in the internal affairs of another nation."

While the father's power of life and death over his children disappeared centuries ago, the principle of non-interference in internal affairs, more honored than ever, amounts in practice to recognizing the state's power of life and death over its inhabitants.

Of course, one state does not "respect" another's sovereignty in the sense that it will refrain from trying to reduce its powers and subordinate it to its own interests. Such efforts have been pursued in a variety of ways going back to earliest antiquity. War is still the primary way of destroying a state, but old-fashioned colonial wars and wars of conquest are rare nowadays. As contemporary examples, however, we can list the Arab states' repeated attempt to destroy Israel, the annexation of Tibet by China and of Sikkim by India, and the latter's long-standing and partially successful effort to overthrow the Pakistani state. Instead of annexation and the elimination of one state by another, war can result in a change of government with the new regime more submissive to the will of the victorious nation; but the institution we find at the end of this process is still and only the state. There are many other means by which larger states have traditionally limited in practice, while respecting in principle, the sovereignty of smaller nations: alliances in which the weak are satellites or clients of the strong, economic agreements favoring one of the partners, unequal treaties, the use of money and agents to intervene in the domestic affairs of another state by bribing newspapers, unions, politicians and criminals. No period of history was free of such practices. Every great power has always tried to create within other states political parties or other sorts of organizations favorable to its own interests (however well or poorly those interests were perceived). Sparta and Athens, Philip of Macedonia and Imperial Rome applied those methods with a mastery rarely surpassed by modern states. I am not referring here to strictly military espionage and counterespionage, which are considered normal and are operated by respected specialists holding semi-official status. I mean participation in another nation's domestic political life, which may range from open, recognized relations with a political party or union movement to assistance extended to subversive groups, guerrillas, military putschists, intellectual extremists, angry peasants or whatever. This sort of interference—at which British and French, Chinese and Russians, Cubans and Americans have all excelled—may simply consist of supporting an authentic local movement, giving it the boost it needs to succeed. Nor is it practiced only by the great powers that personify "imperialism": between 1970 and 1973 the chief of the Libyan government deployed money, threats and terrorists in a dozen African and European states in an effort to frighten public opinion and influence government policy toward Israel. However, such efforts usually fail if they are completely artificial and do not exploit real social conflicts in the nation to be infiltrated or "destabilized." The CIA and the KGB working together, with all the gold of the Transvaal, would not be enough, at least in the present state of things, to establish a military dictatorship in the Netherlands or Sweden.

Precisely because it is clandestine, intervention in the domestic affairs of another nation is an indirect way of paying homage to the principle of sovereignty. Everyone knows that open foreign intervention is unlikely to produce a lasting, acceptable outcome, so it had better be disguised as a domestic event in the target country.

When there is a coup or an insurrection, a foreign government responding to a call for "help" or simply for manna to be spread around at election time can drastically alter the nature of government in that country. The paradox is that such operations, though illegal under the country's constitution, if it has one worthy of the name, are legitimate in foreign eyes provided only that they result in a new state that endures. The sovereign state, the only legitimate entity in international relations, is not itself held to any precise criteria of legitimacy, all that is required of it being that it exercise de facto power for a minimum period over a territory whose frontiers have been recognized over time.

Some alliances are more than guarantees of mutual military assistance and have as their avowed purpose the perpetuation of a certain type of political and social order within each of the member states. Such was the case in the nineteenth century of the Holy Alliance, designed to protect the principle of dynastic legitimacy in Europe. Such is the case today in Eastern Europe, where the Soviet Union's armed intervention in the domestic affairs of its satellites, when revolutions occur there, is explained by the "socialist community's right to intervene" when there is a "counterrevolutionary danger." But this right to intervene is quite poorly defined (at least in theory; in practice it is fearfully explicit). Sometimes the Soviet Union says it is acting because it has undertaken to protect socialism, and sometimes it claims to be responding to an appeal for help from the legal government, that appeal being in response to a subversive plot mounted from abroad. That last explanation revives the classic fiction of an alliance that comes into play only when there is a *foreign* threat to one of the members. Though it is merely a subterfuge, it is interesting to note that this fiction recognizes even as it mocks the sovereignty of the local state as the only authority entitled to settle an internal problem.

Among the Western democracies we have seen the quick failure of the occasional passing impulse to try to limit the principle of state sovereignty according to the nature of the government sheltered by that sovereignty. Certain governments with abnormally refined democratic scruples brought charges against the Athens dictators before the Council of Europe between 1967 and 1974. Some American senators tried to make financial aid to the Greek colonels conditional on liberalization of their rule. The House Committee on Foreign Affairs voted in July 1971 to cut off military aid to Greece and Pakistan. The only outcome of this battle against the executive was that, from 1972 on, American military aid, which had been kept secret by the Defense Department for twenty-three years, was made public, country by country, and listed in the official budget. The U. S. Senate suspended military aid to Turkey after its invasion of Cyprus in 1974, thus opening a breach in NATO's Mediterranean flank. These temperamental actions, like the imposition of economic "sanctions"—on Mussolini's Italy before 1939 and on Rhodesia in the late 1960s—never result in measures that are really troublesome to those at whom they are aimed, except in cases where their moral motivation is reinforced by powerful economic or political interests.

All in all, then, efforts to link the recognition of a state's powers—or simply the granting to it of financial or military assets—to the way it treats its people have seldom been more than symbolic gestures. If such threats and demands for reprisal are ephemeral and limited in effect when they emanate from other states, they are even less effective, indeed completely in vain, when they emanate from individuals or good will groups or indignant "world citizens." Paradoxically, the twentieth century, instead of making the value of a nation conditional on the value of the civilization it houses, has conferred status on the nation as such, free of any moral, political or humanitarian consideration. If you have a nation and a state, you are endowed with all rights, you are above criticism. The absolute nation has succeeded the absolute monarchy.

Or, more accurately, it has contributed to its re-establishment, for one-man rule is the logical extension of the single cult of the nation. "If you have resolved to be a patriot, you must necessarily be a royalist," said Charles Maurras.

Charles Maurras, the theoretician and advocate of monarchy, is forgotten today, and yet his ideas are practiced almost everywhere. Karl Marx is not forgotten, and yet his ideas are not incarnated in any regime, at least not in any form that he would have wished.

Is a political philosopher's influence on people's ideas and emotions likely to be greater if his influence on events is diminished? Perhaps: if his ideas are implemented, he is overtaken by reality and his myth will fade away. If his ideas are unpracticed or impracticable, they will continue to excite the imagination and to provide food for discussion. The name of Karl Marx is no doubt uttered several million times a day in the three thousand-odd languages spoken on our planet, although—perhaps because—no existing society, according to the socialists themselves, is authentically socialist. The name of Charles Maurras is probably not spoken once a week in his maternal tongue, not even behind the nostalgic ramparts of an aristocratic manor house, and yet almost the entire world is governed according to his principles: those of absolute monarchy.

Monarchy, not royalty. Sweden, Denmark, Great Britain have kings or queens, but they are not monarchs in the political sense.

One-man rule or its second-best substitute, the rule of the few—oligarchy—need not follow the principle of heredity essential to royalty. Monarchic political power and hereditary royalty are still found in conjunction in some important states—Saudi Arabia, Iran. But as history has shown, continuity can be assured by other principles of succession. The modern political regimes which seem in practice to be most favored by humanity can be defined as absolute monarchies whose principle of succession is the coup d'état.

Of the 140-odd sovereign states in 1975, only 28 or 30 can be considered democracies. Even some of these are open to doubt: Mexico, for example, regularly holds free elections, but in fact each president co-opts his successor. Sometimes, as in Argentina and Lebanon, democracy gives way to anarchy. We more often see a country go from democracy to monarchy than the opposite, but fortunately the change does not always go in that direction. Since 1973 Chile has become fascist, but Greece and Portugal have emerged from fascism, though the latter country almost traded Salazarist for Stalinist monarchy.

Democratic states are a small minority in the world today. But the full extent of the triumph of monarchy can be seen when we consider, not the number of states, but the number of *people* governed by the two systems. The list of democratic states includes many that have fewer than 15 million or even 10 or 5 million inhabitants—Austria, Norway, New Zealand, Israel. Except for the United States, the demographic giants are found among the monarchies. The 9 million Greeks who returned to democracy would be easily lost among the 600 million Indians annexed by monarchy when Mrs. Gandhi proclaimed her state of emergency in June 1975.

In Mrs. Gandhi's coup, a democratic chief of state succeeded herself by assuming the monarchy when she found the laws of the Constitution to be a hindrance: this is the Bonapartist style of coup d'état. In an already existing monarchy, on the other hand, the coup provides a change in leadership, rotation in office. The machinery is less cumbersome than that of election, it spares the people the time away from his desk that the leader would have to spend campaigning for re-election and it can be used as often as needed.

In 1975 Madagascar, Nigeria, the Comoro Islands, Bangladesh, Chad and Peru all demonstrated how well the system works, whether or not the change-over provides for summary execution of the dethroned monarch.

The coup d'état is superior to hereditary succession in that the pretender runs a risk and must earn his victory. Coups undertaken with various amounts of preparation failed in Libya, Uganda, Sudan and Ecuador. In the latter country, I am pleased to report, French-made tanks prevented the putschists from acceding to legitimacy. In Bolivia, the president staged a simulated coup, analogous to military maneuvers elsewhere, so that all the actors could rehearse their roles. A citizen of Zaire, after being graduated from an American university where he wrote a doctoral thesis on "How to Prepare a Successful Coup d'État in Zaire," went home with the idea of putting his theory into practice, but it was a woeful failure. This sour note was, alas, neither the first nor the last time political science had failed in its practical application.

In Communist monarchies, the coup takes place within the single party. The abrupt and enigmatic changes in personnel within the Chinese ruling elite since the Cultural Revolution are the outward result of coups and countercoups that we can only guess at. In the Soviet Union, the ouster of Shelepin from the Politburo may have been the first step in a coup against Brezhnev, similar to the successful coup that ousted Khrushchev in 1964. The Communist monarchies should, in the spirit of Helsinki, democratize their coup d'état by allowing non-party members to take part and by staging them in the open so the general public can enjoy the show, as is the case in Africa. Is not the coup after all one way to achieve the Helsinki ideal of "free circulation of people and ideas?"

Today all the traditional political, religious, geographic or kinship groupings in which people were joined—tribe, city, region, church—are melting under the pressure of the state, even when they straddle its boundaries or contest its authority. Within the territory it controls, the state tends to try to eradicate a diversity in which it sees only a mosaic of local interests that resist its centralizing authority and are an impediment to "national unity." Abroad, it opposes other states even when they are temporarily its allies, because, being a tool created for rivalry, it sees the world in those terms. Its nature makes it exacerbate what we might call the border mentality. The state works at making the society within its borders at once more homogeneous and more distinct from other societies, increasing the sense of difference between itself and others, between "we" and "they."

That is why so many governments exert themselves to isolate their people from the rest of humanity by prohibiting or strictly rationing their contact with foreigners, limiting the freedom of people and especially of ideas to enter and leave their territory. (In the case of ideas, after a certain amount of time there is little left to export.) They prevent the free circulation of information about the nation itself as well as about other countries and world affairs. Censorship and propaganda collaborate to put forth each day a paranoid fictional vision of the nation and the world, so that little or nothing penetrates the society that is unfavorable to those in power or that fails to do homage to the accuracy of their views and the fruitfulness of their policies. The dream of every state—that no one, at least no one subject to its authority, should be able to verify its claims or judge its works—has become reality over most of the surface of this globe. The great increase in the quantity of information and the speed with which it is disseminated, something we have been hearing so much about since 1960 from media experts, applies only to those 30-odd democratic nations among the world's 140 states. Everywhere else, there is surely quantity and speed, but what is spread is anything but information. There the media are merely extensions of political power, institutions designed to cage the human spirit.

This isolating of human groups from each other is facilitated by the states' accompanying policy of promoting popular nationalism in the form of the most adolescent chauvinist pride, xenophobia and touchiness. This collective megalomania is all the more easily promoted and justified because the state's propa-

ganda machine keeps the people in a state of profound ignorance
—notably of any foreign comparisons to their own society—and
is all the more useful for the goal of keeping society quiet because it relieves the boredom of people for whom the parading
of the grandeur of the state is generally the only show in town.

Nationalism is exploited by the rulers to discourage criticism,
distract people's attention from the internal situation and fasci-
nate them with ambitious foreign-policy objectives, which in
turn provide a new pretext for the omnipotence of the executive.
We know that procuring weapons is the main concern of contemporary governments. The world's military expenses, including
and especially the poorest nations, annually total twice what is
spent on education, three times what is spent on health, and
twenty times the aid extended by the rich nations to the third
world. The normal relationship between the nation and the state,
in which the state is merely an instrument serving the interests
of the nation and the people in it, has been completely reversed.
Now nations and people have been made servants of the state,
usually by means of force, while the state has become an independent organism or apparatus concerned only with its functioning and with the enlarging of its own power.

States as a rule only perceive the search for power among
others. In their own case, it is viewed as a natural desire for independence, a mere resistance to the imperialist trespasses of
others.

But there is only a difference of degree between the goals of
"independence" and "power." A state is a "power" or "superpower" if it can exert influence on a global scale. A state is restricted to a policy of "independence" if its means are limited to
the ability to thwart the global politics of the superpowers in
some perceptible way that may be purely symbolic but psychologically effective. "Independence" is the supergrandeur of the
weak. It does not differ in principle from the aggressive politics
of hegemony of the superpowers: it grows out of the same motives and the same nation-state culture. It is like the team whose
members pass the ball around among themselves, not in the hope
of scoring, but just to keep it out of the hands of the stronger

team and prevent them from scoring. Were they stronger themselves, they would go over to the offensive and try like everyone else to win the championship. Nation-state diplomacy itself being a competitive sport, the politics of "independence" of the weaker states does not represent any advance in civilization nor the beginnings of change in the system that could lead to a broader, more universal view of the interests of the human species, but is rather a defensive position, a substitute for the power politics that is beyond their reach, which they condemn not in principle but because it belongs to others.

Indeed, the politics of hegemony practiced by the superpowers has a better chance of leading to the international management of our planet than does the spawning of more states practicing the politics of independence. For though they are motivated by the expansionist egotism which is the essence of the nation-state, the superpowers nonetheless are forced to assume global responsibilities and to see problems in terms of their worldwide interrelationships. If the world were entirely Soviet, Chinese or American, whatever reservations one may have concerning the quality of life under one or another of these eventualities, we would be rid at least of one absurd aspect of the present situation: the leaving of responsibility for problems whose solution can only be worldwide in design and execution to a scattering of autonomous, disparate, rival decision-making centers that are often intellectually limited and lacking even a common mode of thought.

Since 1945, while we have witnessed the flourishing of the rhetoric of international co-operation and the growth of organizations intended to take on great issues in the interest of all humanity, we have also seen the growing fragmentation of the world into cells that are ever harder and more hermetically sealed. And while we have witnessed the spread of both the ideology of democracy and the parody of its practice, what in fact has occurred is the advent of history's most remarkable horde of new rulers who are freebooters in their origins and authoritarian in their practices. The stronger the nation-state has grown, asserting on the international scene a sacred authority accountable to none for the way it treats that portion of humanity that happens to be under its control, the less the masters of the nation-states are chosen and overseen by the people in whose name they speak.

The indictment of the nation-state can be summarized as follows:

By inciting and sustaining nationalist feelings, the state in variable proportions substitutes false problems for real ones.

The boundaries of the state never coincide with the real economic and cultural boundaries of human societies.

The state stimulates the least critical and most pathological side of human nature in what is said to be the national interest, usually not the case.

The state diverts wealth into armaments.

The state provides the ideological and emotional base for despotism and a stage on which demagogues are invited to star. The conditions under which power is acquired and held in most nations offer no sufficient guarantee of the mental competence and sense of responsibility of the rulers.

The state invites corruption, for it impels those who occupy it (in most cases the state is indeed "occupied" in the sense that a conquered nation is occupied) to practice venality and profiting from office as well as the purely political abuse of their power. We see this in capitalist and socialist, developed and underdeveloped nations alike.

The state can fully realize its potential only at the cost of choking off the flow of information and thereby making the members of each human group ever more invisible to other groups and to each other.

Thus the nation-state, ever more egotistical, is incompatible with those means of action suitable to the global nature of the urgent problems that humanity today must resolve.

In theory a mere instrument of the collective will, the state increasingly defines itself as the end not the means and, in the pursuit of its own interests, advances inexorably toward the limits of totalitarianism at home and imperialism abroad.

14

UNITING THE NINE POWERS

The combination of Stalinism and the division of the world into nation-states gives the Communist powers certain advantages over the free capitalist or social democratic nations. Their principal advantage is that the Communist executive cannot be publicly criticized or legally prevented from acting by other powers, nor forced to reverse itself by the opposition of public opinion. Accordingly, many third-world leaders have found it expedient to mold their states on Stalinist lines. In such a system, only serious economic difficulties can create internal discontent that poses a threat to the authorities. But lacking other outlets, that discontent can only express itself in a rare outbreak of rioting that thanks to effective repression has little chance of success. Even in such circumstances, the Stalinist state has a trump card denied to the free state, for censorship makes it possible, at least in the vast territory of the Soviet Union and China, to conceal the disaster or unrest occurring in one region from the rest of the nation. Aside from that possibility, and the currently non-existent danger of defeat in a foreign war, the Stalinist state has no chink in its armor either with respect to its own people or with respect to its free competitors.

Yet the totalitarian state is fragile to the extent that it cannot satisfy the needs and desires of the society it rules. It tries to destroy the autonomy of private life, which it fears, by constant surveillance; it shows its fear by following each of its members through his work, his entertainment, his travels, his friendships, the raw materials of his thought and his emotions. It is precisely because the state is fragile that it can never relax its vigilance, show no tolerance to criticism or make hardly any concessions in foreign policy. Lacking any degree of elasticity, the state must be rigid in order to survive, always in fear that any indisposition, no matter how minor it may seem, may become a fatal illness. Its very weakness dooms it to being ever stronger.

While the nature of the totalitarian state is that it must continually reinforce itself, the logic of the democratic state makes it evolve in exactly the opposite direction: toward the growing separation, multiplication and diversification of centers of power and decision-making. Indeed, the free state was born out of the idea of the separation of mutually restricting powers. The separation of the three powers as defined by Montesquieu is often derided as "obsolete" when it is being abolished in favor of totalitarianism disguised as socialism or a supposedly modernizing rightest anti-parliamentarianism. In fact, it is extremely difficult to maintain, it requires a high level of civic consciousness and despite its age it remains the basis of every democracy. Whether presidential or parliamentary or mixed, democratic institutions cannot exist if the executive governs beyond limits set by the legislative and without legal mandate, or if the judiciary is subject to the orders of either of the other branches.

But since the eighteenth century other powers have grown independently of those basic three. The economic power of the firm; union power; the power to inform[1]; the police power, which tends periodically to become independent of the judiciary and the legislative and even in the long run of the executive; the military power, increasingly detached from the rest, whose opinions are often decisive even in domestic policy; the imperial power, which is the power to conduct foreign policy. The growing complexity of diplomacy, with its inevitable element of secrecy (and secret services), has made it virtually an independent branch of government, to the point that it shamelessly bypasses the instruments of parliamentary control and sometimes even the titular minister of foreign affairs.

[1] The expression is from the title of Jean-Jacques Servan-Schreiber's book, *The Power to Inform* (New York: McGraw-Hill, 1974). The French title was *Le Pouvoir d'informer*.

I shall not try to deny that my list is heterogeneous, impressionistic and empirical—indeed, that admission is the only scholarly thing about it. Other kinds of powers may come to mind: for example, technological power—but technology and the economy are now inseparably intertwined; or regional power, but in some democratic nations that power existed from the beginning, and recently it has been the setting for a confrontation among the powers listed above, including—what a paradox!—the power of conducting foreign policy. (Thus, Alberta in Canada and Scotland in Great Britain would like to deal directly with the international oil market without going through their respective central governments.) Another objection might be that one cannot put in the same category the army in an underdeveloped nation, whose power is primitively praetorian, and that of the developed nations, where the power of the "military-industrial complex" flows from the increasing specialization of weapons technology and military strategy. Or that one cannot use the same vocabulary for union and police power, because the first is legal and democratic, while the second can only acquire independence at the cost of infringing on democracy. True enough, but in practice the political powers, the executive and legislative, are dealing with resistant organisms (though their reasons for resisting may differ), with power centers with which they must negotiate. The police, whose duties are divided between the maintenance of political order, an area in which citizens always feel it has too much power, and the fight against crime, in which case the citizens feel it never has enough power, is thus periodically motivated to make demands on the state: either abandon political repression, and no state likes that notion, or else close your eyes to some of our methods, which endangers the public's right. If anyone objects, well, let him fight crime on the streets without us!

Whatever the powers involved in any given case, an ever increasing number of groups are competing with the political powers in the democracies. Now, when the general will has been expressed at the ballot box, or the parliament has voted, or the administration has made its decision, nothing as yet has been settled. To the contrary, *that is when the negotiations begin.*

This multiplication of power centers also results in the increasing liberation of society from the guardianship of the state, permitting it to develop an ever more diversified life of its own, in which not only several political galaxies but several cultures and several systems of morality are able to co-exist. To the contrary of what is often asked of it in a spirit of authoritarian paternalism that harks back to religious dogmatism and forward to Maoism in its desire to mold the minds and behavior of the masses, it is not the duty of a free democratic civilization to choose its members' way of life, to hold up an "ideal." Only immature people, not adult citizens, want the state to be a Pygmalion giving them both their "goals" and the means of achieving them. Only in the totalitarian society does the state arrogate to itself the right to give "meaning" to people's lives. The free state, on the contrary, tends to create conditions under which the group imposes no way of life, no form of consciousness, on the individual. Those are the conditions that define every modern revolution, as I argued in another book. One can hardly ask the free society at once to refrain from issuing prohibitions and to preach the truth. Denounced as repressive when it meddles in exercising pressure on the values of the individual, the free state cannot be held derelict in its duty when it refrains from interfering.

This centrifugal trend in the free societies, often sensed as disorder, anarchy, the crumbling of society into ungovernable pieces, loss of any discipline over the individual, gives rise to attempts to return to the womb, to compress all powers into one at the original source. This was the case between the wars in Europe, that cradle of fascism.

Fascism is a reaction to democracy. Fascism is the destruction of democracy, it incessantly and obsessively defines itself by contrast to democracy, that evil fouler of the nest which fascism is proud to have put to death. Hitler was so virulent because he was vomiting up the Weimar Republic. General Pinochet performs against the backdrop of the former Chilean democracy. If he had not dug its grave, he would be classified not among the fascists but among the heads of those archaic authoritarian states which have *not yet* evolved toward democracy, where we would see him alongside such figures as the kings of Morocco and Saudi Arabia. He would be not criminal but *backward*. Mrs. Gandhi would not have been so resented for her coup, which after all just made India conform to all its neighbors, whose systems are not subject to any similar reprimand, had not democracy been previously implanted on the Indian subcontinent. Fascism is the apoplexy of the free society; it disrupts its functions the way apoplexy disrupts the brain, sometimes irreversibly. That is why democrats hate fascist governments more than Stalinist ones, even when it can be shown that the latter have committed as many, or many more, crimes than the former. In their eyes a fascist government is a black sheep of the family, it has betrayed and dishonored the civilization it deserted to take the wrong course; whereas Stalinist regimes are perceived as strangers living on another planet: if those people want to kill each other, that's their business.

A more subtle way of reconcentrating power has occurred since 1945, though in a context that remains democratic, through a kind of overdevelopment of the executive. It has given us most notably Gaullism, which has served many third-world leaders as an excuse to turn to personal power and the political star system with a clear conscience and, of course, without the minimal democratic equipment that was the creative element in the Gaullist design. In the United States, the Tonkin Gulf resolution, which permitted the White House to conduct the war in Vietnam without informing Congress of its bloody and futile exploits, marked the high point of Executive overdevelopment. In 1974 the Watergate affair concluded with the victory of the peripheral powers over the center. The press, public opinion, the judiciary and the Congress forced the resignation for constitutional irregularities of the head of the most powerful state on earth, despite the universal remonstrances heaped on the American people (especially by the Soviet Union) over this new execution of Louis XVI, which, because no blood was shed, was perhaps even more revolutionary than the first. Nixon's forced resignation, obtained in the most juridically scrupulous manner—a "legal" putsch, even if justified, would have been a step backward not forward for democracy—dealt a body blow to an authoritarian deviation that had endowed the executive with dangerous privilege. The counterattack continued with the investigations of the machinations of the CIA and the suspect activities of multi-national corporations, putting in each case the concern for democracy before even the foreign policy interests of the United States—a concern for democracy that at any other time or in any other country would have promptly bowed to reasons of state.

The free societies have thus continued, despite fascism and authoritarianism, to follow a course during which they are becoming more centrifugal and are transcending conventional nationalism. The British author Ghita Ionescu gives an example of this process in his *Centripetal Politics: Government and the New Centers of Power:* "Take, as an example of such a situation in Britain, the problems arising around North Sea Oil. Here the region [Scotland] demands to be given its monopoly; the unions demand that the monopoly should go to the British state; the multinational corporations demand that they should handle the oil since they invested the capital; and the European Community demands that the oil should be shared with the Community."[2]

It is clear that the phenomena of civilization and culture, the power to inform and the power to educate, are progressively escaping from all centralized power in any but a "people's" democracy. That is why the Soviet Union only reluctantly accepted and then enthusiastically sabotaged the clause in the 1975 Declaration of Helsinki on "free circulation of ideas and people," for it knew that its application at home would amount to hurling the Soviet system into the deadly cyclone of centrifugal civilization.

[2] London: Hart-Davis MacGibbon, 1975. The author proposes the idea of "centripetal" government, as opposed to that of centralized government; that is in order to avoid the reciprocal neutralization of all decision-making centers, not the return to the former concentration, but the convergence of peripheral powers within new decision-making structures.

The Totalitarian Temptation

By contrast to democratic civilization, the unity of the nine powers remains the golden rule, not just in the two main Stalinist states and their satellites, but in many new nation-states of the third world. The archaic simplicity of a single and absolute power is more convenient and more comfortable than the headaches of the precarious and scattered powers of the free society. Besides, the majority of nation-states are either already totalitarian or are receptacles just waiting to be filled with the Stalinist stew of reactionary statism and verbal socialism.

Five

NATIONAL TOTALITARIANISM
OR GLOBAL SOCIALISM

OF DOCILITY TOWARD STALINISM: AN ESSAY IN EXPLANATION

"The public likes false novels . . .

"It likes books that have the appearance of being in society . . .

"It likes equivocal little works, girls' memoirs, alcove confessions, erotic uncleanness, the scandals exposed in the windows of bookshops . . .

"The public further likes to read what is soothing and comforting, adventures that end well, imaginings that disturb neither their digestion nor their serenity . . ."

Those words did not issue from the pen of some Maoist or Christian railing against the current flood of pornography; nor do they express a patriotic politician's concern over the fall in the birth rate; nor are they excerpted from an enraged literary critic's diatribe against the grossly commercial practices of contemporary publishing; nor yet are they from a contentious Marcusian poster indicting, in the spirit of the 1960s, our alienating pseudo-culture—the only culture, as we all know, that pseudo-democratic civilization has ever provided to its unhappy charges.

None of the above. Those words date from 1864, and were written by the Goncourt brothers in the preface to *Germinie Lacerteux*, their novel about the life and loves of a servant girl.

Erich Auerbach, in his *Mimesis*,[1] observes about that preface that in the nineteenth century writers developed the habit of flogging their own audience, whom they saw as a motley crew of depraved taste and stunted mind. A rather contradictory accusation, for it was to that same audience that such authors as

[1] Berne: C. A. Francke, A. G. Verlag, 1946.

Dickens and Zola, George Eliot, Flaubert and Tolstoy owed their popular success. So roundly condemned ever since the Romantic era, that reader is essentially bourgeois and therefore the epitome of stupidity and cowardice. Auerbach asks: "Can we subscribe to that opinion? Did not that same bourgeoisie take on the enormous task, the perilous adventure of nineteenth-century economic, scientific and technological civilization? And did not that same bourgeoisie produce the leaders of revolutionary movements, those men who were the first to become aware of the crises, dangers and sources of corruption in that civilization?"

We all know the answer to *that:* economic, scientific and technological accomplishments are due exclusively to the profit motive and the exploitation of the workers, not to the imagination to conceive the new and the skill to make it reality. As I observed earlier, if the desire for profit and the exploitation of the workers were sufficient to produce economic progress and the political freedom that accompanied it, why did those two developments not appear before the end of the eighteenth century? The workers were far more oppressed in undeveloped precapitalist economies than in societies where industrial capitalism had taken root, and the same is true today of underdeveloped societies. Anyone who has spent any time in the third world, unless he is vaccinated against the virus of reality, cannot fail to see that a destitute population does *not* produce economic growth, otherwise those nations would be the richest of all. A kingdom like Saudi Arabia may have virtually the greatest amount of wealth per inhabitant in the world, but it remains nonetheless an underdeveloped country. Changed intellectual attitudes, conceptual perception and above all the ability to translate those into custom are more important to development than exploitation and the greed for profit. How else can it be explained, for example, that so well known a "leftist" as the agronomist René Dumont, after an assignment in India, and "unfamiliar with the society, was shocked at what seemed to him to be a complete disdain for reality?" (As reported by his namesake, Louis Dumont, in his *La Civilisation indienne et nous.*[2] "Changed intel-

[2] Paris: Armand Collin, 1975.

lectual attitudes" does not refer only to science and the scientific method of thought. A society can, like the Soviet Union, reach an advanced scientific level in some sectors while the rest of the society is partially or predominantly underdeveloped. Besides, even if one were to show that science and not greed for profit was the factor that made the difference, the main engine that powered the economic take-off, that would not suffice to absolve industrial capitalism in the eyes of those who consider it the darkest stain on the history of mankind. In fact, hostility toward science and technology in contemporary philosophy is as strong as the revulsion against societies oriented toward economic production, and the two feelings often mingle and become one.

It seems to me that the totalitarian temptation is really driven by a hatred on principle of industrial, commercial civilization, and would exist even if it were proved that people in that civilization were better fed, in better health and better (or less badly) treated than in any other. The real issue lies elsewhere: money is sinful, the root of all evil; and if freedom was born of economic development, then it too suffers from that original sin.

It is significant, for example, that "freedom of the press" is almost always associated with the idea of a "press enslaved by money," which becomes "pseudo-freedom of the press" in the service of "profit." This image is completely contrary to reality, because up till now there has never been a free press, "pseudo" or otherwise, that did not emanate from private investment. Historical experience includes only two kinds of press: the state press and the "money" press. And the institution of the modern press and media, that enormous central fact without which it is impossible to conceive of the world, derives entirely from the money press. The state press has never been more than a pale copy or caricature of the money press, because dictators always emasculate as well as appropriate this new means of influence. Thus it is ridiculous to condemn the press on the grounds that it is a "money press": there has never been any other kind.

Of course, societies with a long democratic tradition may be able to convert a channel of information to public service without subjecting it to political power. But to be successful such a formula must be based on lengthy previous experience with the "money press," in order to develop the critical faculties of the public and the skepticism of journalists. Otherwise the political power will soon gain control, openly or surreptitiously, of the medium in question, which will become subservient to coteries and clans and favoritism.

Besides, the press is not due to money alone. It is also the result, among other things, of the disappearance of illiteracy, for without the generalization of schooling, where would it find its readers, from whom would the profiteers of the rotary press and publishing extract their profits? Only now do we see the lucrative scheme that lay behind capitalism's legislation for compulsory free education.

Attacks on the press are of course vigorously applauded by politicians, always ready to blame it for its "sensationalism" (meaning it raises subjects that disturb them) while in the same breath criticizing the spinelessness of journalists who lack the courage to reveal the incompetence and corruption of rival politicians. The art of the politician, like that of the dentist, lies in convincing the client he is the only trustworthy member of a profession that is full of bandits, all of whom have been recently barred from practice as veterinarians.

Preferring totalitarianism to "money," opting for poverty under dictatorship over freedom with corruption, is a choice that can be argued. It is done so most eloquently by those who have conserved the moral characteristics of the old aristocratic and ecclesiastic culture, the similarity of which to the mentality and behavior of Stalinist bureaucrats has often been noted. An ideology to be effective must be in harmony with a style, a way of being, and that style in turn influences the ideology. Some kinds of personalities aspire to a hierarchical society in which—as in Michel Foucault's nightmare or the all too real India described by Louis Dumont—the individual neither exists nor thinks for himself but only in relation to the group. In the Soviet Union and China, the individual is assigned a job, a standard of living, a home, rights and duties, not by the despicable "market," but by a superior central authority acting in the light of transcendental truth. It is worth noting that the four nations of Western Europe in which communism is a substantial political force (it is insignificant elsewhere in the region) are Latin Catholic nations in which capitalism was late developing and industry still lags behind that of northern Europe; they have had troubled constitutional histories, with many undemocratic interludes.

Communist leaders are not unaware of the ecclesiastical nature of their intellectual and administrative structures. Ceretti, the confidant of Togliatti and Thorez, writes in his memoirs about the latter: "Getting along despite diversity, as Togliatti wants, is an art the Church understands. It is two thousand years old, while we are barely adults. That is the whole problem."[3]

The success of the works of Roger Garaudy, especially since he was expelled from the party, is due without doubt first of all to his great talent, but also perhaps to his effort to fuse into one the two great dogmatisms of the West. During one of his visits to the United States, a mutual friend, the philosopher John Wilkinson, affectionately called the brilliant author of *The Alternative Future* "half Marx and half Jesus." That quip effectively summarizes the goal of people who feel a need to enclose themselves in an edifice built according to a doctrinal blueprint rather than floating loose in a society constantly rocked by the waves of change—the "achieving society," as David McClelland called it.[4]

It is symptomatic that the entrepreneurs were the first ruling class in history to be despised as well as condemned. The member of the pre-revolutionary French clergy living on ecclesiastical stipends and benefices, and noble at the court of Louis XIV who spent his nights playing backgammon might be the subject of moral disapproval, but he was not *despised*—not so much in any event as the members of the bourgeois ruling class, who work harder, whether industrialist, shopkeeper, doctor or engineer, and under whose reign the exploited masses are less badly off than they were under any previous ruling class.

Many are attracted to Joseph Schumpeter's prediction, in *Capitalism, Socialism and Democracy*, that capitalism and the po-

---

[3] Quoted by Robrieux, *Maurice Thorez*, op. cit., Philippe p. 463.
[4] David C. McClelland, *The Achieving Society* (Van Nostrand, 1961).

litical democracy that clings to its back (for no other form of economy has borne democracy) will be done in not by its technological failures or its moral failings but by its intellectuals. Works inveighing for or against the "intellectuals" are a favorite item on the sales counters of the publishing world: it is a kind of mental falsie that requires little material and can be filled by a brain of modest size while still conveying to the viewer a flattering impression of its dimensions. But Schumpeter's hypothesis is unconvincing. While Romain Rolland, Pound, Brecht, Aragon, Sartre rejected capitalism as criminal and democracy as illusory, Bergson, Günter Grass, Orwell, Keynes and Thomas Mann did not. The incidence of irresponsibility and fanaticism among intellectuals is about the same as in any other socioeconomic group, and lunacy is equitably distributed across the political horizon, as Alfred Kazin showed us in his biting and impartial 1973 *Playboy* article, "The Writer as Political Crazy." Scientists are equally eclectic: Joliot-Curie served Stalinism, Einstein democracy, Heisenberg Nazism. Doubtless some intellectuals feel it is bound to be a winning gamble because you cannot lose by being a Marxist-Leninist or a Stalinist in a free society. If the society remains free, you will be in the opposition, with all the guarantees democracy provides to that status, without any great practical risk, and with the prestige of being a nonconformist. If it becomes a totalitarian society in which opposition is no longer tolerated, you will be among the masters or their house servants, in any event one of the beneficiaries of the new order. But you do not have to be an intellectual to calculate the odds on betting on the red. As an entity, the "intellectual" seems to me as unmonolithic in the present and as versatile in the long run as the "bourgeois."

Free societies are much more likely, I believe, to disintegrate under the pressure of nationalism. Capitalism has produced an obsession with success and failure, with being the most or least "advanced" nation. The wounds that daily comparisons of one's nation's "performance" with that of others can inflict on the collective pride may make people wish for a world in which national competition is outlawed. The error here lies not in wanting to end national competition—an ambition I wholeheartedly share—but in wanting to do it by destruction rather than creation, not by outgrowing the nation-state but by the collective suicide of totalitarianism. As if it is better to blind yourself rather than try to change the show! The underdeveloped nations can only bear their backwardness by blaming it entirely on the imperialism of the rich nations, on the "looting of the third world." Industrial nations, in a more subtle sort of rivalry, contend for first place. In their hearts many feel that it would be better to destroy the developed world rather than not be number one. Before 1940 Britain was number one; today it is the United States. The most powerful among us bears all our guilt and is responsible not only for all our misfortunes but also for all the harm we do to the third world.[5]

[5] A poem by León Felipe (1884–1968) forcefully expresses the hatred of which Britain was the object between the two world wars. Note that Felipe, who opposed Franco and after the civil war was a refugee in Mexico, so detested the British that he found them more contemptible than the Italian Fascists and the German Nazis! Here is the first part of the poem.

RAPOSA

Inglaterra,
eres la vieja Raposa avarienta
que tiene parada la Historia de Occidente hace más de tres siglos,
y encadenado a Don Quijote.
Cuando acabe tu vida
y vengas ante la Historia grande
donde te aguardo yo,
¿qué vas a decir?
¿Qué astucia nueva vas a inventar entonces para engañar a Dios?
¡Raposa!
¡Hija de raposos!
Italia es más noble que tú
y Alemania también.
En su rapiña y en sus crímenes
hay un turbio hálito nietzscheano de heroísmo, en el que no pueden respirar
    los mercaderes,
un gesto impetuoso y confuso de jugárselo todo a la última carta, que no
    pueden comprender los hombres pragmáticos.

FOX[*]

England,
you are the hungry old Fox,

[*] Translated by Electa Arenal, from the manuscript *Oh! This Anguish of Spain!*, a bilingual anthology of Spanish Civil War poems of León Felipe.

I set forth in *Without Marx or Jesus* what I mean by revolution and "world" revolution. The French subtitle of that book, "De la seconde révolution américaine à la seconde révolution mondiale" ("From the Second American Revolution to the Second World Revolution"),[6] indicated that my primary intent was to revise and redefine the idea of revolution. But the fact that I built my case around the United States, arguing that it was the setting for a new kind of revolutionary process, brought forth impassioned outcries from all quarters (as indeed does any mention of American civilization today). Some realities so torture people's cultural egos as to exceed their capacity for impartiality (so limited even in the best of circumstances).

I was a sympathetic witness to that troubled state of mind in Italy between 1952 and 1956, but in that case with respect to France. I often discussed aesthetic questions with writers and artists and with my students. But no general discussion of aesthetics could really be general because it would stir up memories of an unbearable fact: that virtually all aesthetic revolutions since the eighteenth century have originated outside Italy; French painting in particular had been bruising the Italian cultural ego for two centuries. It was of course painful to admit that the creative imagination had forsaken Italy of all places, the civi-

---

you have stalled the History of the West for more than three centuries,
and held Don Quixote in chains.
When your life ends
and you come before Great History
where I await you,
what will you say?
What new stratagem will you invent then to deceive God?
Fox!
Daughter of Foxes!
Italy is nobler than you.
And Germany too.
In her plunder and in her crimes
there is a turbid Nietzschean breath of greatness in which merchants can't
    breathe,
an impetuous confused gesture of playing it to the last card that pragmatic
    men can't understand.

[6] The American edition was subtitled "The New American Revolution Has Begun."

lization that along with Greece and China has left the most beauty on the surface of this planet. Thus any seemingly general discussion of aesthetics was in fact motivated by the burning need to prove that nothing that had happened since 1800 was really original and in fact was no more than imitation or a passing fancy.

That same need, but on a global scale, motivates debate on any political, cultural, economic or moral issue that to any degree involves the example of America. The result in the case of *Without Marx or Jesus* was an armful of misunderstandings that seemed only to be aggravated by my many efforts at explanation. As Ludwig Wittgenstein said in the preface to his *Philosophical Investigations,* "My vanity was hurt, and I had some difficulty soothing it." Yet I had had the opportunity to learn through previous books that, by virtue of some bizarre effect, possibly even a law, the reasons for which escape me, the comprehension of an idea decreases as its circulation increases.

That led me to meditate upon the riddle of our modern sphinx, mass communications. And to ask myself by what inversion the rather wide circulation of a book, the numerous commentaries it provoked, the many opportunities the author was afforded to explain what he meant, all conspired to produce an ever more fallacious idea of that book's basic thesis. In one sense, that idea became more blunt, more black and white, when it should have become more shaded, more complex; in another, it grew ever more remote, at times to the point of contradiction, from what the author had said.

On one of the recent occasions the sphinx interrogated me it assumed the austere features of *Playboy,* which only a few years ago was considered merely a gutter magazine, combining the cheerful merchandising of an ostentatious hedonism with the diabolical misuse of cultural alibis: excerpts from books, theater and film reviews and, most notably, in-depth interviews with writers, actors, sociologists, philosophers, politicians, economists, theologists, promoters of new forms of consciousness. So many people whom position or talent have charged with shaping or expressing any slice, no matter how thin, of the events, ideas, moods and dreams of our times have accepted the offer (misled no doubt by the contradictions of capitalism) of the deceptive pulpit of *Playboy* and its repressive tolerance—including Herbert Marcuse himself,[7] and Sartre besides—that it would surely be easier to understand the decade of the sixties without delving into the *American Journal of Sociology* or the *Revue française de science politique* than without the regrettably notorious lightweight magazine from Chicago.

Today *Playboy* is no longer really lightweight, at least by comparison with films and other magazines in the 1970s. Still, it continues heroically to put forth its highly original mixture of pictures of a Victorian sexuality and frankly cynical text.

Since the act of speaking out is more cynical than anything we admit to in what we say, forgive me for reproducing an excerpt from my ramblings about *Without Marx or Jesus* in particular, and generally about anti-Americanism, its causes and the purposes it serves. The following is from the French edition of *Playboy*, May 1975:

Q: Is there any connection between the anti-Americanism of the Left, that of the Communists, and of the Right, that of General de Gaulle?

A: The two have the same root—failure. The European Right failed in the sense that it did not succeed in preserving for the European nations the world role they played until 1939. The European Left failed on an even larger scale: at the time of the Great Depression between the wars, Europe reacted by going to the Right, while the United States went to the Left. In Europe, we had fascism and Nazism, Pétain in France, Franco in Spain. In the United States, there was Roosevelt's New Deal. That's something Europeans won't admit. Subconsciously they are well aware of it and they cannot be proud of it. All the more since the Europeans are responsible for the two world wars, European civil wars which degenerated into world conflicts. Those two world conflicts bled Europe white, completely dislocated its poli-

7 "Portrait of the Marxist as an Old Trooper," interview of Herbert Marcuse by Michael Horowitz, *Playboy*, September 1970.

tics and reduced its territory. The Europe of before 1914 stretched from the Atlantic to the Urals: it was possible to communicate with tsarist Russia, there were trade and cultural exchanges. By 1920 Europe only extended from the Atlantic to the Carpathians, and after 1945 it only reached to the Tyrol. Western Europe today is a rump continent. Among the consequences of those two wars are a number of political monsters. It was Europe, after all, that invented Stalinism, anti-Semitism, organized mass extermination. Stalinism, Nazism, fascism, Francoism, Pétainism—it adds up to a lot! The main aberrations of the twentieth century were born in Europe. Thus the Europeans lost in terms of both power and morality. So they attribute to some sort of American malevolence the power of the United States that is the direct consequence of their own mistakes: American power grew out of the collapse of Europe, which in turn was brought on by Europe itself. The cause is mistaken for the result: American superpower and Soviet superpower as well are direct consequences of the internal failures of European political civilization in the twentieth century.

Q: In your view what is the meaning of the expression "American imperialism," used by the Communists, and "American hegemony," used by the Gaullist Right?

A: We are in a new world. The United States has really become a world power, like Britain in the nineteenth century, like France until 1939, though the latter's role was not as easy as Britain's because its economy was less strong. Throughout history some power has played a predominant role: the Roman Empire, the Spanish and Japanese monarchies, Germany at the time of Wilhelm II . . . It is a historical constant. What is not a constant is that, here again, it is seen as a specifically American phenomenon, as if one could become the world's most powerful state in sheer self-defense. (In 1939 the Americans wanted neither army nor foreign policy.) The superpowers of the presidency—pretty much of a cream puff at the moment—date from Roosevelt; in 1939 progressives opposed the powers of Congress. This nation which by 1945–46 had become the world's greatest economic and military power, again somewhat in spite of itself, was led by the cold war, which was then beginning, to take on world responsibilities, for better or for worse.

Q: What do you have in mind by "better" or "worse"?

A: "Better"? I mean, for example, the Marshall Plan. "Worse"? I mean all sorts of semi-colonial activities in Latin America, usually linked to the classical kind of economic imperialism. It was the British and the French who invented the "hidden empire," as an addition to traditional colonialism. There was the British presence in Greece, and the French in Romania between the wars. I do not approve of that system, but what interests me is why people think it was invented by the United States. Actually the Americans have tended in some cases to restrain that system, for a greater opposition to imperialism in foreign policy has grown up in American public opinion than there was toward our own imperialism in British or French public opinion. America's behavior is that of a great power. What we call American imperialism is sometimes intervention to protect or develop economic positions or a global security system, and sometimes a sort of automatic result of power. Behavior that is considered a kind of imperialist American plot would in our own case be considered the legitimate defense of our interests. Once you have the nation-state, you have the imperialism that of necessity derives from it, regardless of political systems. And the strongest nation-states are the most imperialist, according to a natural political law to which I see no historical exception. If you want to destroy imperialism, you must destroy its source—the nation-state. I find it comical when Gaullists rage against American imperialism while at the same time they exalt the nation-state and nationalism to the point of frenzy. If you put Calvados in the baby's bottle, you shouldn't complain about alcoholism.

Q: But shouldn't a responsible, mature political civilization restrain its own imperialism?

A: Yes, it should; but it rarely does. Note that the United States did so, at a time that is little considered except in cold-war terms: the period from 1945 to 1951, when only the Americans had atomic weapons. No power in all of history had ever held such an absolute monopoly of force, theoretically enabling it to subdue the entire world. Did the Americans abuse that power? I don't think we can say they did . . . Many of the problems now being discussed in France were settled seven or eight years ago in the United States. For example, a Gallup poll in June 1974 showed that what in 1967 were called the values of the "counterculture" had become the values of the average bourgeois.

Q: The leftists call that co-optation.

A: In any co-optation, the co-opter is changed just as much as those who are co-opted. If giving the land to the French peasants in 1789 was co-optation, then I'm all for co-optation.

Q: Your *Without Marx or Jesus* was published in France in 1970. You announced to the Europeans, who were somewhat startled, and to the French, who were flabbergasted, that the next world revolution—the first having been the Anglo-French-American one of the seventeenth century—could only begin in the United States. Do you still hold to that opinion?

A: More than ever. Besides, what I said was not that the world revolution would take place in the United States. I went further: I said it had already begun. In fact, the exportation of all the ideas linked to what we call change in contemporary societies has already begun; their application may be more or less successful . . . All the ideas that consist of calling into question the relationships between men and women, between adults and children, between political power and the people, between economic power and the consumers and the workers; the responsibilities of industry for the environment, for housing, for continuing education, the world responsibilities of the great powers, their responsibilities toward the third world—all these ideas were born in the United States during the 1960s. The first "Minister of the Third World" was McGovern, in the Kennedy administration. (I'm not saying he did anything spectacularly effective, but the idea was there.) I never said that this revolution would take place automatically. Besides, I wrote that revolutions that fail are far more numerous, in human history, then revolutions that succeed. I am no longer Marxist in that I no longer believe that revolution is automatic.

Q: You don't believe in historical determinism?

A: I don't believe in *historical certainty;* there is no process that can only lead to a single outcome. On the other hand, in every period there is what I call a "laboratory society" where most of the new concepts, the new or renovating forces, either are born or acquire their international dynamism. Thus, it is obvious that certain ideas concerning the organization of work in the factory originated in Sweden, not in the United States. But Sweden is not such an attention-getting monster that events there are immediately contagious elsewhere, except to visitors who go to study them; while American society contaminates those who do not even study it, even those who are against it. For example, youth in Eastern Europe is crazy about rock and jeans, if not about the Supreme Court, which is beyond their interests. Another example: the European industrial nations are discovering racial tension because of their foreign workers. Their superiority complex about how America has handled its black and Puerto Rican problems should be healed by that, and they should study the efforts the Americans made to solve the problem: school integration, quotas in the universities and the political parties, the media, management, etc. There again America has been a laboratory for the best and the worst, like Athens in the fifth century B.C. and Paris in the nineteenth century A.D. Revolution can be broken down into two words: crisis and innovation. America invented the idea of the future. Until then, every society chose its models from the past: the French in the eighteenth century wanted to imitate the English in the seventeenth; the French revolutionaries wanted to imitate the Roman Republic; the national liberation movements of the nineteenth century wanted to imitate the French Revolution; the Russian Revolution wanted to imitate the Paris Commune and the French Left. The models were always in the past. The United States is the first society whose model has become the year 2000, by asking: toward what goal are we heading? That is revolutionary behavior.

Q: Has anti-Americanism diminished in France, qualitatively as well as quantitatively?

A: No. On the contrary, it is stronger.

Of Docility: An Essay in Explanation

Q: Even in politics? President Giscard d'Estaing is less quarrelsome with the "Anglo-Saxons," especially the Americans, than President Pompidou and certainly General de Gaulle.

A: That's certainly true of French government policy. Giscard is not insane on that subject, and de Gaulle of course was obsessive about the Americans. But if we are talking about French society, I find anti-Americanism all the time even in the smallest details.

Q: In all circles? Among the academics as well as among the workers?

A: Especially in university circles! Read the papers, watch the television, listen to the radio: if you blot out the anti-Americanism, you've erased 80 per cent of French political thought, left or right. Anti-Americanism is a symptom of disguised self-accusation: Europeans project onto the United States the accusations they make against themselves, including the war in Vietnam, which would never have happened if the French had not set foot there first. Since it is self-accusation projected abroad, anti-Americanism is of necessity ambiguous: a combination of hostility and infatuated imitation of the United States, both in great excess.

Q: Did you have any examples from the 1975 crop?

A: Of course! For example I read in *Le Nouvel Observateur* for January 20, 1975: *"The Americans, being incapable of reorganizing their economy, are forced to make their partners pay for their recovery."* Such is the theoretician Jacques Attali's diagnosis of the world recession.

That is the summary in the table of contents of an interview with that young economist, who is both a lecturer at the École Polytechnique and inspirational adviser to the Socialist party. Note the usual ambiguity: The Americans are incompetent asses who can't even set their own house in order, repeat offenders in the bankruptcy courts; but at the same time they are such devilishly sly swindlers that they always manage to make the rest of the world pay for their prosperity or, as the case may be, their recovery. I would not dare bring up the fact that at times the

Americans have paid a little toward the recovery of others[8]; for, coming from them, that pseudo-generosity cannot be other than a particularly sordid form of imperialism.

But I am somewhat disturbed by the low esteem in which the Socialist theoretician holds the human race: for to show on the one hand that Americans are idiots and on the other that they are crafty enough to deceive the whole world does not speak very well for the mental ability of other peoples.

Shortly thereafter Jacques Attali enriched his analysis during a radio broadcast[9]: America has every intention of becoming, or rather of continuing to be, "Europe's economic enemy." After sorrowfully acknowledging that the Americans were "discovering" (in 1975!) the problems of pollution and the cities, this most brilliant of French economists under forty years of age then revealed that it was "not excluded" that the United States would become "fascist one day or another." Coming right after Watergate, that best and rarest example of how an entire people can block a fascist plot, that prophecy was at least provocative and certainly symptomatic of profound sociological insight. But let us be kind: the usually keen mind of the Socialist theoretician was at that moment possessed by a recurring fantasy, in which Europeans see fascism in one of the few countries (among those with democratic traditions) where it has never triumphed. Note that I said "triumphed." I do not mean that there are not and never have been fascists in the United States, but that the nation and its government have never become fascist. Between the two wars and during World War II the state became fascist in Italy, Ger-

---

[8] According to a 1973 report of the House Appropriations Committee, the United States since 1946 had spent $164 billion in foreign aid, to rebuild Europe and Japan and to help the third world. Part of that aid, of course, was military, notably the $12 billion allotted to South Vietnam starting in 1966. But it is far from being the largest part: for example, the 1974 budget included $2.8 billion in foreign aid, of which $490 million was for weapons. The committee calculated that, by adding interest on the money since 1946, one arrives at a total cost of $270 billion. Contrary to common belief, these credits do not always go to one side. Thus, in 1974 Israel received $324.5 million in aid, Egypt $250 million, and $100 million was divided between Syria and the Palestinian refugees.
[9] "France-Inter," Sunday, April 20, 1975, at 1 P.M.

many, Romania, Poland, Hungary, Spain, Portugal, France, Japan and Greece[10]; but *never,* before or after this golden age of fascism, has there been a totalitarian government in the United States. Yet it is there and there alone that we Europeans perceive the danger of fascism. Such vigilance is praiseworthy! No need to have read Freud (the fables of La Fontaine would suffice) to see that this is a case of massive guilt transference. The same is true of the war in Vietnam. There we held a better hand, since the American war in Vietnam was a real atrocity, in contrast to the imaginary American fascist government which our augurs have been seeing in the entrails of the last thirty years. Alas, what we forget is that the American war in Vietnam was *an extension of European imperialism.*

Thanks to that opportune oversight, the war has served as a scapegoat for all the sins of the West, a lightning rod for our guilt. White Europeans have laid all the sins committed against the rest of the world for five centuries on the shoulders of the United States. We Europeans have assigned America a power of attorney for all the harm done humanity by the West, just as, for that matter, the victims of white expansion all over the globe have developed the habit of heaping on America alone the curses and hatred earned by their invaders. Since 1973, anti-Americanism has found a new war horse—the multi-national corporations, identified of course with American capitalism. But they forget just two things. First, the multi-nationals of American origin are under greater fire in the United States than anywhere else. Second, I can name ten multi-nationals, among the most powerful on earth, that are not American: Ciba—Swiss; Nestlé—Swiss; Philips—Dutch; Unilever—Anglo-Dutch; Michelin—French; Fiat—Italian; Erikson—Swedish; Mitsubishi—Japanese; Bayer—German; and Saint-Gobain—French. And that's without counting the most secretive, invulnerable, omnipresent and powerful multi-national of them all—the Swiss bank. Every major firm has always had foreign branches, but the novel aspect of the multi-national

[10] I am referring to the pre-1939 Metaxas dictatorship which, to my surprise, has not yet been attributed retroactively to the CIA, created in 1947.

is that it shifts its centers of production according to the location of raw materials, the availability and price of labor, and its differing ability in different states to raise capital and negotiate low taxes. Thus there is no longer a center; the center is everywhere.

It's old-fashioned to go on hammering away at the multi-nationals. I have an idea in the back of my head that the multi-nationals are in many respects a progressive factor, just as the nation-state was in its opposition to feudalism in the beginning of the sixteenth century. Anyone with a bit of revolutionary spirit should be interested in the multi-nationals instead of warding off the evil eye by sprinkling himself with holy water blessed by Marx. The multi-national is reshuffling the economic deck, in ways that are perhaps not entirely negative.

Q: In your opinion, are negative facts about the United States overemphasized, while the good is passed over in silence?

A: Yes. The news that the Supreme Court had banned the death penalty got little attention in the French press. Had the court decided for the death penalty, it would have appeared on the front page.

Q: How do you explain that, given that information is more widely disseminated?

A: It's more available if you read English. But if you only read the French press and listen to our television and radio, I don't see how you can be informed about America. I remember seeing a French program about television news in the United States, which was described with a note of contemptuous self-satisfaction, notably by a former French television correspondent, whom I had never seen do any more than show us his face against a background of the White House or the Capitol while he rattled off a few trivialities lifted from two-day-old newspapers. No one seems to understand in discussing American television that it is not nationalized. The emphasis is always on too much advertising, on poor taste in entertainment programs, on soap operas. On the other hand, no one observes about Watergate that the Ervin Committee hearings were broadcast live for six hours a day, and that this was also the case with the House Judiciary Committee hearings on Nixon's impeachment. I can imagine no

greater lesson in democracy, in political participation . . .
Among recent American measures that might serve as useful examples to France or Italy I would list controls on campaign
funding; Watergate, which was not simply a matter of eavesdropping but rather was a historic body blow, delivered by legal
means, to the omnipotence of the state and the abuse of reasons
of state. It was more like our Dreyfus case, except that it is more
serious for a people to indict a chief of state than to acquit an ar-
tillery captain.

Q: Is it your impression that anti-Americanism has reached its
peak?

A: I don't believe that anti-Americanism among the people is
about to diminish. It is going to increase all over the world. We
are going to see more occasions—in Cyprus, Brazil, Bali or
wherever—on which the Americans are going to be blamed for
whatever goes wrong in the country. They will be blamed if they
are not involved, and if they are, their involvement will be exag-
gerated.

Q: For example?

A: The Communists tried to seize power in Portugal. If there
had been any sort of counterattack, it would have been attributed to the CIA rather than to other Portuguese citizens. In
economic affairs, inflation is blamed on America; the energy crisis is blamed on America. In the French press in 1974 you could
read this truly demented reasoning: Kissinger deliberately provoked the Yom Kippur War of 1973 in order to set off the energy
crisis and bring Europe and Japan to their knees! More and more
I see people blaming everything that happens on the evils of the
American "presence." Again, such behavior is always ambiguous.

Q: Why is it ambiguous?

A: We are fated to collaborate with the United States. That is
one of the main reasons for anti-Americanism. The world is still
divided into two major blocs. On each side people complain
about the dominant power. But even if people in the Communist
bloc attribute their misfortunes to Soviet influence—which is in
fact the case—they cannot do so openly because they do not

have freedom of speech. So the only noise we hear in the world is that of anti-Americanism.

Q: You mean that if, say, the East German press were free it would be as opposed to Soviet as to American imperialism?

A: More so, no doubt. Do you think that the inevitably moderate anti-Americanism of a West German can even come close to the hatred a Czech feels for the Soviet Union? In the nations of the third world, the problems of population and hunger can be attributed in part to the selfish policies of the rich nations, and in part to barriers within those third-world countries: political barriers, the weight of religious and family tradition, superstition, resistance to change, corruption. In Bangladesh the government admitted that all the relief food they had gotten for a year had been sold in India by the officials who were supposed to distribute it to the people! In the market in Calcutta I saw cans of cooking oil labeled: "Not for Sale. Gift of the American People." They were selling for 200 rupees a gallon.

The Americans will be blamed when they are responsible; they will be blamed when the Europeans are responsible; they will be blamed when the third world is responsible. That clears the conscience of Europe and the third world, so it seems to me that anti-Americanism can only increase. If—and that seems at the moment to be the trend in American opinion—the Americans decided to suspend their aid to some third-world nations, even if there are "strings," that is, political and military conditions, on that aid, then again the Americans will be accused. Look at those big international conferences which tried to resolve problems of vital importance to the whole world: the conference on the environment, in Stockholm in the fall of 1972; the rights of the sea, in Caracas in the summer of 1974; population, in Bucharest in the fall of 1974; food, in Rome at the end of 1974. Without a doubt those four conferences were supposed to deal with problems that concern all mankind. But all four turned into anti-American diatribes, including among their targets the presentations of American experts who had nothing to do with the American government—their studies were rejected simply because they were American. If they suggested limiting population growth in some part of the world, the reaction was: "On the contrary! We need more children! Your position is imperialist!"

So I foresee a continuing growth of anti-Americanism among popular attitudes, which makes more difficult the solution of the world's great problems, those that can be undertaken only on a global scale—ecology, the oceans, population, food, the international monetary problem—and require agreement between the major industrial powers, thus first of all the United States and the developing nations. Such negotiations can only be embittered by systematic anti-Americanism. But on the other hand, governments do have to practice a minimum degree of realism. Take for example the OPEC nations, which have already come to realize that they cannot make unrestrained use of oil as a weapon of political vengeance—right or wrong, that's not the issue—because it might boomerang, and that the imperialist nations were not the only ones whose economies were in danger of being strangled by the high price of oil. In that case, some realism was shown. I believe that many of the problems humanity now faces cannot be resolved unless the United States plays an important role, for good *or* ill, which was also the case of the Roman Empire. In any event, the United States will be found morally at fault: if they continue to play a leading role in the world, it will be held against them; and if they abandon that role, that will be held against them too.

Democracy will lose ground as long as the system of nation-states endures. And if democracy loses ground, socialism cannot come into being.

Already a small minority in this world, the democratic nations will be progressively devoured by Stalinism and all its totalitarian and authoritarian variants, that is by a system that is of necessity stronger than democracy. Stalinism aims not at human well-being but at domination of its people at home and of other states abroad, and it devotes all its energy to those goals, whereas democracy usually gives well-being priority over political security. The totalitarian world would be undermined by democratization, but its rulers are completely aware of that threat. It is a vicious circle: nationalism arms dictators and bureaucrats with the perfect weapon to resist democratization; they reject any questioning of their regime by the international community in the name of the principle of non-interference in internal affairs. Dictatorial at home and revolutionary abroad, national totalitarianism sounds all notes simultaneously.

Nationalism has a pre-eminent part in this process because, as I observed earlier, in the democratic nations it makes resentment of a stronger nation seem more important than guaranteeing the survival of free societies as a whole. And among people living in the world of poverty, nationalism incinerates the political and cultural roots of democracy by emphasizing xenophobia over development. The third world feels the need to believe that the only reason for its backwardness is capitalist imperialism, primarily American—and it is vigorously encouraged in that obsession by, of course, the Communist states, but also and more seriously, by democratic nations other than the United States that calculate that they can exploit anti-Americanism to win markets and guarantee their oil supplies.

But as long as the world remains divided into nation-states, it will always be the turn of one of those nations to be economically and militarily predominant. The nationalist illusion consists of believing that, in order to rid the world of imperialism, we must rid ourselves of *that nation* rather than ridding ourselves of the system of nation-states.

Unless we break the mold, we will always be confronted with "that nation"—yesterday Britain, tomorrow perhaps Brazil, Canada, Iran, Japan or Australia. When they pander to the most myopic chauvinism wherever it is found, the world's pseudo-socialists help create the conditions for a general anti-democratic reaction, for, under the guise of "independence" in foreign policy, they promote the idea that any state with any sort of rulers should be considered sacred. As long as they are against "imperialism," tyrants and oligarchs are granted absolution by progressives. Their reasoning is that of a simpleton, for, in historical time American power is a transitory event, while the systematic abandonment of democracy which nationalism and anti-Americanism serve to justify will be an enduring reality.

There are two reasons why the world made up almost entirely of anti-democratic and chauvinist states toward which we are heading is incompatible with the birth of true socialism.

The first is that it will continue to be an imperialist jungle in which the goal of power will always take precedence over that of well-being, the spirit of domination over that of stewardship, individual ambition over the vision of the whole. When I say imperialism, I mean *all* its manifestations: that of the capitalist nations toward the third world; of the third world toward the fourth world; of the Communist states toward those two worlds and toward the capitalist nations; of the Communist states toward each other, the capitalist states toward each other, and the underdeveloped nations toward each other and toward the first two worlds when they have the means to exert power over them, oil being the primary such means at the moment.

The second reason is that nationalism impels socialism in a single direction toward a bottleneck in the way of any true economic democracy—I mean the obsession with nationalizing the economy. Up till now socialists in practice have been unable to think of anything better than to make the means of production the property of the holy state as the incarnation of the society and guardian of the "general interest." Although experience has amply demonstrated that a state monopoly over the economy is harmful to both industrial and agricultural production,[11] the ravages of fascination with totalitarianism, hatred for private enterprise and regression toward pre-logical nationalist thinking have all conspired to guarantee that our torpid socialists do not seriously search for any means other than that primitive alchemist's potion, that master key that opens the door to totalitarian poverty. Besides the economic disaster assured by any Stalinist

[11] And to the workers' standard of living. It is shocking to learn, for example, that the wages of miners in Bolivia's nationalized tin mines are lower, in terms of purchasing power, now than they were fifty years ago under the "barbaric" capitalist Simón Patiño. (Figures in Norman Gall: *Field Reports, West Coast, South American Series*, Vol. 21, Nos. 1 and 2, 1975.)

management, how can the nationalizers speak of democratic socialism? Anyone who is even vaguely familiar with Marx—and *some* of them must be—must know that in his view there is a necessary relationship between the economic infrastructure and its political superstructure. If that is so, how can the economy be totally managed from the top down unless political power is a carbon copy of that economic power, in other words how can there be a state-owned economy without political dictatorship?

Thus, aided by the enduring system of nation-states, it would seem that the Communist counterrevolution can succeed quite rapidly in simultaneously eliminating capitalism, democracy and socialism.

The appearance of communism on the scene blocked the evolution of free capitalist nations toward democratic socialism after 1920. Communism's historical role has been counterrevolutionary. It is no accident that it triumphed in Russia and China, those two empires with histories of xenophobia and totalitarianism, in which the state had always imposed the cult of personality of the monarch, bureaucratic despotism and a dictated culture. If Europe, especially, wants to resume its progress toward the Left, it must first rid itself of the notion that communism belongs to the Left.

TOWARD A NEW SOCIALISM?

I had thought of giving this book a frankly uninviting and inten-
tionally didactic title: "Of the Inevitable Advance of Stalinism in
the World and the Sure Failure of the Efforts That Will Be
Made to Oppose It." The consternation that always appeared on
the faces of those on whom I tried out that title convinced me to
abandon it.

Yet it pretty well summarizes the evolution of power relationships in the world. Stalinism's inevitability is due to its being the
first regime in history to be reactionary at home and revolutionary
abroad, oppressive in its domination and liberating in its propaganda. Those who experience it would certainly like to escape it,
but they cannot. Those who wish for it have never experienced
it; all they see of communism is its critiques, some of them well
founded, of the capitalist system and of free democracy. That is
what enables a totalitarian machine having nothing in common
with any possible form of socialism to advance in its name and
by usurping its appeal.

Socialism can only take root in capitalism and develop by
outgrowing—not destroying—capitalist civilization, while preserving its two cornerstones: the capacity to produce, and political, individual and cultural freedoms. Up to now every revolution
made or attempted under the socialist label has failed to preserve those two cornerstones, and that is the reason, the only
sure reason, their authors have been ousted or have had to resort
to police-state methods to stay in office. The only regimes that
are related to the socialist ideal as it has been formulated since
the beginning of the nineteenth century and that can be consid-

ered to have taken the first tangible steps toward implementing that ideal are the social democratic states, and they grew only out of the most developed form of free capitalism. That does not solve the problem of the third world,[1] but, for the industrial nations, it is the only way without inviting disaster to transcend the capitalist system of production, which at the cost of constant correction will remain ours for a long time to come, barring outbreaks of Stalinism.

It will be said that this thesis is not very original and that after all I have gotten bogged down in the muddy waters of reformism. I have two replies to that objection.

First, politics is the domain not of the *theoretical* imagination but of practical creativity, *which means* the accurate perception of reality. Other fields are available for the exercise of theoretical imagination: literary criticism, theology, chess, mathematics, basic research in the natural and behavioral sciences. Political thought consists of learning not to see what does not exist and to see what does exist, in order, when the occasion arises, to act accordingly. In Antonio Gramsci's elegant phrase, it requires "pessimism of the intelligence and optimism of the will."

Secondly—and this point is even more important than the first —it is impossible to conceive of any road to democratic socialism except via reformism. If we think for a moment about how the issue of respecting the rights of the individual arises when one wants to change society, it will seem astonishing that people have been able to discuss and debate for so long without putting an end to that old cliché about "reform" being the "opposite of revolution." All socialists and most Communists—in nations where they do not rule the state—agree in saying that socialism must have its birth in and with *pluralism*. The concept of pluralism appears constantly in debates on "the democratic path to socialism" and was at the heart of the polemic between Socialists and Stalinists in Portugal.

But the safeguard of pluralism excludes anything but re-

[1] On this subject I will postpone discussion to a future book, which will deal with the "war of the worlds" and the exacerbation of imperialisms in relation to the failures of development.

formism. Those who condemn the latter in effect give up the former. The total transformation of a society implies the elimination of recalcitrant minorities, or even the imposition of dictatorship on the majority when that majority opposes change (which was the case, as we saw, in Chile). Any sudden and complete substitution of one social system for another requires, if it is to be accomplished democratically, a new social contract, and that requires unanimity. As Rousseau wrote, only the social contract itself must be unanimously adopted, because it is the pact by which each individual commits himself *for the future* to submit to laws voted by the majority, even if he himself did not vote for them. But it is obvious that no individual will enter into such a contract against his will. The same is true of creating a supranational European government: the rule of the majority will have to be adopted unanimously. In practice, most nations adopt a new constitution by a two-thirds majority. But, also in practice, history has abundantly shown that the revolutionary method rules out pluralism. If, on the other hand, you choose pluralism, you must choose reformism, there is just no other way.

Does that mean the Communists have become reformists? Are we witnessing the development, centering on the Italian party, of what Arrigo Levi of *La Stampa* calls "neo-communism?"[2]

In international relations, the inspiration of that neo-communism would seem to be the spirit of Helsinki. In the relations of national Communist parties to the Soviet party the new rules would leave each party free to analyze its situation and determine its policy in any given situation. How real is this neo-communism at this time, and what is its future?

We can observe differences among the Eastern European satellites as well as among the various Western parties, and, in the West, these differences sometimes reach the level of polemics. The over-all picture is not uniform. The Polish formula is total diplomatic submission to the Soviet Union in exchange for a small amount of domestic liberalization. The Romanian formula, on the contrary, involves less diplomatic dependency, accompa-

[2] See his "A Communiqué from World War III," *Newsweek*, July 14, 1975.

nied by uncompromising domestic discipline, so that the Soviet Union should never think it its duty to send troops to Bucharest to save socialism. In the West, the year 1975 was marked by an increasing contrast between the Stalinist-impregnated rigidity of the French and Portuguese parties and the more broad-minded views of the Italian party, adopted also by the Spanish party as it emerged from its underground existence during the Franco years. What lessons can we draw from these developments and dissonances?

The most important interested party, the Soviet, showed no sign of believing that the international Communist movement should no longer be directed by Moscow, nor that there was any reason to modify, in the light of local circumstances, the Leninist doctrine of the dictatorship of the proletariat, which translates into the seizure of power by the party apparatus, no matter how small a minority the Communists may be in that country. Since the summer of 1974 there has been a fresh wave of Soviet articles and statements attacking polycentrism, the idea that the international Communist movement can have several truly autonomous decision-making centers; and attacking pluralism, that is, the Western style of democracy, and reformism and social democracy as well. Even before Constantin Zarodov's article (in *Pravda,* August 6, 1975) condemning the tainted alliances of the French and Italian parties and their "erroneous conception" of democracy, that same general line had appeared elsewhere, as in Boris Ponomarev's article in *Problems of Peace and Socialism*[3] and, in May, an editorial in the magazine *Politiceskoe Samoobrazovanie* (addressed primarily to Soviet party functionaries) denouncing the "overestimation of the importance of national characteristics" and "the imperialist ideologues who invented the concept of supposed pluralism, whose goal is to divide the Communist parties and the socialist states." Thus, if the Western parties claim freedom of action, it is not because Moscow willingly

[3] An international journal, published in several languages, aimed primarily at the non-Russian parties. Its editor is the previously mentioned Constantin Zarodov; Ponomarev is the Soviet leader in charge of relations with other parties. The French, Italian and Spanish editions did *not* include his article. The English language edition is also titled *World Marxist Review.*

granted them that freedom. Quite the contrary. The result can only be sniping and even conflict.

That in fact is what happened after the *Pravda* article of August 6. It was no longer cause for surprise that the organ of the Italian party, *L'Unità,* very calmly refuted *Pravda,* citing its own "rejection of the principle of dictatorship." However, the sharp reaction of the secretary-general of the French party was applauded as a considerably greater novelty. But it seemed that Marchais had taken offense more at form than at content, just as he had when the Soviets had rudely cut short François Mitterrand's visit to Moscow. The French party could not allow its Socialist ally to be treated so cavalierly without losing face, nor could it remain silent when accused of an "opportunist" policy of "unity at any price," causing it to become "an ideologically amorphous organization," in the almost insulting words of Constantin Zarodov in *Pravda.*

But on the fundamentals—and this is why Zarodov's insults were unjustified—the French party remains faithfully orthodox, even if its critical views extend to saying that Lenin could not have foreseen all the subsequent history of humanity. (Zarodov's article began by stressing the urgent and imperative necessity of celebrating the seventieth anniversary of the publication of a small pamphlet by Lenin entitled *Two Tactics of Social Democracy and the Democratic Revolution.*) In Marchais's June 29, 1972, report, published by Étienne Fajon in his book *L'Union est un combat,* we can find lines worthy of Zarodov: "It would be dangerous to have the slightest illusions about the sincerity or the firmness of the Socialist party . . . The Socialist party's ideology today is and remains absolutely reformist . . . It is totally foreign to scientific socialism." And that was in the euphoria of unity on the Left, before relations between the two parties cooled at the end of 1974.

In Portugal the French party energetically supported Cunhal's classic line, in strict application of the principle that everywhere practical priority should be given not to democracy but to seizure of power by the party, which must get rid, especially, of socialists and centrists. When Cunhal's bid for power failed, the

Portuguese Communists, supported by the French, made an appeal for holy unity on the Left against "pogroms," "burning at the stake" and "witch-hunts" which they blamed on a fascism whose revival they themselves had provoked. What can you expect to have left if you try to annihilate all the democrats who are not Communists?

But the Russian theoreticians of international communism adopted the opposite point of view: the "revolution" failed in Chile and Portugal *because* the Communists there were too tolerant. It is necessary, Ponomarev wrote, "to neutralize the political line promoted by the ultras of anti-communism within social democracy . . .

"It is necessary to know how to defend the conquests of the revolution, to be ready rapidly to modify the form that the struggle takes, both peaceful and not peaceful, to respond with revolutionary violence to the counterrevolutionary violence of the bourgeoisie . . .

"The big information media play, in the social and political struggle of our times, a role for which there is no analogy in the history of past revolutions. The experience of Chile convinces us that, in order to triumph, it is necessary to put an end to the class enemy's domination of the principal means of information and propaganda . . .

"Even when the revolution comes about peacefully, it is indispensable to put an end to the hold that representatives of the old regime have on so essential an instrument of power as the army, and to create a new state apparatus."

Zarodov's article proclaims the same points of view. Evidently we cannot consider these to be the opinions of a group of hardliners hostile to Brezhnev and détente, since Brezhnev himself received Zarodov and elaborately congratulated him on his noted *Pravda* article, in order to make a public display of his support for the article's contents.

Neo-communism in the Italian party seems more tangible than in the French party, since, unlike the latter case, it does not consist merely of making promises about non-existent situations and of continuing to behave in a Stalinist manner in all existing situations where it is possible to take immediate concrete action. The Italian party does not limit itself to stating that its policy is set in Rome, not Moscow; it sets policies that are different from those of Moscow.

In foreign policy, the Italian party opposed the Soviets on Portugal, supports Italian membership in the Atlantic alliance and NATO and supports the ideal of supra-nationality in Western Europe—against which *L'Humanité* and *Pravda* inveigh on all occasions. In domestic affairs, the Italians express respect for pluralism in politics, in the unions and in intellectual life. But they go further: they advocate co-operation with management in an economy in which capitalism would continue to play a role. The industrialist Umberto Agnelli declares that "Fiat is ready to collaborate with the Communist party for the good of Turin," and in return Giorgio Amendola, one of the "historic leaders" of the Italian party, hastens to reply that he wants to "emphasize once more the importance of private enterprise."

Of course, the Italian party is favorable to democracy because it has benefited from it, and it respects elections because it wins them. But in its opinions it has moved so far from Marxist-Leninist dogma that it will have either to retreat or else to break completely with the Communist International. Its platform today is, both in its content and its guiding principles, a purely social democratic platform: a prudent Atlanticism, political democracy, compromise with capitalism. After the disaster of Portuguese communism, due to obtuseness and sectarianism, the future of Europe depends in large measure on the authenticity or lack of it of Italian neo-communism.

Still, we should not exaggerate the novelty of dissension among the various Communist parties. As long ago as 1956, when Khrushchev denounced Stalin's crimes at the Soviet 20th Party Congress, the French party reacted with great hostility to this unaccustomed frankness. For years the French party stubbornly resisted the de-Stalinizing slogans issued by Moscow. Maurice Thorez, its secretary-general, plotted with what was known as the "Molotov faction" to thwart Khrushchev's "liberalization"—which itself was quite relative, since it did not prevent the sending of Soviet tanks to Hungary in late 1956 to suppress the popular uprising in Budapest (with the advice and consent of Mao Tse-tung, then on friendly terms with the Kremlin rulers). Their rejection of the "thaw" put the French Communists at odds not only with Khrushchev but also with the Italians, who supported the new line without reservations. In this period Thorez and Togliatti came close to a complete break. Thus it is false to say that the French party is always unconditionally faithful to Moscow: after 1956, it was faithful to Stalin, but not to Moscow.

Nonetheless, these differences within its ranks do not mean that the Communist International has ceased to be a reality. People disagree within the camp, but it remains a camp. Since the capitalist nations began experiencing social and economic difficulties in 1973, Moscow apparently expects the Communist parties in those countries to devote their energies to destabilizing the West rather than entering into coalition governments. Those parties, on the contrary, seem eager to achieve power by means of alliances with the non-Communist Left, or even—in the case of the Italian party's offer of a "historical compromise"—with the center and the Right. Doubtless that solution would be inopportune in the eyes of the Kremlin, at a time when it wants to make use of the grave economic, social and political ills of Italy and Britain (where the official Communist party is negligible, but a "destabilizing" Marxist minority is very active) and exploit the fragile internal situations of Portugal, Spain, Greece and Turkey, to make of non-Communist Europe a continent in chaos, unable to unite or even to preserve the minimum degree of cohesion necessary to organize its defense under the American nuclear umbrella. A weak and divided Western Europe, not annexed but docile, more and more separated from the United States, has always been one of the goals of Soviet foreign policy. The Soviet Union fears the success of social democracy, in substance if not in rhetoric, for it takes place in orderly fashion, with the agreement of the local Communists, and furthermore threatens to advance the construction of European unity. It is in this sense that the anti-reformist prejudice of the pseudo-revolutionary ideologues of unofficial Stalinism effectively serves totalitarian objectives. Détente to Brezhnev consists of obtaining economic advantages from the capitalist world while continuing to destabilize it and without making any major concession in the realm of human freedoms.

We can only be glad to hear the Western Communists' recent professions of faith in those freedoms. In the case of the Italians, their sincerity will only be tested if and when they come to power in the national government. Until such time, they have every interest in projecting a liberal image, for it wins them votes. We must never forget this peculiar trait of Communist parties: they are the only ones who insist on being judged on their words alone, while all other political parties are judged on their deeds. In the realm of words, the Italian Communists have indeed made great progress in their advocacy of political and cultural freedom. But in the actual practice of government, we remain completely ignorant of their future behavior.

The methods of the French Communists are little changed: they verbally defend freedom, but they do it in totalitarian fashion. Their proclamations of fidelity to pluralism are always larded with virulent invective against those whom they suspect of not wanting it. Like the "moderate" South American party which chose as its slogan "Death to the extremists!", the French Communists in the name of tolerance sling mud at all those who do not share their self-appraisal that they respect all opinions. For example, an article in *L'Humanité*, after a remarkably unequivocal condemnation of the internment in a psychiatric prison of the Soviet mathematician Leonid Pliouchtch, is suddenly transformed into a harangue against those who exploit the Russian action as being "motivated only by anti-Soviet resentment" and against socialists who join with the "extreme Right" and "follow in the emigrés' footsteps." Thus, the "total disapproval" of Pliouchtch's possible murder by chemistry became a kind of ultimatum demanding silence on the part of anyone who might claim to draw some sort of lesson from that event.[4]

[4] René Andrieu, "De grâce, pas de leçon!", *L'Humanité*, October 25, 1975.

Nonetheless, Western Communists are well aware of the weakness in Zarodov's line when he writes in *Pravda* that "no revolution is possible except under the hegemony of the proletariat." In the first place, the industrial "proletariat" is going to make up less and less of the working population in developed societies; secondly, only a minority of the workers are Communist. While half the Communist vote is cast by industrial workers, two out of three of those workers do not vote Communist. The Communist share of the workers' vote has steadily diminished. As Jean Charlot observed in an article titled "Who Votes Communist?" (*Point*, February 5, 1973): "The records of the French Institute of Public Opinion on this point are clear: in June 1946, 43 per cent of French workers voted Communist, 31 per cent in March 1967, 33 per cent in June 1968, 34 per cent in December 1972."[5]

We can also to a certain degree go along with Milovan Djilas when he says that "Communism is a spent force." Djilas continues: "Look at the Communist-run countries—they are backward, both economically and culturally. When has communism inspired the last major work of art? Stagnation has been the key characteristic of Eastern Europe for years. What the past has proved is that communism is not a new sort of religion but merely a different kind of dictatorship."[6]

This book was written with the aim of bringing out that truth, but also and alas the little effect it has on people's attitudes and on world policies. The desire for dictatorial power is usurping the image of the Left and is widely overflowing the limits of organized Stalinism. The totalitarian temptation may well prove more powerful than the yearning for socialism, the hatred of capitalism violent enough to make acceptable the destruction of freedom, the fervor of nationalism so fanatical that it will engulf this earth in eternal civil war.

[5] Charlot adds: "Communism is only gaining ground among the retired and non-workers (11 per cent of the vote in 1946, 20 to 22 per cent today) and among small-business men and industrialists (up from 5 to 13 per cent); it is stagnant among upper-echelon employees and the professions and is falling among wage earners."
[6] Quoted in *Newsweek*, European edition, September 1, 1975.

A NOTE ON
EUROCOMMUNISM

THE "HISTORICAL COMPROMISE" AND THE DEMOCRATIZATION OF WESTERN COMMUNISTS

Two expressions have recently entered with perturbing effect into Western political commentary: "historical compromise" and "Eurocommunism." The first has a legitimate birth and father, Enrico Berlinguer, leader of the most important of the Communist parties functioning in democratic nations; it dates from the fall of 1973. The second expression, whose origins are bourgeois and anonymous, appeared in 1975. It was not conceived by the Communists, but the contagious force of its immediate success quickly caused them to adopt it. Enrico Berlinguer first used it in a public speech in June 1976 in Paris, during a turbulent joint rally of French and Italian Communists.

What general impression does the public get from the surprising repudiations and declarations that make up the offer of the historical compromise and Eurocommunism, also known as neo-communism? What the Western Communist chiefs would like the citizens of their countries to be convinced of by their new line comes down to two main ideas. In foreign affairs, the Western Communist parties say they have become independent of Moscow; at home, they henceforth accept democracy, pluralism in political parties and those basic freedoms that in Marxist-Leninist tradition had previously always been dismissed contemptuously as "formal." In short, they promise not to take power unless they win it by universal suffrage, to respect the rights of their opponents while they hold it and to surrender it if they are beaten in an election.

Thus proclaiming themselves purged of their Stalinist essence, the Western Communist parties offer their candidacy for normal participation in political responsibilities, "normal" meaning compatible with the rotation of different majorities in power without the risk of an irreversible and authoritarian change of regime. In fact, since the Second World War, the exercise of power in countries with a strong Communist party has been radically warped by the anomaly of opposition without alternation in office. In France and Italy especially, the Communist parties can achieve considerable electoral success, but an invisible barrier stands between them and power: for to give them power would amount to taking a one-way ticket for an unknown social system that *perhaps* would be managed from Moscow. That invisible barrier also blocks the route to power for those who are too intimately allied with the Communists.

Are the Communists of Western Europe sincere in their recent profession of faith in democracy? Since for sixty years they have practiced deceit and the sudden reversal of the party line all over the world, we have the right to be particularly skeptical in their case. And yet, strangely enough, doubting their honesty is today viewed in the West as being in poor taste (not just in Europe, but among political science practitioners in the United States and Canada). Not to believe them is said to amount to "a return to the cold war." In this sense, the Communists have already won the psychological battle, and in any event their democratic overture is a perfect public relations operation.

What can we say with certainty about neo-communism, if we judge it on its performance?

A first observation is that no Communist party has ever democratized power, when it held power, in the country in which it held it. Furthermore, on the only occasion in the West when a Communist party had the opportunity to offer solid proof of its good will by participating in the construction of a pluralist democracy—the case of Portugal—the Communist minority (about 10–12 per cent of the vote) used illegal and violent methods in an all-out attempt to win total power. Those socialist regimes, like Algeria, which though not Communist follow the principles of economic collectivism also seem unable to do without a totalitarian political organization. Communist promises to respect democratic methods in the exercise of power have to this date never been put to the test. Those promises emanate from Communist parties which have never held power, or at least not enough power to eliminate other political forces.

Yet the will of the Western Communists to be independent of Moscow seems authentic. It is not new among the Italians, but rarely has it been as clearly stated as it was by Berlinguer in his speeches to the 25th Congress of the Communist party of the Soviet Union in February 1976 in Moscow, and to the summit conference of European Communist parties in East Berlin in June. Among the French, by contrast, it is very recent. It dates from the fall of 1975 and, as always with them, it took the form of a sudden shift. The recognition of the right to autonomy in "national ways" to achieve socialism and the rejection of the "single Soviet model" were clearly affirmed, against the desires of Moscow ideologues like Suslov and contrary to the wishes of Leonid Brezhnev, in whose mind this summit, so laboriously prepared for two years, was to confirm the authority and the primacy of the Soviet Communist party over all others. It was a serious setback for the Soviets, so much so that the Soviet press printed expurgated versions of the speeches of the Western Communist leaders and of the final statement, eliminating the most heretical passages, so that the people of the Soviet Union and Eastern Europe remain unaware that Moscow is no longer the capital of world or even European communism and that its regime is challenged in the West by the Communists themselves.[1] But the

---

[1] The Italian Communist daily, *L'Unità*, printed in boldface type the passages that *Pravda* had censored from the speeches of Berlinguer and other Western leaders.

seeking of national autonomy in regard to Moscow is not the same thing as democracy at home—de-Russification does not by itself constitute democratization. The "nationalizing" of a Communist party does not mean it has been liberalized. The two ideas are often confused. But the Chinese, the Albanians, the Yugoslavs, the Romanians have been able to win total or partial independence from Moscow without democratizing their domestic rule; indeed they have become much *more totalitarian* at home than some docile satellites like Hungary or Poland. How would the Western Communist parties govern in their own countries? That is now the question.

If the Western Communists are holding the Soviet Union at arm's length, it is because they have become convinced that the Russian leaders do not understand how Western societies function and that remaining faithful to the old Marxist-Leninist gospel would doom communism in the West to a role of eternal and hopeless opposition. In these societies, they have concluded, one must accept the rules of democratic pluralism, based on elections and alternation in power of majorities with different programs, which naturally entails freedom of speech, of information and of culture, and (as Berlinguer said at the Berlin summit) "the non-ideological character of the state." The leaders of the Western Communist parties do not limit themselves, as did Tito, Mao and Ceauşescu, to demanding the right to oppress their fellow citizens in their own rather than the Russian manner; they define their "national way" as democracy and the rejection of oppression. The question then is whether this democratic way is compatible with the substance of Marxism. Are the Western Communist parties in the process of being transformed imperceptibly into reformist, social democratic parties? Or have they merely understood that they can put the electoral system to intelligent use to win office under perfectly legal conditions, and establish solid, incontestable bases with a view to later achieving a monopoly on power? If the first hypothesis is accurate, then they must be allowed to participate in government in Western nations on the same terms as other political parties. But if the second hypothesis is correct, they must be denied that participation. But then the Western democracies would be betraying their own basic law, their reason for being, by discriminating against certain of their citizens, a discrimination that would poison public life. Which of the two hypotheses is the right one?

Let us first consider to which countries the idea of Eurocommunism can be applied. The situations to which it would supposedly apply are so incomparably different that the idea appears to be a phantom. Greece has two Communist parties, one hostile to Moscow and the other favorable; between them they drew less than 10 per cent of the vote in the most recent elections. They seem unlikely to be candidates for power for a long time, as do the Portuguese Communists (7 per cent of the vote in the presidential elections of June 20, 1976). The Spanish Communist party, which is at once banned and tolerated, has slowed the country's evolution toward democracy by demanding immediate legalization, a demand that is unacceptable for the time being to the heirs of Franco. Although Santiago Carrillo, secretary-general of the Spanish party, is liberal in his statements, it must be observed that by his intransigence he has to the best of his ability pushed Spain toward a dangerous internal fragmentation. In order for the Spanish Communist party to participate someday in Spanish democracy, there must first *be* a Spanish democracy. To prevent its birth by making maximum demands, while at the same time proclaiming ultra-liberalism, is to double-cross democracy. By opposing centrist solutions, Carrillo has produced guilt among the parties of the non-Communist Left, to the point of inspiring in them that servility toward Stalinism that one finds also among the French Socialists. Here is an example:

In the March 27, 1976, issue of the Spanish magazine *Cuadernos para el Diálogo* (*Notes for a Dialogue*), the following appeared under the name of a non-Communist writer, Juan Benet: "I firmly believe that as long as people like Alexander Solzhenitsyn exist, the concentration camps will and must continue to exist. Perhaps they should even be under better surveillance, so that people like Alexander Solzhenitsyn cannot leave them without having acquired some education. But the mistake of letting them out having once been made, nothing seems to me to be more hygienic on the part of the Soviet authorities (whose tastes and criteria concerning subversive Russian writers I often share) than to seek a means of ridding themselves of such a plague." Now, *Cuadernos para el Diálogo* (a strange kind of dialogue!) is the organ of the *left wing of the Christian Democrats* in Spain! Recently it has allied itself with the Socialists and Communists. The editor of the magazine, Joachin Ruiz Gímenez, is the leader of the "left" Christian Democratic movement, and he is also the vice-president of the Institute of the Rights of Man, Institut des Droits de l'Homme, in Strasbourg (the René Cassin Foundation). Juan Benet's article followed a Spanish telecast (March 20, 1976) on which Solzhenitsyn dared to say that the Spanish in 1976 enjoyed greater freedom, or endured fewer shackles on their freedom, than the Soviet people, a statement which is both accurate and easily proved, but which constitutes ideological heresy. In choosing what they call a "strategy of rupture," that is, a test of strength with the regime of King Juan Carlos and with the army, the Spanish leftist parties by their actions are contradicting the basis of the "Eurocommunist" strategy—even if Carrillo defends that strategy in speeches in Berlin, Paris and Rome.

The situations of the French and Italian Communists, which have little relation to that of the Spanish, also differ greatly one from the other. French and Italian Communists agree on the "national way" as against the Soviet model and on the acceptance in theory of the rules of pluralist democracy. But beyond those two general principles, they agree on hardly anything else. The Italians are against extending the role of the public sector in the economy, while the French back a program of extensive nationalization. The Italians want to form a coalition with the Christian Democrats, a government of national union (minus the neo-fascists); the French, by contrast, reject not only any collaboration but even consultation with the majority of President Giscard d'Estaing and with the "reformers" of the center-left, in short with any political party which does not subscribe to the joint platform of the Left, which foresees the abolition of capitalism by means that explicitly reject social democracy (accused of collaboration with capitalism). The Italians are Atlanticist, advocates of European political unity and the election of the Parliament of Europe by direct universal suffrage; the French vehemently oppose that idea, waving the specter of "abandoning national independence" and seizing every opportunity to make of themselves, in opposition to Atlanticism and Europe, the champions of a kind of Red Gaullism.

In reality, therefore, there is no such thing as Eurocommunism. There is only Italocommunism.

In Italy the Communists propose not "rupture" but an *alliance* with the *adversaries* of Marxist socialism. This idea of the "compromise" came to Berlinguer from pondering the events in Chile. The fall of Allende, Berlinguer explained in a series of articles,[2] demonstrated that a Marxist coalition, even though victorious at the polls, could not manage society democratically without concluding a kind of pact of non-aggression and even of co-operation with its adversaries, at home as well as abroad. Even if the general elections of June 20 and 21, 1976, had made the Communists Italy's leading party, Berlinguer said he still would have sought an association with the Christian Democrats. Thus his analysis ruled out in advance any *complete* overturn in Italian politics. Besides, the election results made such an overturn impossible, at least in a democratic context. The Communists continued to gain ground after their success in the June 1975 regional elections, for their vote rose in twelve months from 32 to 34.4 per cent of the total. But the Christian Democrats gained more ground, so that their lead over the Communists rose from barely 1.9 per cent in 1975 to 4.3 percent in 1976.

But the heart of the matter lies elsewhere: if one wants to understand the historical compromise, one must examine areas other than government and the legislature. What matters much more is the *unofficial compromise which already exists in the nation*. The Communists may well come to control all Italy without having a single minister in the Cabinet. First of all, virtually three quarters of the laws adopted since the 1946 origin of Italy's present institutions were drafted in consultation with the Com-

2 Enrico Berlinguer, "Riflessioni sull' Italia dopo i Fatti del Cile," *Rinascita*, September 28, October 5 and 9, 1973.

munists. Furthermore, for a long time, but especially since the regional elections of 1975, the Communists have held power in the main provinces and in almost all the major cities. Even Rome now has a Communist city administration. This regional power carries a lot of weight in a nation where the central administration has far fewer prerogatives than it does in France, and besides is operated by a totally ineffectual bureaucracy.

As for the economy, the big industrialists are the first to say that Communist participation is indispensable to the management of Italy. The best-known among them, Giovanni Agnelli, repeated that belief after the 1976 elections in a striking interview published in four languages in four European papers.[3] And why should Berlinguer demand nationalization when the Italian economy is already in the process of nationalizing itself, spontaneously and on the sly? In fact, Italian capitalism is dying; for a long time it has been incapable of capitalist "accumulation." Shareholders and entrepreneurs no longer hold power. Firms live on their loans from the banks, which in the last resort means the Bank of Italy: on the one hand, then, they are increasingly at the mercy of credit accorded by the state; on the other, they are ever more under the control of the unions, which in turn are largely controlled by the Communists.

In May 1976, for example, the industrial association of Bologna published a report in which it deplored "the sort of crusade against management as such, a crusade carried on not only by certain politicians or union leaders, but also by part of the intellectual and cultural world, and even the judiciary." In support of that view, the report told about the landmark case of a judge who convicted the head of a business of "anti-union behavior" because he had anticipated his employees' demands and thus had cut the ground from under the unions' feet![4] Here again, why should the Communist party mount a violent assault on the means of production and distribution? It would be superfluous: Italian business already is almost in a situation of direct management by the unions, subsidized by the state, which in turn is sub-

[3] *The Times* of London, *Le Monde, La Stampa, Die Welt,* July 6, 1976.
[4] Quoted in *Il Sole 24 Ore,* May 15, 1976.

sidized by foreign capitalism. Thus in a sense the Italian Communists are *already in power,* and they are adopting a conciliatory stance to avoid a "backlash." They have succeeded in dominating the society rather than seeking in vain to gain control of the state. In so doing the Italian Communists have only been following, to the letter and for a long time, the teaching of their great theoretician, Antonio Gramsci. Gramsci's principle was that the Italian Communist party must begin by influencing the culture, winning the intellectuals, the teachers, implanting itself in the press, the media, the publishing houses. The party has been doing just that since 1945 and it has been spectacularly successful. A majority of the most prestigious names in art, film and literature are Communists or Communist sympathizers. But, more profoundly though less visible to foreigners, the fundamental establishment of the Communist view of the world and of history will become evident to anyone who takes the trouble to study schoolchildren, for example, and to examine the textbooks they currently use.

In Gramsci's view, the state will become separated from the ruling class when the latter is no longer capable of managing it, and then it will fall like a ripe fruit. So there is no reason to seek combat. As a strategy, that isn't "Leninist," but it certainly is effective.

In order to help win acceptance of their omnipresence within the nation, the Italian Communists are careful not to challenge foreign policy. The historical compromise can be stated as follows: the state to the Christian Democrats and the nation to the Communists. Which amounts to saying: foreign policy to the Christian Democrats and domestic policy to the Communists. Five days before the 1976 elections, Enrico Berlinguer declared that, as of June 1976, he felt more at ease building Italian socialism under the protection of NATO than if Italy were a member of the Warsaw Pact.[5] By contrast, the French Communists want to change the fundamentals of French foreign policy.

[5] Interview in *Corriere della Sera,* June 15, 1976. This statement was omitted from the text of the interview published the following day by the Communist paper *L'Unità,* probably to avoid shocking the party rank and file.

After "Eurocommunism," the "historical compromise" and the demand for "national ways to socialism," the great sensation of the beginning of 1976 was the French Communist party's repudiation of the "dictatorship of the proletariat." That alone was enough to make many exclaim as if they had seen a miracle. They forget just two things. First, no Communist party *actually holding power* has ever renounced dictatorship; the Western parties at the moment are renouncing a power they do not have. Secondly, the "renunciation of the dictatorship of the proletariat" is a theme that appears periodically in the history of communism, as does the proclamation of independence from Moscow.

On this subject Kostas Papaïoannou, whom I have often cited in this book, reminds us of some damning evidence:

"As early as 1946 all the Communist parties in the world (including the Chinese) had discovered the virtues of 'democracy' ('progressive,' 'people's' or 'new') as well as the relativity of the Soviet 'model' and the plurality of 'national ways.' As Mathias Rákosi, the well-known apostle of the independence of the Hungarian nation, said, 'in the last twenty-five years the Communist parties of the world have learned that there exist several paths that lead to communism.' Another important 'democrat,' George Dimitrov, said in his turn, 'Bulgaria will not be a Soviet republic, but a people's republic, in which the governing role will be played by the great majority of the people. There will be no dictatorship.'

"But doubtless the prize goes to Klement Gottwald, the future president of the people's republic of Czechoslovakia. In a report he made on September 25, 1946, to the central committee of the party, he went so far as to say, 'As experience has already shown, and as we have been taught by the classics of Marxism and Leninism, the dictatorship of the proletariat and the Soviets is not the only way to socialism. Given the presence of certain forces in the international sphere (the proximity of the Red Army) and in the domestic sphere (a position in the Ministry of the Interior), we can envisage still another path leading to socialism . . . that is equally true for our country.' (*Rude Pravo,* September 26, 1946.)

Several days later, and after recalling that the means by which the Soviet Union blazed its trail to socialism do not represent the only possibility, Gottwald added, ". . . Marxism conceived in a creative spirit always takes into account the concrete situation, the time and the place, when it determines its attitude toward a given problem . . . A new kind of democracy is born, we call it people's democracy. Thus life in practice has confirmed the theoretical provisions of the Marxist classics, according to which there exists a way to socialism other than that which passes by way of the dictatorship of the proletariat and the Soviet regime. Yugoslavia, Bulgaria, Poland and also Czechoslovakia have engaged themselves on this other way. (*Rude Pravo*, October 5, 1946.)"[6]

There were many then who thought the Communists had changed. In France, Maurice Thorez, secretary-general of the party, who had spent the entire war in Moscow, gave on his return to Paris in 1946 a resounding interview to *The Times* of London in which he explained that the French party would henceforth establish its political line in complete independence, without letting itself be influenced by Moscow.

Three years later, all these positions were in their turn repudiated, and the victims of the Budapest and Moscow trials paid for the new line with their lives.

" 'We continually emphasized and spread the theory of Czechoslovakia's supposed special path toward socialism,' 'confessed' Josef Frank, assistant to the secretary-general of the Communist party and one of the victims of the Slansky trial. For his part, Ludvik Frejka, Gottwald's chief economic adviser, 'confessed' that '. . . to achieve our conspiratorial designs, more precisely, to achieve the plans of the Western imperialists, especially the American monopolists, we spread among the Czechoslovak people our opportunistic theory, according to which it is possible to build socialism without the dictatorship of the proletariat.' "

Papaïoannou reaches this unarguable conclusion:

"We know what followed: the hangings, the terror, the total

[6] *L'Express*, January 26, 1976.

loss of national independence, the cultural stagnation, the transformation of Czechoslovakia into an underdeveloped country . . ."

Since 1920, there have always been two phases in Communist party tactics: the open phase of the extended hand, and the closed, hard phase of the "class front" or "class struggle." The two alternate with punctual regularity. As I have often said in this book, the great skill consists of finding a new vocabulary for each return to the open phase. Political propaganda depends on the shortness of memory; it gambles on the amnesia of the masses, and even more incredible, that of many "specialists."

Thus, in order to evaluate the import of any new Communist party line, one must consider, *as one does for any other political party,* not declarations of intent but actual behavior. Now, in practice the French Communist party remains Stalinist. Since its switch in favor of pluralist democracy, the party has loosed on the public an avalanche of books on liberty, laborious homework essays, schoolchildren's term papers written on management orders, by the young, by the old—unaware of the comic implication of these manifestoes for freedom, all written on command and pouring forth within a few months, fruits of the marvelous spontaneity of minds working in a harmony as close as the co-ordination between the hand and the eye. But in spite of this feverish libertarian output, the methods of *L'Humanité* remain Stalinist: it never discusses a point of view, it only discredits the person. Even those journalists who are sympathetic to the Communists, if they are unfortunate enough to differ even in the slightest degree from the positions taken by the party, are accused of being "agents of the Minister of the Interior," that is police collaborators, a level of political discourse that is purely Stalinist. Here is one example among many (from *L'Humanité,* May 13, 1976):

"*Le Monde* never marks time in its anti-communism. Under the signature of Thierry Pfister, *Le Monde* writes that in view of the supposed 'many reservations provoked by the line adopted by the 22nd Congress . . . the political bureau of the French

Communist party decided at its meeting May 11 to mark time.' This pseudo-information calls for just one comment. Does the fact that this paper and/or this journalist are lending a helping hand to operations aimed at the Communist party and its policies mean that they *now are in the service of M. Poniatowski?*"[7] (*Le Monde* made no protest.)

Within the French Communist party, the voting in the party organizations, the elections to positions of leadership, the ban on factions within the party, the always unanimous votes in support of the leadership, the bureaucratic authoritarianism in the Confédération Générale du Travail, the union run directly by a member of the party political bureau (and the brutality of the CGT's thugs)—all these show that the French Communist party's basic personality remains totalitarian, despite its rhetorical efforts to disavow it. As Branko Lazitch, one of the most encyclopedic experts on communism, wrote: "Why should the French Communist party, if tomorrow it is in the government, respect the freedom of action of the *anti-Communist* opposition when it does not tolerate the slightest Communist opposition within its own ranks?"[8]

Nor is there any democracy *within* the Italian Communist party. Thus Lazitch's quite accurate observation applies equally to Italy. If the Communists have become sincerely democratic, why do they not prove it *right now?* Instead, they prove the contrary every day.

Furthermore, their totalitarian philosophy has spilled over onto the French Socialists, for while the latter have become more numerous at the polls than the Communists, they have on the other hand become ideologically submissive to them. Their intolerance is in no way inferior to that of vintage Stalinists. Thus, the Socialist philosopher François Chatelet, a member of the "study group" formed by François Mitterrand to draw up the "Socialist charter of freedoms," stated that: "The fascist state is

[7] The Minister of the Interior. Emphasis added. Can one imagine the howls of rage from the Communist leaders should one or another of them be accused of being in the service of the KGB?
[8] "Les Communistes et la liberté," *Le Figaro,* February 10, 1976.

the free state reduced to its essence."[9] That is the most orthodox of Marxist-Leninist views on the state. If, then, *for the Socialists* (not just the Communists), there is *no essential difference* between a fascist state and a free state, how can we believe that they will vigorously defend the latter? It would seem logical that other objectives would have higher priority. In addition, a delegation of the French Socialist party invited in 1976 by the Hungarian government declared that it was "favorably impressed by the successes in the building of socialism by the Hungarian people *under the direction of the working class and its party*,"[10] thus adopting as its own a Stalinist formula, without the slightest reservation, to praise a party that governs alone and by totalitarian methods.[11]

The political analyst must follow the historian's procedure of affirming nothing that is not based on documents that are verified and authenticated. History, of which political analysis is a branch, is based not on favorable or unfavorable prejudices but on distinguishing facts that can be confirmed from conjectures that cannot. A politician has the right to *bet* on unconfirmable conjectures, at his own risk (or rather at the risk of others); the analyst must refuse to do so and must limit himself to facts that can be confirmed.

What are the facts about Eurocommunism that can be confirmed? In summary:

1) The Communists in all the nations that they govern maintain the structure of the totalitarian state, that is a total monopoly over the economy, politics, the police, unions, culture, the legislature, the judiciary, the military, information and education.

[9] *Éléments pour une analyse du fascisme* (Paris, 1976). (Seminar by M.-A. Macciochi.) The sentence above was quoted and approved by the Socialist weekly *Le Nouvel Observateur*, June 21, 1976.
[10] *Le Monde*, June 1, 1976.
[11] We might add that the failure of Hungary's "new economic structure" as well as the people's absolute contempt for the system, socialism in general and Marxism in particular, are known to all visitors and observers. So why should the French Socialist party act as propagandist for a regime that the Hungarians only endure under Soviet compulsion?

2) The proclamation of "national ways" to achieve socialism independently of Moscow in no way changes that state of things. The Chinese and the Albanians have long since broken with Moscow, but they remain no less totalitarian.

3) In the case of the Communist parties that are not in power and that operate in the West, the theme of renouncing the dictatorship of the proletariat is not new, and furthermore is not accompanied by any democratization within those parties. At the present time, taking a rigorously historical view, we lack decisive proof as to how they would wield power were they in office.

4) If Eurocommunism and the "renunciation of the dictatorship of the proletariat" mean anything, they must lead to an open and avowed transition from a Marxist-Leninist character to a reformist and social democratic character. Without that, the purported new line of the Communist parties *has no logical coherence and no practical possibility of being implemented.* But no Western party has yet dared to break ranks in that direction, because to do so would threaten with disintegration the internal cohesion of the party, which is based on centralism and obedience.

5) The meaning of this tactic thus is limited. Without denying that there may be a sincere evolution toward social democracy among some *individuals,* like Dubček and probably Berlinguer, one must not lose sight of the fact that the essential thrust of Communist *movements* is still toward monopoly power. Up to now, their behavior makes sense only in terms of the conquest of monopoly power, whatever "ways" or means may be considered most likely to result in that conquest.

September 26, 1976